AWS Certified Solution Architect - Professional

Study Guide with Practice Questions and Labs

Volume 2

www.ipspecialist.net

Document Control

Proposal Name	:	AWS Solution Architect - Professional
Document Edition	:	Third Edition
Document Volume	:	Volume 2
Document Release Date	:	16th September 2021
Reference	:	SAP-C01

Feedback:

If you have any comments regarding the quality of this book, or otherwise alter it to better suit your needs, you can contact us through email at info@ipspecialist.net

Please make sure to include the book's title and ISBN in your message

About IPSpecialist

IPSPECIALIST LTD. IS COMMITTED TO EXCELLENCE AND DEDICATED TO YOUR SUCCESS.

Our philosophy is to treat our customers like family. We want you to succeed, and we are willing to do everything possible to help you make it happen. We have the proof to back up our claims. We strive to accelerate billions of careers with great courses, accessibility, and affordability. We believe that continuous learning and knowledge evolution are the most important things to keep re-skilling and up-skilling the world.

Planning and creating a specific goal is where IPSpecialist helps. We can create a career track that suits your visions as well as develop the competencies you need to become a professional Network Engineer. We can also assist you with the execution and evaluation of your proficiency level, based on the career track you choose, as they are customized to fit your specific goals.

We help you STAND OUT from the crowd through our detailed IP training content packages.

Course Features:

❖ Self-Paced learning
  • Learn at your own pace and in your own time
❖ Covers Complete Exam Blueprint
  • Prep-up for the exam with confidence
❖ Case Study Based Learning
  • Relate the content with real life scenarios
❖ Subscriptions that suits you
  • Get more and pay less with IPS subscriptions
❖ Career Advisory Services
  • Let the industry experts plan your career journey
❖ Virtual Labs to test your skills
  • With IPS vRacks, you can evaluate your exam preparations
❖ Practice Questions
  • Practice questions to measure your preparation standards
❖ On Request Digital Certification
  • On request digital certification from IPSpecialist LTD

About the Authors:

This book has been compiled with the help of multiple professional engineers. These engineers specialize in different fields e.g., Networking, Security, Cloud, Big Data, IoT, etc. Each engineer develops content in its specialized field that is compiled to form a comprehensive certification guide.

About the Technical Reviewers:

Nouman Ahmed Khan

AWS-Architect, CCDE, CCIEX5 (RandS, SP, Security, DC, Wireless), CISSP, CISA, CISM is a Solution Architect working with a major telecommunication provider in Qatar. He works with enterprises, mega-projects, and service providers to help them select the best-fit technology solutions. He also works closely as a consultant to understand customer business processes and helps select an appropriate technology strategy to support business goals. He has more than 14 years of experience working in Pakistan/Middle-East and UK. He holds a Bachelor of Engineering Degree from NED University, Pakistan, and M.Sc. in Computer Networks from the UK.

Abubakar Saeed

Abubakar Saeed has more than twenty-five years of experience, Managing, Consulting, Designing, and implementing large-scale technology projects, extensive experience heading ISP operations, solutions integration, heading Product Development, Presales, and Solution Design. Emphasizing on adhering to Project timelines and delivering as per customer expectations, he always leads the project in the right direction with his innovative ideas and excellent management.

Dr. Fahad Abdali

Dr. Fahad Abdali is a seasoned leader with extensive experience managing and growing software development teams in high-growth start-ups. He is a business entrepreneur with more than 18 years of experience in management and marketing. He holds a Bachelor's Degree from NED University of Engineering and Technology and a Doctor of Philosophy (Ph.D.) from the University of Karachi.

Mehwish Jawed

Mehwish Jawed is working as a Senior Research Analyst. She holds a Master's and Bachelors of Engineering degree in Telecommunication Engineering from NED University of Engineering and Technology. She also worked under the supervision of HEC Approved supervisor. She has more than three published papers, including both conference and journal papers. She has a great knowledge of TWDM Passive Optical Network (PON). She also worked as a Project Engineer, Robotic Trainer in a private institute and has research skills in the field of communication networks. She has both technical knowledge and industry-sounding information, which she utilizes effectively when needed. She also has expertise in cloud platforms, as in AWS and Microsoft Azure.

Rafia Muzaffar

Rafia Muzaffar is working as a Technical Content Developer. She holds a Bachelor's of Engineering degree in Telecommunication Engineering from NED University of Engineering and Technology. She possesses exceptional research and writing skills. She is enthusiastic and passionate in her academic pursuit. She has a sound knowledge of Networking, IoT, and Cloud and also knows multiple programming languages, including MATLAB, HTML, CSS, React. Js, C# and Java.

Mohammad Usman Khan

Muhammad Usman Khan is a Technical Content Developer. He holds a Bachelor's Degree in Telecommunication Engineering from Sir Syed University of Engineering and Technology. He holds First Position Telecommunication Engineering and received two Gold Medals, the first from Sir Syed University of Engineering and Technology. He worked on many Deep Learning projects. He is certified by the National Center of Artificial Intelligence (NCAI), which is a research institute of the Government of Pakistan in the field of Artificial Intelligence. He is also certified by the Nvidia Deep Learning Institute in Deep Learning with Computer Vision.

Syeda Fariha Ashrafi

Syeda Fariha Ashrafi is working as a technical content developer. She has completed bachelor's degree in telecommunication engineering from NED University of Engineering and Technology. She has also completed the CCNA (Routing and Switching) course. During her bachelor's program, she has worked on the project "Smart metering using PLC (Power Line Communication).

Free Resources

For Free Resources: Please visit our website and register to access your desired Resources Or contact us at: helpdesk@ipspecialist.net

Career Report: This report is a step-by-step guide for a novice who wants to develop his/her career in the field of computer networks. It answers the following queries:

- What are the current scenarios and future prospects?
- Is this industry moving towards saturation, or are new opportunities knocking at the door?
- What will the monetary benefits be?
- Why get certified?
- How to plan, and when will I complete the certifications if I start today?
- Is there any career track that I can follow to accomplish specialization level?

Furthermore, this guide provides a comprehensive career path towards being a specialist in networking and highlights the tracks needed to obtain certification.

IPS Personalized Technical Support for Customers: Good customer service means helping customers efficiently, in a friendly manner. It is essential to be able to handle issues for customers and do your best to ensure they are satisfied. Providing good service is one of the most important things that can set our business apart from the others of its kind.

Excellent customer service will result in attracting more customers and attain maximum customer retention.

IPS offers personalized TECH support to its customers to provide better value for money. If you have any queries related to technology and labs, you can simply ask our technical team for assistance via Live Chat or Email.

Our Products

Study Guides

IPSpecialist Study Guides are the ideal guides to developing the hands-on skills necessary to pass the exam. Our study guides cover the official exam blueprint and explain the technology with real-life case study-based labs. The content covered in each study guide consists of individually focused technology topics presented in an easy-to-follow, goal-oriented, step-by-step approach. Every scenario features detailed breakdowns and thorough verifications to help you completely understand the task and associated technology.

We extensively used mind maps in our study guides to visually explain the technology. Our study guides have become a widely used tool to learn and remember information effectively.

vRacks

Our highly scalable and innovative virtualized lab platforms let you practice the IPSpecialist Study guide at your own time and your own place as per your convenience.

Exam Cram

Our Exam crams are a concise bundling of condensed notes of the complete exam blueprint. It is an ideal and handy document to help you remember the most important technology concepts related to the certification exam.

Practice Questions

IP Specialists' Practice Questions are dedicatedly designed from a certification exam perspective. The collection of these questions from our Study Guides is prepared keeping the exam blueprint in mind, covering not only important but necessary topics as well. It is an ideal document to practice and revise your certification.

Content at a glance

Table of Contents

AWS Cloud Certifications

AWS Certifications are industry-recognized credentials that validate your technical cloud skills and expertise while assisting in your career growth. These are one of the most valuable IT certifications right now since AWS has established an overwhelming lead in the public cloud market. Even with the presence of several tough competitors such as Microsoft Azure, Google Cloud Engine, and Rackspace, AWS is by far the dominant public cloud platform today, with an astounding collection of proprietary services that continues to grow.

The two key reasons as to why AWS certifications are prevailing in the current cloud-oriented job market:

- There is a dire need for skilled cloud engineers, developers, and architects – and the current shortage of experts is expected to continue into the foreseeable future.
- AWS certifications stand out for their thoroughness, rigor, consistency, and appropriateness for critical cloud engineering positions.

Value of AWS Certifications

AWS places equal emphasis on sound conceptual knowledge of its entire platform, as well as on hands-on experience with the AWS infrastructure and its many unique and complex components and services.

For Individuals

- Demonstrates your expertise to design, deploy, and operate highly available, cost-effective, and secure applications on AWS.
- Gain recognition and visibility for your proven skills and proficiency with AWS.
- Earn tangible benefits such as access to the AWS Certified LinkedIn Community, invite to AWS Certification Appreciation Receptions and Lounges, AWS Certification Practice Exam Voucher, Digital Badge for certification validation, AWS Certified Logo usage, access to AWS Certified Store.
- Foster credibility with your employer and peers.

For Employers

- Identify skilled professionals to lead IT initiatives with AWS technologies.
- Reduce risks and costs to implement your workloads and projects on the AWS platform.
- Increase customer satisfaction.

Types of Certification

Role-Based Certifications:

- *Foundational* - Validates overall understanding of the AWS Cloud. Prerequisite to achieving Specialty certification or an optional start towards Associate certification.
- *Associate* - Technical role-based certifications. No prerequisite.
- *Professional* - Highest level technical role-based certification. Relevant Associate certification required.

Specialty Certifications:

- Validate advanced skills in specific technical areas.
- Require one active role-based certification.

About AWS – Certified Solutions Architect Professional Exam

Exam Questions	Case study, short answer, repeated answer, MCQs
Number of Questions	100-120
Time to Complete	170 minutes
Exam Fee	165 USD

The AWS Certified Solutions Architect – Professional exam validates advanced technical skills and experience in designing distributed applications and systems on the AWS platform. Example concepts you should understand for this exam include:

- ➢ Designing and deploying dynamically scalable, highly available, fault-tolerant, and reliable applications on AWS
- ➢ Selecting appropriate AWS services to design and deploy an application based on given requirements
- ➢ Migrating complex, multi-tier applications on AWS
- ➢ Designing and deploying enterprise-wide scalable operations on AWS
- ➢ Implementing cost-control strategies

Recommended AWS Knowledge

- One or more years of hands-on experience developing and maintaining an AWS based application
- In-depth knowledge of at least one high-level programming language

- Understanding of core AWS services, uses, and basic AWS architecture best practices
- Proficiency in developing, deploying, and debugging cloud-based applications using AWS
- Ability to use the AWS service APIs, AWS CLI, and SDKs to write applications
- Ability to identify key features of AWS services
- Understanding of the AWS shared responsibility model
- Understanding of application lifecycle management
- Ability to use a CI/CD pipeline to deploy applications on AWS
- Ability to use or interact with AWS services
- Ability to apply a basic understanding of cloud-native applications to write codes
- Ability to write codes using AWS security best practices (e.g. using IAM roles instead of using secret and access keys in the code)
- Ability to author, maintain, and debug code modules on AWS
- Proficiency writing code for server-less applications
- Understanding of the use of containers in the development process

	Domain	Percentage
Domain 1	Design for Organizational Complexity	12.5%
Domain 2	Design for New Solutions	31%
Domain 3	Migration Planning	15%
Domain 4	Cost Control	12.5%
Domain 5	Continuous Improvement for Existing Solutions	29%
Total		100%

Chapter 06: Architecting to scale

Introduction

In this chapter, we will discuss the Auto-Scaling feature available for different resources in AWS.

Concepts

Architectural patterns are the suggested ways to design any architecture.

Loosely Coupled Architecture

In this type of pattern, every component can stand independently, and they can even work without the knowledge of other components working.

Advantages

- This architecture introduces layers of abstraction
- It permits more flexibility
- Its components can be interchangeable
- The functional units are more isolated
- It helps in independent scaling

Tightly Coupled Process vs. Loosely Coupled Process

In a tightly coupled process, there are three steps in the process, which step1 and step3 take 5 seconds to complete, and step2 takes 20 seconds. If your goal is less than 15 seconds, you cannot achieve your goal.

To achieve the goal, you have to provide more computing power in step2 so that it would take maximum of 5 seconds.

The problem with this architecture is that you cannot scale only one step. Therefore, other steps computing power will be excess because other steps are already completing in 5 seconds (they do not need more computing power).

In a Loosely Coupled Process, you can easily scale any of the steps because all of the components are independent of each other. Step2 can be scaled vertically (increasing computing power/RAM), or it can be scaled horizontally (increasing number of instances working in step2) if supported by the application.

Horizontal Scaling vs. Vertical Scaling

Horizontal Scaling	Vertical Scaling
Adding more instances	Adding more CPU and/or RAM
No downtime is required for scale in or scale out	Downtime requires as a restart of instance is required
Automatic using Auto-scaling groups	Scripts are required for automation
Theoretically unlimited	Limited due to instance size

Table 6-01: Horizontal vs. Vertical Scaling

Scale-Out, Scale-In, Scale-Up, Scale-Down

Scale-Out: Add an instance

Scale-In: Remove an instance

Scale-Up: Add a resource to an existing instance

Scale-Down: Remove resource to an existing instance

Sample Message Processing Architecture

In the given architecture, m5.2xlarge instance is used to process the messages and save them into the S3 bucket

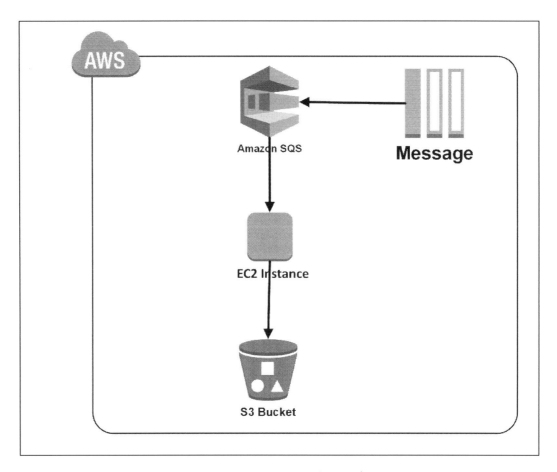

Figure 6-01: Message Processing Architecture

By using Scale-Out Architecture, more m5.2xlarge instances can be used.

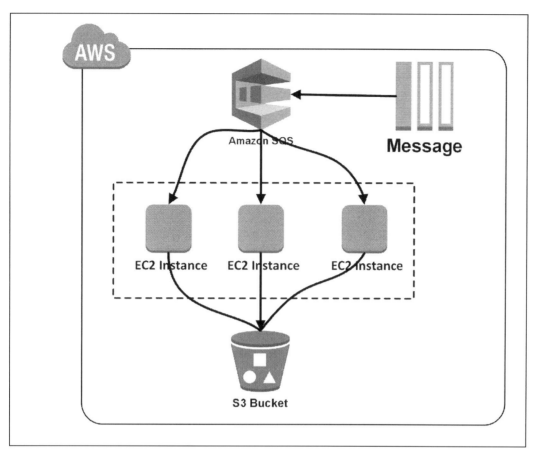

Figure 6-02: Message Processing Architecture (Scale-out)

Scaling to Match Demand

You can scale in and scale out to meet the changing demand each day. If you use one large instance, its price will be the same, no matter what the demand is.

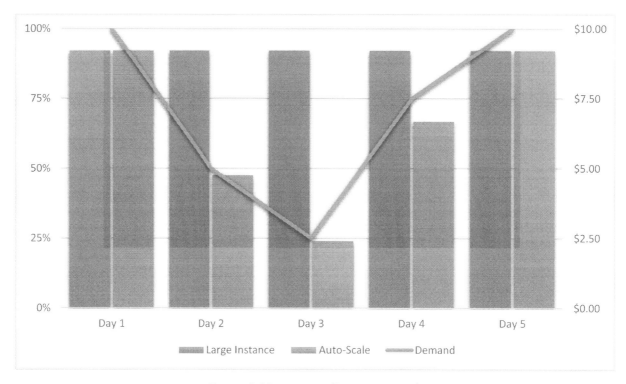

Figure 6-03: Auto-scaling vs. No-scaling

Scaling Economics

You can save your cost by using Scaling

No scaling	$46.08
Auto-scaling	$32.26
Savings	$13.82

Table 6-02: Scaling Economics

Auto scaling

Name	What	Why
Amazon EC2 Auto scaling	It belongs to EC2 instances auto scaling	You can setup scaling groups for EC2 instances; also perform health checks to remove unhealthy instances.
Application Auto scaling	There is an API to control scaling for resources other	Provides a common way to interact with the

	than EC2 such as Dynamo, ECS, EMR	scalability of other services
AWS Auto scaling	Provides a centralized way to manage scalability for stacks; Predictive scaling feature	The console that can manage both of the above from a unified standpoint

Table 6-03: Auto scaling in AWS

EC2 Auto-Scaling Groups

Auto-Scaling group is a group of Amazon EC2 instances, which is managed by the Auto-Scaling Group service. It provides automatic horizontal scaling.

Scaling Policy

You can adjust Auto scaling dynamically by associating scaling policies and Amazon CloudWatch alarms with an Auto-Scaling group. When the threshold is crossed, Amazon CloudWatch automatically sends alarms to trigger scaling in or out to the number of EC2 instances that are currently receiving the traffic behind the load balancer. When the message is sent by the Amazon CloudWatch alarm to the Auto-Scaling group, Auto scaling executes the associated policy to scale in or out of your group. The policy is a set of instructions that defines whether to scale out or launch a new instance, terminate the instance, or scale-in.

There are four scaling options:

Maintain: Keep a specific or minimum number of instances running

Manual: Use maximum, minimum or specific number of instances

Schedule: Increase or decrease instances based on schedule

Dynamic: Scale based on real-time metrics of the systems

Launch Configurations

Every Scaling group has launch configuration options, which control when Auto scaling should terminate and launch new instances. An Auto-Scaling group must contain a minimum and a maximum number of instances and the name of instances that can be in the group. Desired capacity can be specified, which is the number of instances that should be in the group all the time. By default, desired capacity is a minimum number of instances you specify. You should specify VPC and subnets for the scaled instances as well as specify whether you want to attach the instance with ELB. Also, you have to specify Health Check Grace Period.

Scaling Types

You have to select any of the scaling types to define the group size.

Scaling Type	What	When
Maintain	Hands-off way to maintain X number of instances	You need the same number of instances always
Manual	Manually change desired capacity via console or CLI	Your requirements change rarely that you can manually add or remove instances
Scheduled	Adjustment of min/max instances on specific time	Your website has high traffic on weekends
Dynamic	Scaling due to some specific elements in the environment	CPU utilization increases, then you require to scale up

Table 6-04: Scaling Types

EC2 Auto Scaling Policies

In Dynamic scaling type, the following scaling policies are provided

Scaling	What
Target Tracking Policy	Scaling based on the set target value for any predefined or custom metrics
Simple Scaling Policy	Wait until the health check and cool down period expires before evaluating the new requirement
Step Scaling Policy	The more sophisticated and logical response to scaling requirement

Table 6-05: Scaling Policies (Dynamic Scaling Type)

Scaling Cool down Concept for EC2

The difference between Health check and cooldown is that health check gives the resources some time to stabilize before checking their health, whereas cooldown period is a duration that provides scaling a chance to "come up to speed" and absorb the load. This period is configurable. The default cool down time is 300 seconds. Cooldown is applied automatically to dynamic scaling and is optional for manual scaling, however, it is not

supported for planned scaling. You can alter the default cooldown duration, for example, if you are utilizing scale down policy and do not need any wait time for termination.

If there is no cooldown period, many instances will be launched that are not actually needed because no instance will be stable enough to absorb load, and auto scaling will assume that the resource isn't enough to handle the current load.

AWS Application Auto scaling

APIs that are used to control scaling of resources other than EC2 have some scaling policies.

Scaling	What	When
Target Tracking Policy	Initiate scaling events to try to track as closely as possible a given target metric	You want your ECS host to stay at or below 70% CPU utilization
Step Scaling Policy	Based on metrics, adjusts capacity on the basis of given certain defined threshold	You want to increase EC2 Spot Fleet by 20% whenever another 10000 connections are added to ELB
Scheduled Scaling Policy	Scaling events are initiated on the basis of predefined time, date, or day	Every Monday, you want to increase Read Capacity Units of DynamoDB to 20000

Table 6-06: Application Scaling Policies

AWS Auto scaling

AWS Auto scaling is a single console from where you can perform both EC2 and Application Auto Scaling. It allows you to automatically discover or select resources manually to add in your scaling plan.

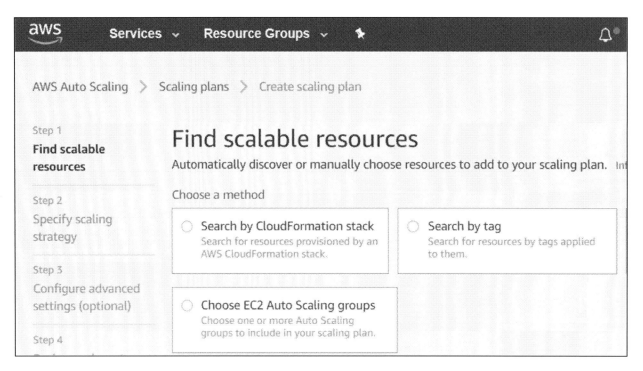

Figure 6-04: AWS Auto Scaling Console

AWS Predictive Scaling

It uses machine learning algorithms to learn your data and predict when scale up or down is required. If you have privacy issues with your data, then you can also opt-out from this option.

 ElastiCache

We can offload the heavy lifting that is included in the deployment with the help of Amazon ElastiCache. Amazon ElastiCache is a web service that allows us to store in-memory data or cached data in the cloud by creating, maintaining, and scaling cache clusters efficiently. This service also improves application performance by quickly retrieving data from in-memory data stores. This enables providing a high-performance and scalable caching solution for your cloud apps simple and cost-effective. The ElastiCache supports two open-source in-memory engines:

1. Memcached
2. Redis

Because Amazon ElastiCache is a fully managed service, you can utilize either Memcached or Redis by simply changing the endpoints in configuration files. Memcached is the most widely used engine for storing simple data types, whereas Redis is used for complicated data types such as strings, hashes, and so on. It is an adaptable engine. With the help of

these engines, you can deploy and manage cache environments. With Amazon ElastiCache, you can add an in-memory layer or cluster to infrastructure within a minute.

There are number of caching patterns, which we can implement by using Amazon ElastiCache, but the most common pattern is a cache-aside pattern that is used to read and operate data from data storage.

To optimize the performance of your application, caching is one of the best tools for less frequently accessed data. Querying a database is expensive as compared to retrieving data from the in-memory cache. The in-memory Cache improves application performance by giving frequent access to the data or storing the data. It also enhances latency and responsiveness for heavy applications, such as gaming, Q&A portals, and social networking data stored in an in-memory cache rather than storing in the database.

Cache Engines

With the help of Amazon ElastiCache, you can deploy two different types of cluster cache engines.

1. Memcached
2. Redis

Both of them are quite similar, but they provide different functionalities and different types of support.

 Memcached:

It is frequently used as a memory object caching system. When you wish to cache objects like a database, ElastiCache is the simplest model. It can scale, add, and remove nodes in response to your system's needs. When you need to run huge nodes with several cores and threads, you can use it. When you wish to distribute data across numerous nodes, you can use Memcached. You can partition your cluster into small sections and run them all at the same time for high throughput. The cluster in Memcached is distributed over numerous machines. When the number of nodes in the cluster grows, auto-discovery becomes more useful. The configuration endpoint and other nodes register the new node. When we remove that node, it automatically deregisters; in both scenarios, other nodes update their cache node metadata. It also detects node failure automatically and replaces it. Auto-discovery is enabled in all ElastiCache Memcached cache clusters. It simplifies code without any need to know about infrastructure topology. To put it another way, auto discovery detects nodes in the cluster, puts them up, and manages their connections.

Redis:

It is an open-source, in-memory object caching system that supports data structures like sorted sets and lists. It is used when you need to sort and rank datasets, which is an advanced feature. It replicates data from primary storage to one or more read replicas for availability. It provides automatic failover if any of your primary nodes fail by making a replica for a new master by using Multi-AZ. It has published and subscribe capability, which allows you the flexibility of changing consumption of messages in the future without any modification in the component of the message producing in the first time.

Redis can back up your data to restore the cluster or provide that data to the new cluster. In the Memcached engine, a backup of data does not exist because it starts empty. Backing up of data starts by preserving data in the disk and creating a snapshot, which is a complete replica of original data that is used later as per our requirement. Redis backed up data is stored in Amazon S3. Then this data is managed by ElastiCache API, AWS management console, and AWS CLI.

Requirement	Memcached	Redis
Simple Cache to offload database	Yes	Yes
Ability to scale horizontally	Yes	No
Multithreaded performance	Yes	No
Advance data type	No	Yes
Ranking/sorting data sets	No	Yes
Pub/Sub capabilities	No	Yes
Persistence	No	Yes
Multi-AZ	No	Yes
Backup and restore capabilities	No	Yes

Table 6-07: Memcached vs. Redis

EXAM TIP: According to your requirement, Amazon ElastiCache allows you to choose the cache engine. Memcached is used in the case of simple storage of in-memory objects, which are scaled horizontally. Redis engine is used in case of backup and restore data. It needs a large number of read replica, and it is used for data structures like sorted sets and lists.

Scaling

Amazon ElastiCache allows resizing of the environment according to the demand of workload as per time. You can scale in or scale out, by adding or removing the cache node from the cluster. Horizontal expansion is easy while scaling vertically; you can use different classes of cache nodes.

1. Horizontal Scaling:

Amazon ElastiCache allows you to scale your cache environment horizontally depending upon the cache engine. As we know, Memcached performs partitioning of data, so it is easy to scale horizontally because it has 1 to 20 nodes. Through auto-discovery, it automatically discovers the added or deleted nodes in a cluster.

Redis contains only one cache node, which performs both read and write operations. In Redis, there is master/slave replication, so you can add additional read-only slave nodes. In this way, you have replication of your data while you have only one write node.

2. Vertical Scaling

Amazon ElastiCache has limited support to vertical scaling. Without the help of vertical scaling, you cannot perform scaling in the cluster. It creates a new cluster according to your desired node type and alters the traffic towards the new cluster. The Memcached cluster starts out empty while in Redis cluster, it is initialized with backup.

> **EXAM TIP:** Memcached engines can be scaled horizontally by simply adding and removing nodes in the cluster. Auto-discovery discovers new nodes that are added or deleted from the cluster. Redis Engine can be scaled horizontally by creating a replication group first, then creating an additional cluster, and adding the cluster to the replication group.

> **EXAM TIP:** To back up a cluster running Redis, you need to create a snapshot. It can be created automatically or manually on demand. Memcached does not support backup and recovery features.

Use of Memcached

1. In cases when you need the simplest model for caching.

2. To distribute your data over multiple nodes. It is also useful in those cases where you need to run large nodes with multiple cores and threads.
3. For caching objects like the database, you can use Memcached.
4. To increase or decrease your system by scaling out and for the addition and deletion of nodes, you can use Memcached.

Use of Redis

1. For complex data types like hash, strings, etc.
2. To sort and rank in-memory datasets.
3. Automatic failover in case of failover.
4. For replication of data to one or more read replicas from primary for availability.
5. Backup and restore features are required in caching.
6. Pub and sub-capabilities are required.
7. Persistence of key stores.

Kinesis

To know about Kinesis, you must know about streaming data. Streaming data is the type of data, which is continuously generated by a huge number of data sources and is sent simultaneously to the data stored in small size (in KBs). Examples of streaming data are games data, the stock market, social networks, IoT sensor data, etc.

> **EXAM TIP:** Consider the use of Kinesis in a scenario where streaming of a large amount of data is needed.

Kinesis is the platform, which is used to send your streaming data. You can load, process, and analyze the streaming data cost-effectively. Through Kinesis, you can also build your customized application according to your requirements. Kinesis is basically short-term storage for data.

> **EXAM TIP:** Kinesis is not persistent storage, it basically stores streaming data, and then The Kinesis application queries this data for analysis. After analysis, it stores that data in long-term storage like S3.

Types of Kinesis

There are three services for real-time streaming data provided by Amazon Kinesis:

- ✓ Amazon Kinesis Firehouse
- ✓ Amazon Kinesis Streams

✓ Amazon Kinesis Analytics

Each service can handle unlimited data streaming.

Amazon Kinesis Streams

It is the most scalable and durable streaming data service, which brings a large amount of data and processes this stream of data in real-time. In Amazon Kinesis, streaming of data is weightless, and you can scale an unlimited amount of data by distributing it in shards. In the Kinesis stream, you can add on any type of data like application logs, click streams, etc., from various sources, and then that data will be available within seconds for the Kinesis application. If any shard is too large, it is then further distributed in shards to share the load; then the process begins by reading data from shards and running it in the Amazon Kinesis stream application. In figure 6-05, the data is generated by producers, then it is sent to Kinesis Stream and stored there for 24 hours by default, but this duration can be increased to 7 days maximum. The data is stored in shards in the Kinesis stream. The consumers then take the data from shards, and by processing the received data, consumers create some information and store this informative data in different AWS services.

In Amazon Kinesis Data Streams, the data is encrypted at the time when the producer enters data into the stream. AWS KMS master keys will do encryption in Kinesis Stream.

EXAM TIP: In Kinesis Stream, data is stored for 24 hours by default and can be extended to 7 days at maximum.

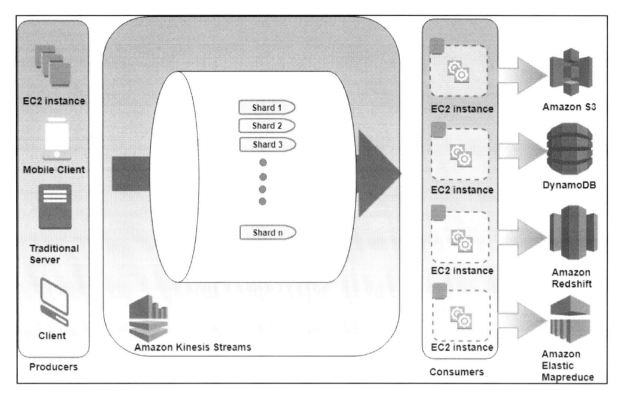

Figure 6-05: Amazon Kinesis Streams

In the given diagram, you can see the producers that are called agents that pump data to Kinesis streams where shards are present. In kinesis stream, multiple shards are present as it is a store for streaming data. Now the EC2 instances, which are consumers, pick that data and perform their own query or analysis or directly push data to S3, DynamoDB, Amazon Redshift, or EMR. For example, if you have a task for logging data, then in the **producers** side, you have a fleet of 5000 EC2 instances, 1 PutRequest per instance that pushes data into kinesis streams, where 5 shards are present because each shard support 1000 PutRequest /sec. After that, the consumers side performs analysis and forwards process data to any of the persistence storage.

Key Concept in Kinesis Streams:

1. Data Producers
2. Shards
3. Records
4. Data Consumers

Data Producers

Data Producers means that these can put data in Kinesis streams. It can be done in three ways:

1. By the use of Kinesis Streams API (which calls API to Amazon). For a single log file or single data record, it uses PutRecord and for multiple log files or multiple data records, use Put Records.

2. By the use of Amazon Kinesis Producer Library that is on Github. Through this library, the client does not need to produce the same logic every time when they create a new application for data insertion. You only need to install that library in your application and customize it according to your need.

3. In terms of logging data, you can use the Amazon Kinesis agent that is a built-in Java application. When you install that in your Linux, it puts logs into kinesis streams.

Shards

Shards in Kinesis are units of measurement for data. The capacity of one shard in terms of input is 1MB/sec, and in terms of output, it is 2MB/sec. In a single shard, you can support maximum of 1000 PUTS record/sec. Depending upon the requirement, you can specify the number of shards during the creation of streams. Via re-sharding, you can add or delete shards from streams dynamically for the desired throughput.

Records

Records are units of data that are put into streams. It has three different elements:

1. Partition Key is used to define which data relates to which shards. As you know, Kinesis streams are comprised of multiple shards, so via partition key, you can group the data for specific shards. It is defined by the application while putting data into the stream.

2. The sequence number in the Kinesis stream is the unique key, which belongs to each data record. It is assigned to data by the stream after data is put into the stream via the use of the client.PutRecord or Client.PutRecords. With the use of sequence numbers, you can pull the data. However, to identify which data belongs to which shards can be done by partition key.

3. Blob is the data blob that is inserted by the producers into the streams. The maximum size of data is 1MB.

Data Consumers

They are the Kinesis stream applications that are EC2 instances, which perform processing and querying of data via multiple applications running on it. Then they put that processed data into some persistent storage.

Amazon Kinesis Firehose

It is the easiest way of load streaming data in data storage. That data is analyzed by Lambda in real-time then sent to Amazon S3, Amazon ElastiCache and Amazon Redshift. It does not require any administration and gives you output by automatically scaling it according

to your data. To minimize the storage and increase the security of data, it makes streaming data compressed and encrypted. In Kinesis Firehose, there is no retention window when data comes into it; it starts analyzing the data and directly stores it to Amazon S3, or first it stores it in Amazon S3 than in Redshift or either store in Amazon ElasticCache and backs it up in Amazon S3. In Kinesis Firehose, you do not need to worry about data consumption.

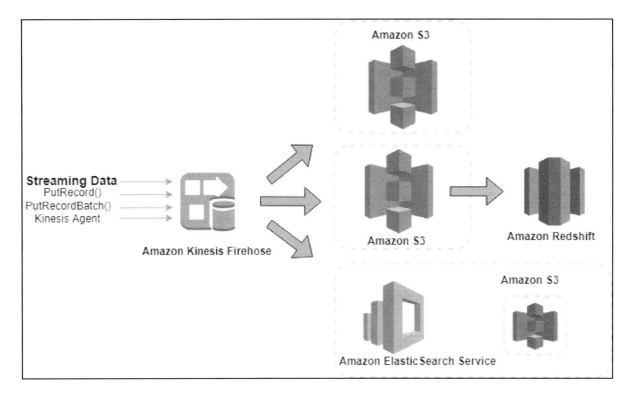

Figure 6-06: Amazon Kinesis Firehose

EXAM TIP: Amazon Kinesis Firehose is used in those cases when they need to analyze data automatically by using Lambda and not worry about consumers. Amazon Kinesis streams are used in scenarios when they talk about shards.

Amazon Kinesis Analytics

Amazon Kinesis Analytics allows you to run SQL Queries of data that exist in Kinesis Firehose and Kinesis Streams. Amazon Kinesis Analytics uses that SQL queries to store data in Amazon S3, Amazon Redshift, and ElastiCache. It is used when you need to use standard SQL to build the streaming application for process streaming data instead of another Programming language. It automatically scales your throughput according to the rate of your data.

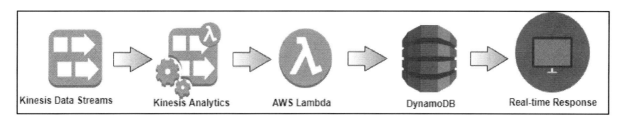

Figure 6-07: Kinesis Analytics

DynamoDB Scaling

DynamoDB Scaling is divided into two dimensions, i.e., Throughput (Read/Write Capacity Units) and Size (Single item can be maximum 400KB).

Terminologies

Term	Description
Partition	It is a physical space to store DynamoDB data
Partition Key	It is a unique identifier for every record and sometimes also known as Hash key
Sort Key	It is the second part of a composite key, where the first part is Partition Key. It defines the storage order. Sometimes it is also known as Range Key

Table 6-08: DynamoDB Scaling Terminologies

Scaling

DynamoDB adds partitions for scaling (Scale out).

Partition Calculations	
By Capacity	(Total RCU* /3000) + (Total WCU** /1000)
By Size	Total Size /10GB
Total Partitions	Roundup for the MAX(By Capacity, By Size)

Table 6-09: Partition Calculations

*RCU is Read Capacity Unit

**WCU is Write Capacity Unit

For example, you have a 10 GB table and have 2000 RCU and WCU.

Partition Calculations	
By Capacity	(2000 RCU* /3000) + (2000 WCU** /1000) = 2.66
By Size	10 /10GB =1
Total Partitions	MAX (2.66, 1) = Roundup (2.66) =3 Partitions

Table 6-10: Example Partition Calculations

DynamoDB allocates equal Read and Write Capacity Units for each partition. It also allows some burst capacity, which is the single partition; it is available if you are not using the other partitions.

Hash Keys

Partition 1
Hash 00xxx – FFxxx

Partition 1	Partition 2
Hash 00xxx – 80xxx	81xxx - FFxxx

Partition 1	Partition 2	Partition 3
00xxx - 55xxx	56xxx – Aaxxx	ABxxx - FFxxx

For example, a data collection system is designed to collect data from sensors. If you choose the partition key of "date", a number of readings are collected in a day; therefore a lot of data will be stored in one partition because the date Hash will be the same. Other partitions will be unused, and only one partition WCU will be filled. When you read the data, only a single partition will be scanned. This is known as the hot partition or hot key issue.

To solve this issue, you can choose "sensor_ID" as a partition key and date as the sort key. When sensor IDs are hashed out, they can be stored in different partitions. Through this, write capacity is used in a better way and also, read capacity is utilized evenly.

DynamoDB Auto scaling

It allows you to define the limits of WCU and RCU; when the limit is reached, DynamoDB is scaled up.

When DynamoDB reaches the specified limit, the DynamoDB configuration triggers the CloudWatch notification. This notification tells the application for auto-scaling process to update the DynamoDB table. CloudWatch notification also enables SNS notification sent for the user knowledge.

Important Points

- Try to stay close to target utilization when using the Target Tracking method
- Recently, DynamoDB does not scale down if the table's consumption drops to zero because DynamoDB cannot figure out that whether the demand is gone down or the table is not used
  - ✓ Workaround 1 is that you can send requests at a minimal level so that DynamoDB can get that the average load is dropped
  - ✓ Workaround 2 reduces max capacity manually to the min capacity
- Auto Scaling also supports the Global Secondary Indexes. It acts as a copy of the original table

DynamoDB On-Demand Scaling

It is an alternative to Auto scaling and is useful when you cannot figure out the anticipated capacity requirement. You can allocate the capacity whenever required; no provisioned capacity is required. It is more expensive as compared to traditional provisioning and Auto scaling.

DynamoDB Accelerator (DAX)

DAX is the in-memory cache that is placed in front of the DynamoDB table. It provides caching in the DynamoDB API supported format. This will boost up the response time.

Use Cases

- You can use DAX when you require the fastest response time
- Use DAX when using read-intensive applications
- Do not use DAX if your application is write-intensive
- Do not use DAX when you are already using client caching methods

CloudFront Part 2

Amazon CloudFront is AWS global CDN. Once a user requests for the content that Amazon CloudFront is serving, the user is moved towards the edge location where the content is

cached. You can get the content in the best possible way with lower latency. If the content is in an edge location, it will be delivered to the user but, if it is not in edge location, it will be taken from the origin. CloudFront caches both static and dynamic content at edge locations.

Dynamic content delivery is achieved via HTTP cookies that are forwarded from your origin. CloudFront supports Adobe Flash Media Server's RTMP protocol, but you must select the RTMP delivery method.

Web distributions use HTTP or HTTPS but also support media streaming and live to stream.

Origin and Behaviors

Origins can be any web server like S3, ELB, or EC2. Multiple origins can also be configured. You can use behaviors to configure serving up origin content based on URL paths.

For example, a word press site, where Route53 is coming to the CloudFront distribution. Static content is in the S3 bucket, and the dynamic content is coming to ELB and then directed to the EC2 fleet.

Invalidation Request

1. You can delete the files from the origin and wait for the TTL to expire.
2. You can use the AWS console to request invalidation either for all contents or specify the path.
3. To submit an invalidation request, you can use CloudFront API.
4. Third-party tools are also available for invalidation of caches, such as CloudBerry, Ylastic, and CDN Planet.

Zone Apex Support

CloudFront supports Zone Apex DNS entries. It is a domain name without www or any subdomain.

Geo-Restrictions

CloudFront also supports Geo-Restrictions. It is useful when you want to restrict some countries or geography to view your content.

Amazon Simple Notification Service

Amazon SNS (Amazon Simple Notification Service) is a cloud-based web service that makes it easy to set up, run, and provide notifications. It gives developers a highly scalable, versatile, and cost-effective way to send messages from an app and have them sent to subscribers quickly.

Amazon SNS follows the "publish-subscribe" messaging paradigm, with notifications being delivered to the subscriber using a "push" mechanism that excludes the need to check again and again or "poll" for new data and updates.

Simple APIs requires no development effort, have no maintenance or administrative cost, and are priced on a pay-as-you-go basis. Amazon SNS provides a straightforward way for developers to integrate a robust notification system into their applications.

In SNS, there are two sorts of clients:

- Publishers
- Subscribers

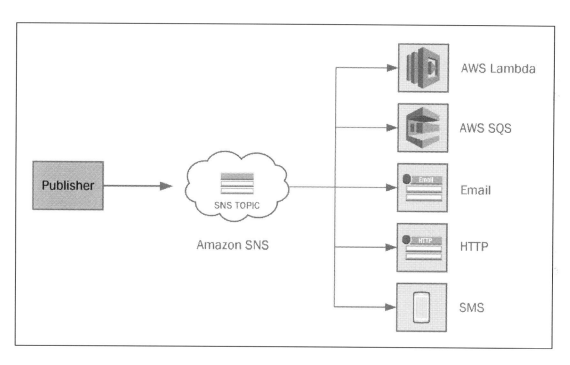

Figure 6-08: Simple Notification Service (SNS)

Common Amazon SNS Scenarios

Amazon Simple Notification Service can fulfill a huge variety of needs, including monitoring applications, workflow systems, time-sensitive data updates, mobile applications, and any other application that make or utilize notifications.

The following sections describe some common SNS scenarios:

- Fanout scenarios
- Application and system alerts
- Push email & text messaging

- Mobile push notifications

Fanout Scenarios

A fanout scenario is when SNS sends the message to a topic. Once a message is sent, then it is replicated and pushed to multiple Amazon Simple Queue Service (SQS) queues, HTTP endpoints, or email addresses. This allows parallel nonsynchronous processing.

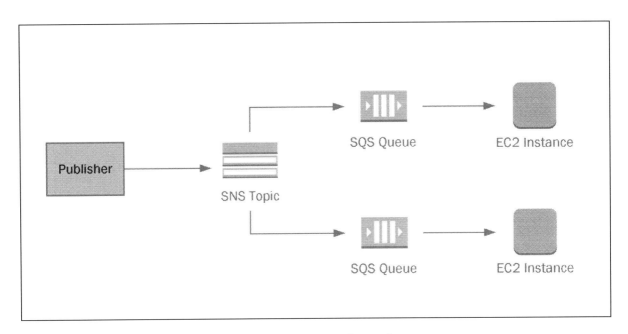

Figure 6-09: Fanout Scenarios

Application and System Alerts

Application and system alerts are SMS or email notifications that are produced by pre-defined thresholds.

Push Email and Text Messaging

Via Push email and text messaging, you can convey messages to a single person or group via email or SMS.

Mobile Push Notification

You can send messages straight to mobile applications via mobile push notifications. You may use this to send messages to Facebook, WhatsApp, and other mobile and desktop applications.

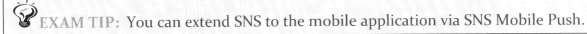
EXAM TIP: You can extend SNS to the mobile application via SNS Mobile Push.

Push Notification Supported Services

1. Apple Push Notification Service (APNS) for both iOS and MAC
2. Amazon Device Messaging (ADM)
3. Windows Push Notification Service (WPNS)
4. Baidu Cloud Push
5. Microsoft Push Notification Service for Windows Phone (MPNS)
6. Google Cloud Messaging for Android (GCM)

Steps for Mobile Push Notification

1. Request for Credentials from the Mobile Platform to connect it with push notification service.
2. Request for Token by using credentials from the mobile platform; token represents mobile app and device.
3. Create a Platform application object. The credentials stored in SNS is as Platform application resource.
4. Create a Platform endpoint object. The Token in SNS serves as an object called platform endpoint.
5. When SNS is configured then send a push notification to mobile endpoint.

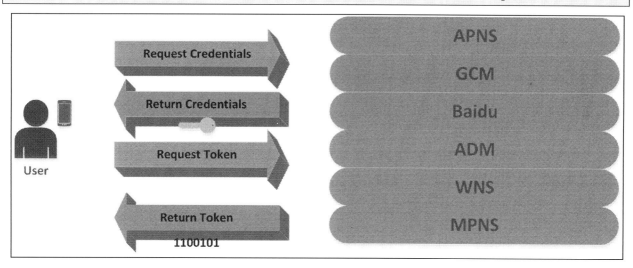

Figure 6-10: Request Messages to Mobile Platform

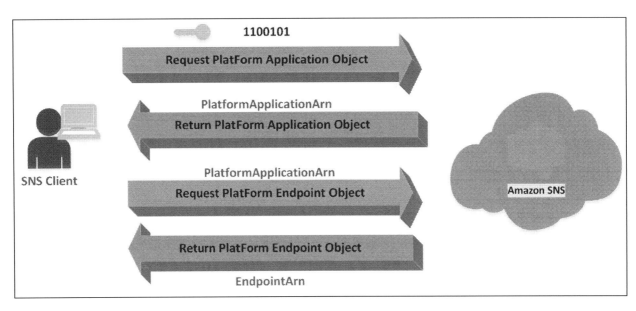

Figure 6-11: Requests Messages to SNS

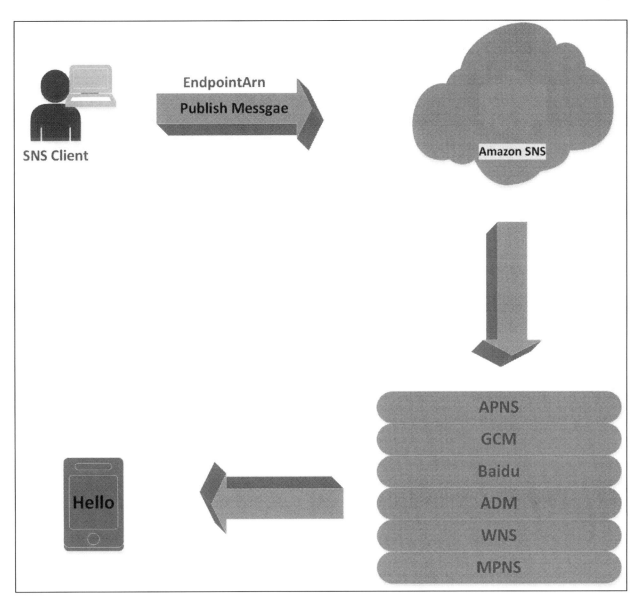

Figure 6-12: Push Message

EXAM TIP: In SNS push notification, each platform endpoint correlates to a single specific platform application. By using credentials that are stored in correspondence, platform applications can be used to communicate each platform endpoint.

Amazon SQS*

The Amazon Simple Queue Service is a fully managed message queuing service that is quick, dependable, and scalable. It is the first AWS service that is open to the public. For encrypted messaging, it supports connections with KMS. Amazon SQS is a distributed

queuing system that allows web applications to queue messages so quickly that they are consumed by another component in the application.

Amazon SQS is a cloud service that provides access to a message queue that may be used to save messages while they are being processed by a computer.

Amazon's SQS makes it simple and profitable to decouple the items of a cloud application. You can use Amazon's simple queue services to transfer any volume of data, at any level of throughput, without any loss of messages or requiring other services to be continuously available. It can also be used to store a message of a distributed application, which can be up to 256KB of text in any format, and then you can retrieve that message through Amazon SQS API. The message size can be increased to 2GB by using a special Java SQS SDK. By default, the message stays in SQS for 4 days, and it can be configured for up to 14 days.

Loosely Coupled

A significant benefit of a queuing pattern is that you can create more loosely coupled architectures. This will help the architecture components work independently even if any of the components face downtime or any outage.

In the given architecture, the ERP system is generating messages. Middleware sends these messages to the SQS queue, which are then fetched by the EC2 instance. After the processing, they are then updated into the DynamoDB table. If the message traffic increases immediately, you need to scale horizontally (adding more EC2 instance), and this will not affect the whole architecture.

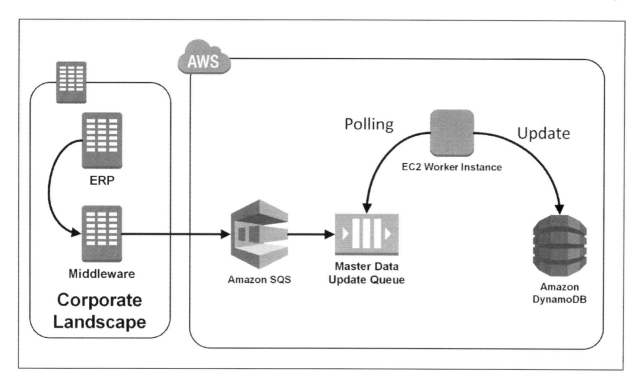

Figure 6-13: Loosely Coupled Architecture

Standard Queue

In the standard queue, there is no assurance that the messages are in order. This is because it will deliver the message according to the arrival of any message. If messages are according to the order, this will create a problem. If the first message arrives after the second message, the queue will store it as it (in incorrect order).

FIFO Queue

FIFO (First In First Out) queue is the solution for the above problem. Sequence order is maintained in it because the message is delivered according to the order. If one message is taking time (failed or stuck), other messages are held until the first message is ready, and this may include some latency but keeps the order as it is.

Lab 6-01: Scaling EC2 Using SQS

Introduction:

Amazon Elastic Compute Cloud (EC2):

Amazon Elastic Compute Cloud (Amazon EC2) is a cloud computing service that gives the durability of computing power. It is intended to make web-scale computing more accessible to IT engineers.

Amazon EC2 offers "compute" in the cloud, much as Amazon Simple Storage Service (Amazon S3) enables "storage" in the cloud. The easy web service interface of Amazon EC2 allows you to obtain and configure capacity quickly. It gives you complete control over your computing resources and will enable you to run on Amazon's tried-and-true computing infrastructure. The time to buy and boot new Amazon EC2 server instances is reduced to minutes, allowing you to scale up quickly and down capacity as your computing needs change. Amazon EC2 revolutionizes computing economics by enabling you to pay only for the resources you utilize.

Amazon Simple Queue Service (SQS):

SQS is a fully controlled message queuing tool that allows microservices, distributed systems, and serverless applications to be decoupled and expanded. SQS removes the complexity and overhead of message-based middleware management and operation, enabling developers to focus on their best actions.

Amazon SNS enables applications to deliver time-sensitive messages to multiple subscribers using a "push" technique, removing the requirement to regularly check or "poll" for updates. Amazon SQS is a queuing request service for decoupling components sending and receiving. It is used by distributed applications to exchange messages using a polling approach.

Amazon CloudWatch:

Amazon CloudWatch is a tracking service for Amazon Web Services (AWS) cloud services and software. Amazon CloudWatch may be used to collect and monitor data, monitor log files, and trigger alarms. Amazon CloudWatch can monitor AWS resources such as Amazon EC2 instances, Amazon DynamoDB tables, and Amazon RDS DB instances, as well as custom metrics and log files created by your applications and services. You can watch the resource use, application performance, and operational health throughout your system using Amazon CloudWatch. These insights might help you react and keep your app working smoothly.

Scenario:

Assume you are a solution architect at an e-commerce company that sells books just like IPSpecialist. The organization runs flash sales from time to time. When there is an increase in orders, the fulfillment backend may struggle to keep up. One method to solve the issue is to overuse EC2 instances in the fulfillment system to provide headroom to process all the orders. However, this may be quite expensive because you would have unused capacity when the traffic dies down. What if there is a better way?

Solution:

Well, there is a solution. This is what you will learn here. In this lab, you will learn to build Auto Scaling rules for EC2 based on most messages in the SQS queue, as shown in the figure.

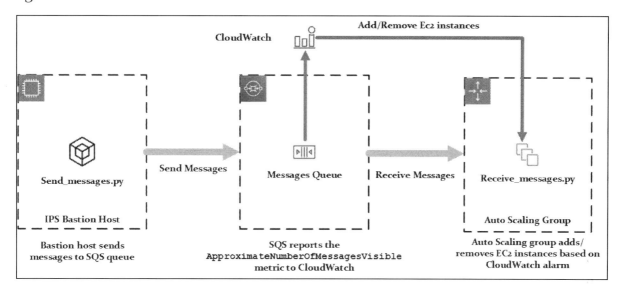

Figure 6-14 Scaling EC2 Using SQS

Follow the given steps to Scale EC2 using SQS.

Before deep-diving into the lab, create EC2 instances and Auto Scaling Groups.

1. Login into the 'AWS Console.'
2. Click on 'Services.'

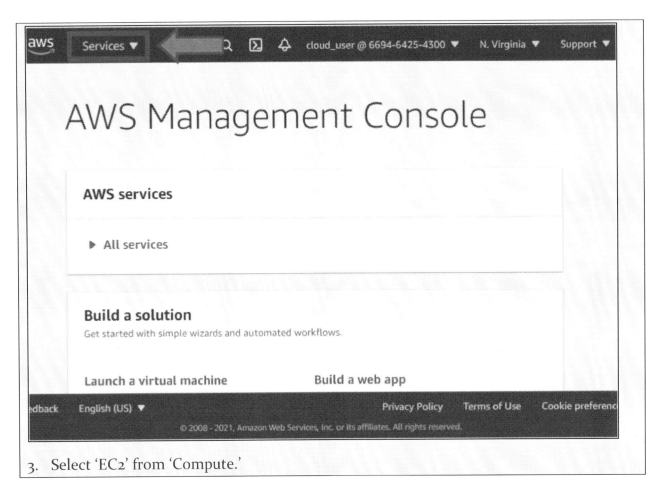

3. Select 'EC2' from 'Compute.'

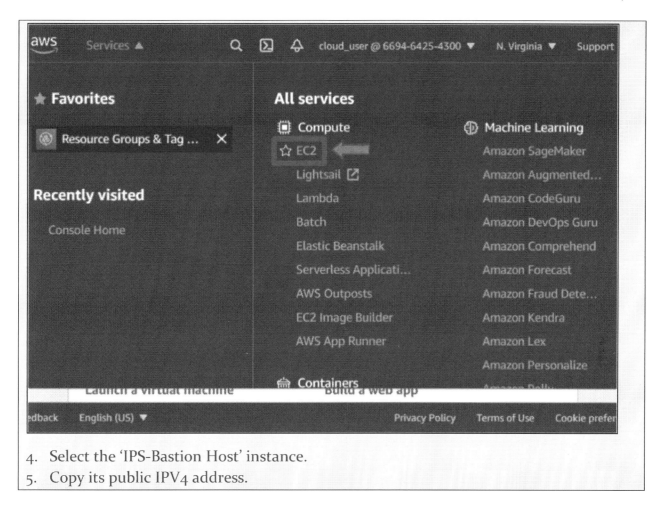

4. Select the 'IPS-Bastion Host' instance.
5. Copy its public IPV4 address.

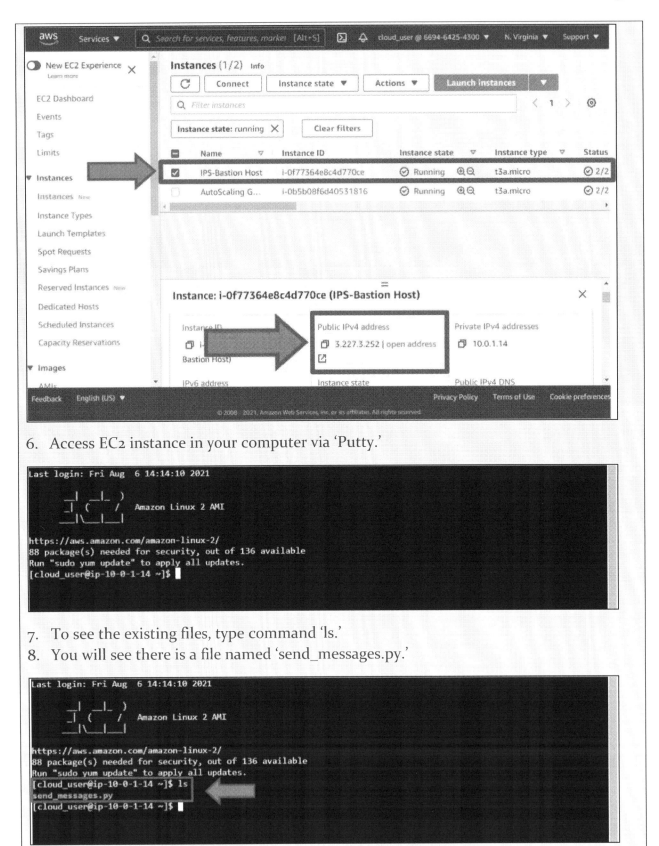

6. Access EC2 instance in your computer via 'Putty.'

```
Last login: Fri Aug  6 14:14:10 2021

     __|  __|_  )
     _|  (     /   Amazon Linux 2 AMI
    ___|\___|___|

https://aws.amazon.com/amazon-linux-2/
88 package(s) needed for security, out of 136 available
Run "sudo yum update" to apply all updates.
[cloud_user@ip-10-0-1-14 ~]$
```

7. To see the existing files, type command 'ls.'
8. You will see there is a file named 'send_messages.py.'

```
Last login: Fri Aug  6 14:14:10 2021

     __|  __|_  )
     _|  (     /   Amazon Linux 2 AMI
    ___|\___|___|

https://aws.amazon.com/amazon-linux-2/
88 package(s) needed for security, out of 136 available
Run "sudo yum update" to apply all updates.
[cloud_user@ip-10-0-1-14 ~]$ ls
send_messages.py
[cloud_user@ip-10-0-1-14 ~]$
```

9. Execute that script by typing the command '.⁄send_messages.py'. It will send messages continuously into the SQS queue, simulating a large volume of orders.

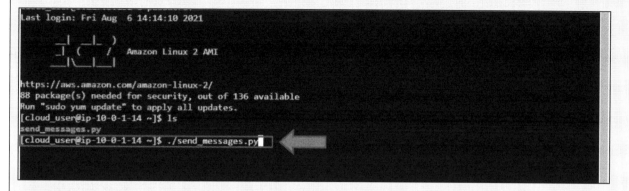

10. Go back to the AWS console. Select the 'Autoscaling Group' instance.
11. Copy its public IPV4 address.

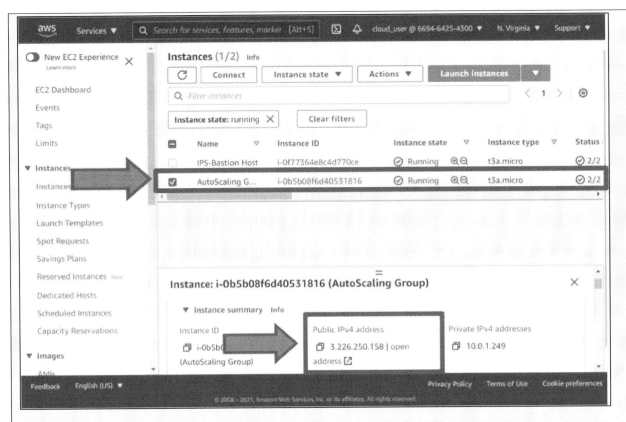

12. Access this instance via a Putty in your computer.

```
Last login: Fri Aug  6 14:14:34 2021

       __|  __|  )
       _|  (     /   Amazon Linux 2 AMI
      ___|\___|___|

https://aws.amazon.com/amazon-linux-2/
88 package(s) needed for security, out of 136 available
Run "sudo yum update" to apply all updates.
[cloud_user@ip-10-0-1-249 ~]$
```

13. To see the existing files in this instance, type command 'ls.'
14. You will see a file named 'receive_messages.py,' which is already running in the background. Hence, do not execute it.

```
Last login: Fri Aug  6 14:14:34 2021

       __|  __|  )
       _|  (     /   Amazon Linux 2 AMI
      ___|\___|___|

https://aws.amazon.com/amazon-linux-2/
88 package(s) needed for security, out of 136 available
Run "sudo yum update" to apply all updates.
[cloud_user@ip-10-0-1-249 ~]$ ls
receive_messages.log  receive_messages.py
[cloud_user@ip-10-0-1-249 ~]$
```

15. To see what is in the log file, type command 'tail –f receive_messages.log'.

16. You will see this instance is retrieving messages from the queue.

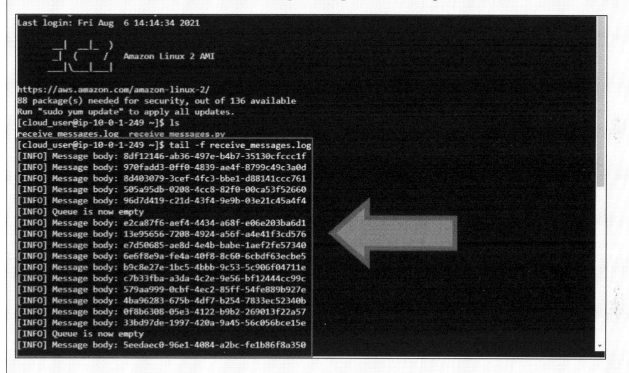

17. Leave the terminals open and running.

18. Now, create a Scale-Out Alarm.

19. Go back to the AWS console. Then go to CloudWatch. On the left-hand side, select Alarms.

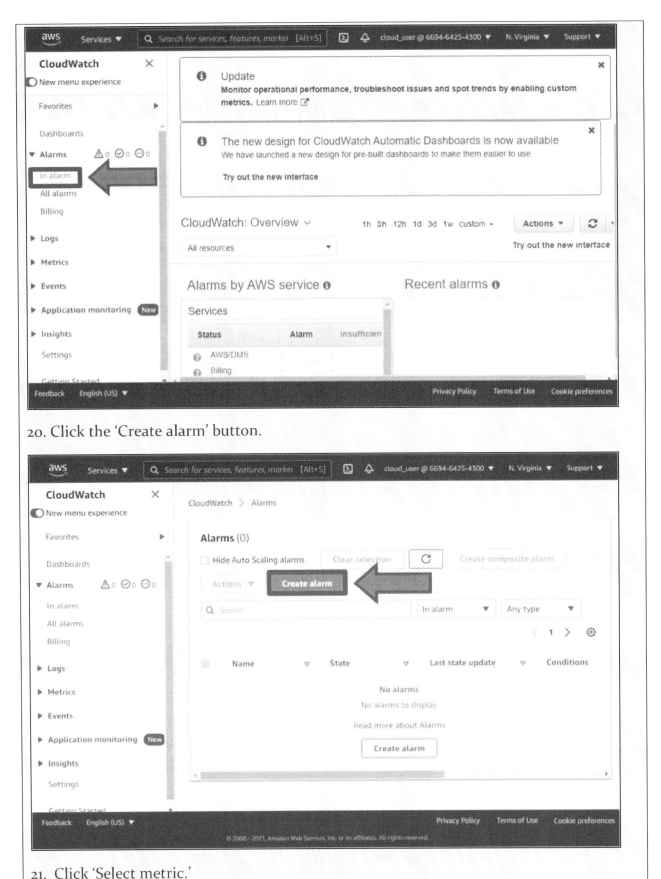

20. Click the 'Create alarm' button.

21. Click 'Select metric.'

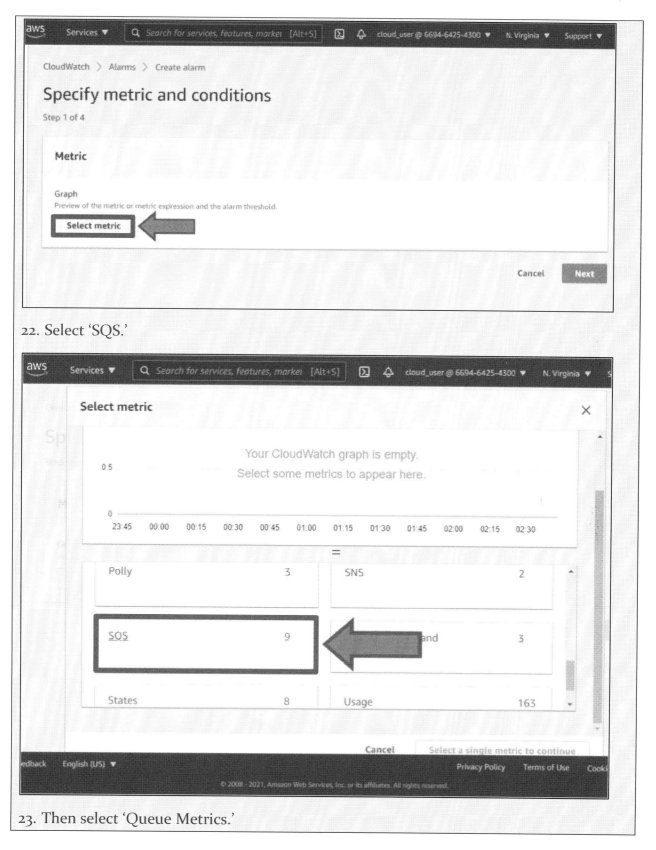

22. Select 'SQS.'

23. Then select 'Queue Metrics.'

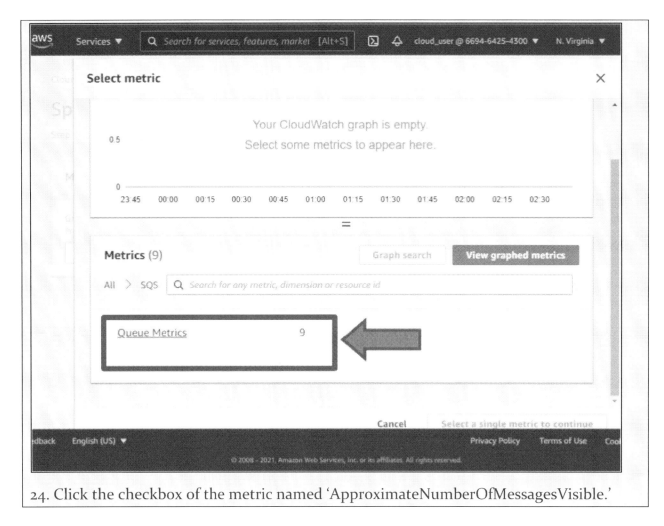

24. Click the checkbox of the metric named 'ApproximateNumberOfMessagesVisible.'

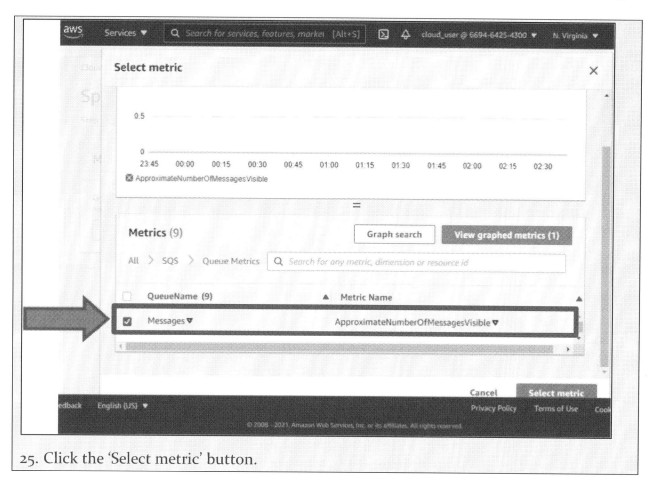

25. Click the 'Select metric' button.

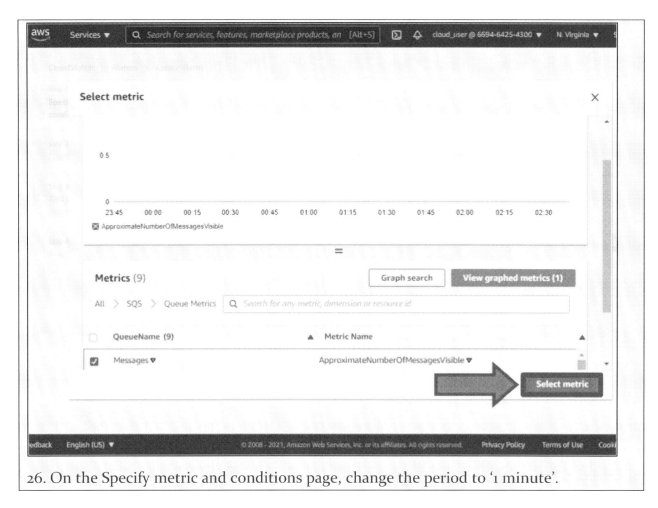

26. On the Specify metric and conditions page, change the period to '1 minute'.

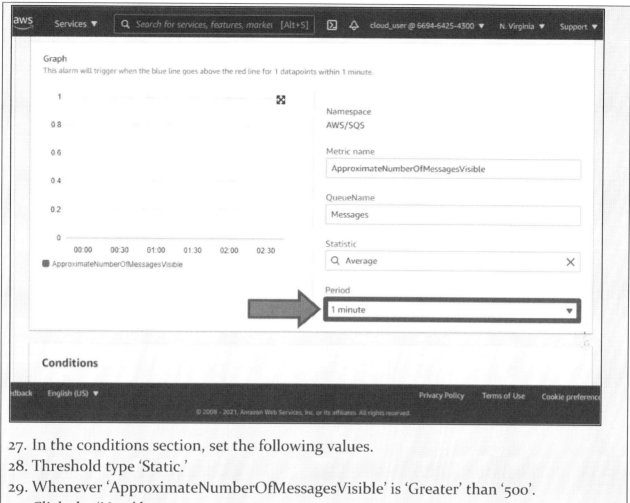

27. In the conditions section, set the following values.
28. Threshold type 'Static.'
29. Whenever 'ApproximateNumberOfMessagesVisible' is 'Greater' than '500'.
30. Click the 'Next' button.

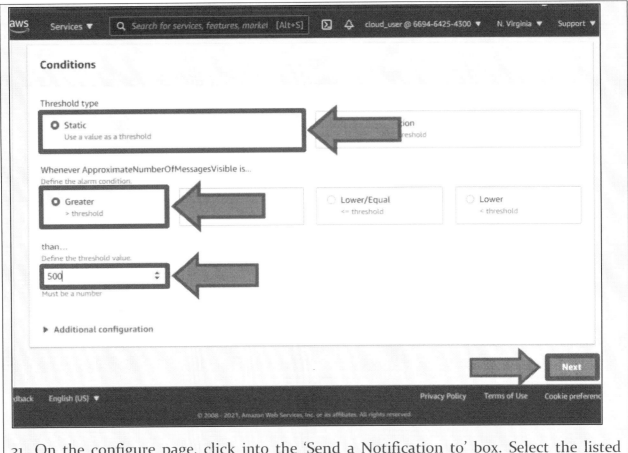

31. On the configure page, click into the 'Send a Notification to' box. Select the listed 'AutoScalingTopic.'

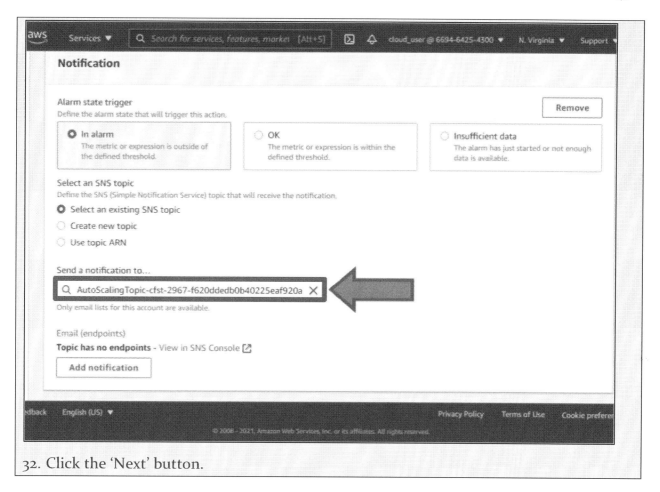

32. Click the 'Next' button.

33. For the Alarm name, enter 'Scale Out.'
34. Click the 'Next' button.

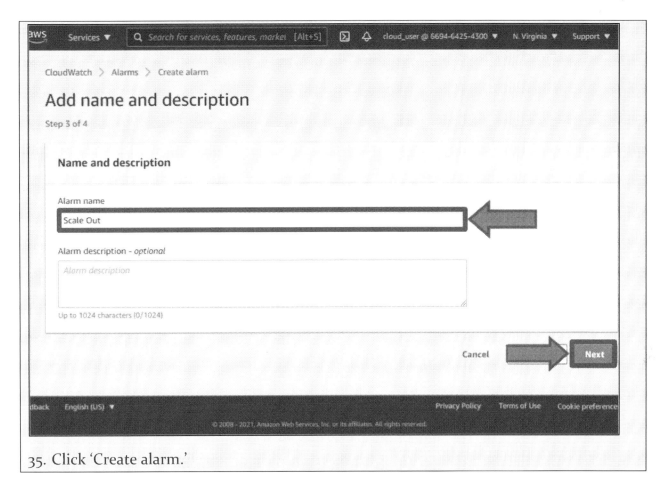

35. Click 'Create alarm.'

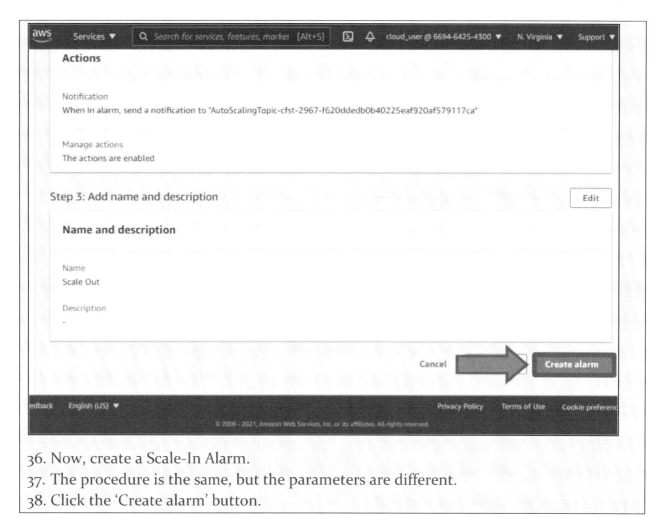

36. Now, create a Scale-In Alarm.
37. The procedure is the same, but the parameters are different.
38. Click the 'Create alarm' button.

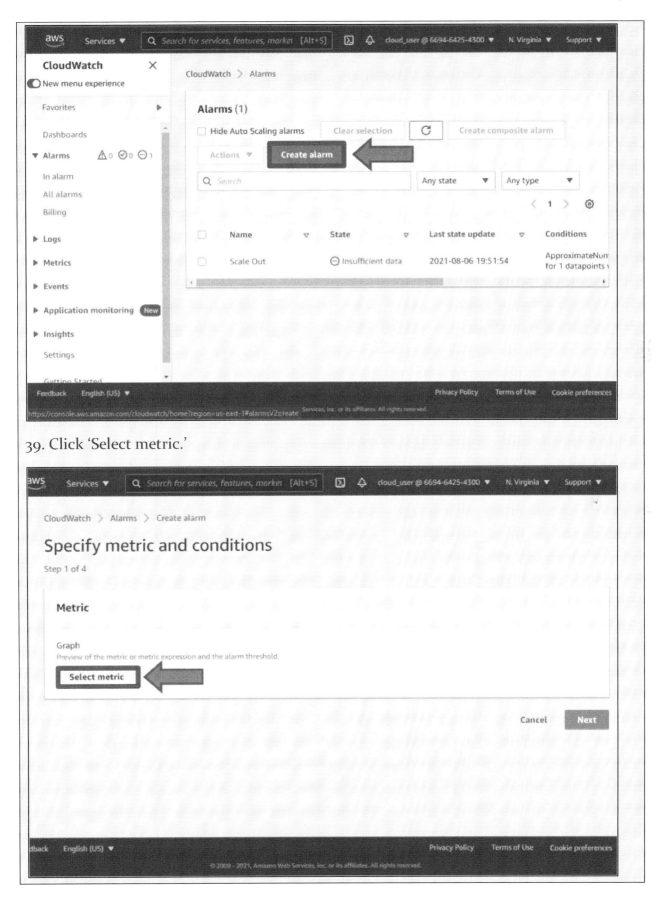

39. Click 'Select metric.'

40. Select 'SQS.'

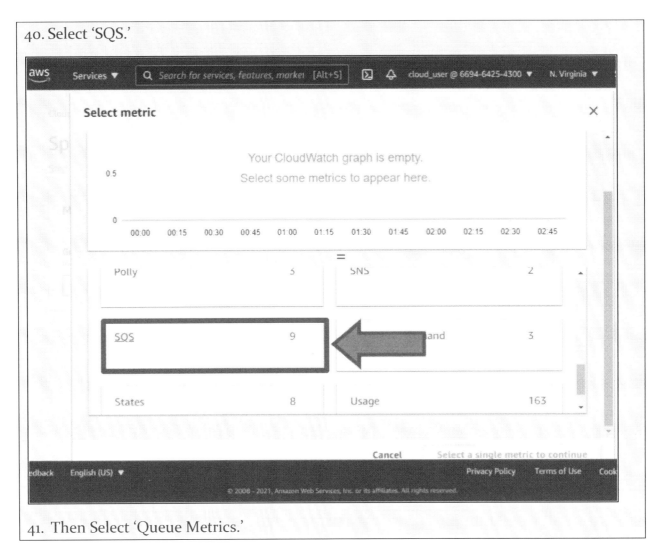

41. Then Select 'Queue Metrics.'

42. Click the checkbox of the metric named 'ApproximateNumberOfMessagesVisible.'

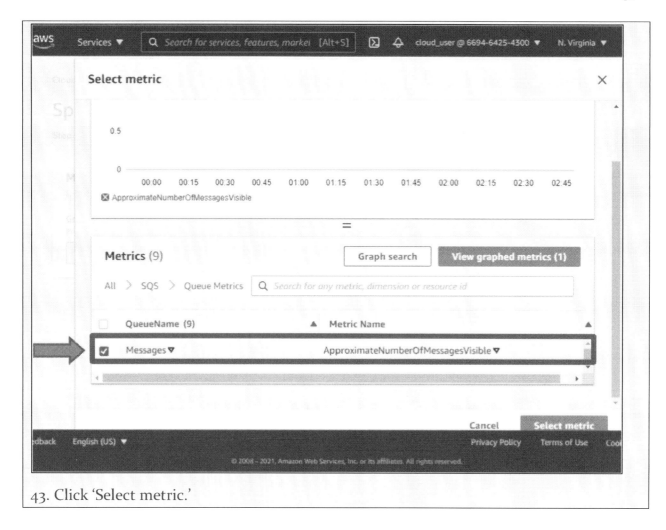

43. Click 'Select metric.'

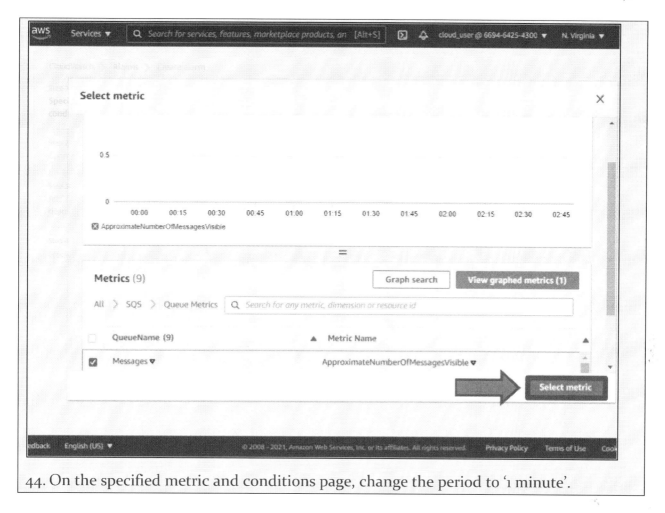

44. On the specified metric and conditions page, change the period to '1 minute'.

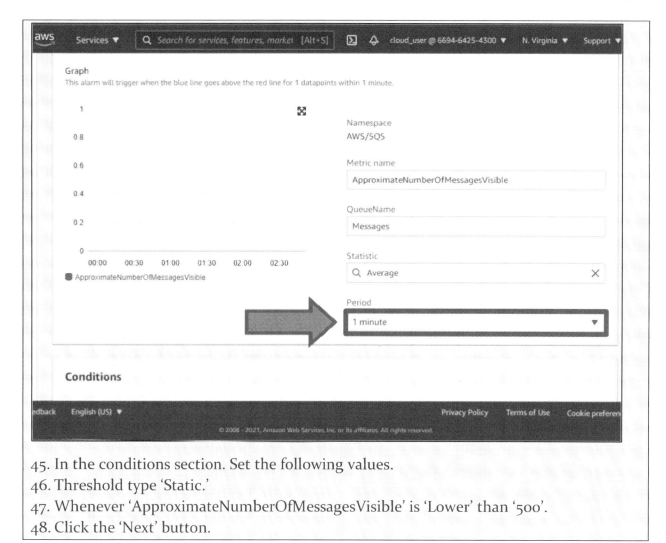

45. In the conditions section. Set the following values.
46. Threshold type 'Static.'
47. Whenever 'ApproximateNumberOfMessagesVisible' is 'Lower' than '500'.
48. Click the 'Next' button.

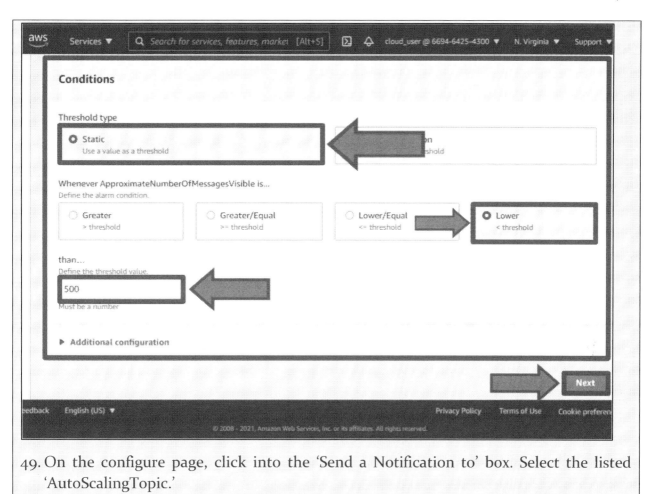

49. On the configure page, click into the 'Send a Notification to' box. Select the listed 'AutoScalingTopic.'

50. Click the 'Next' button.

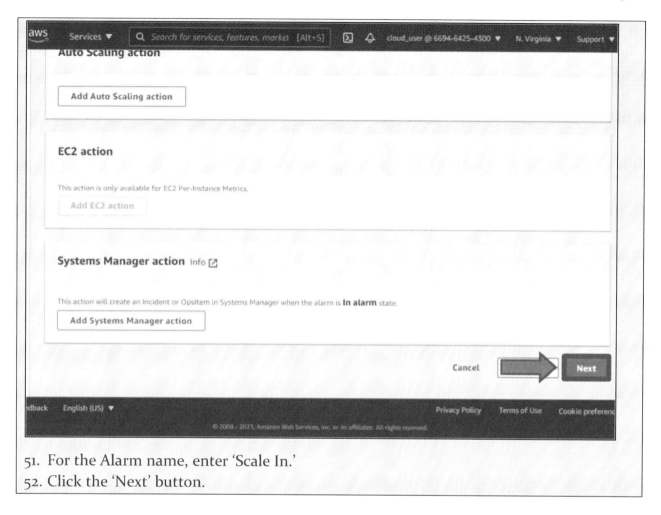

51. For the Alarm name, enter 'Scale In.'
52. Click the 'Next' button.

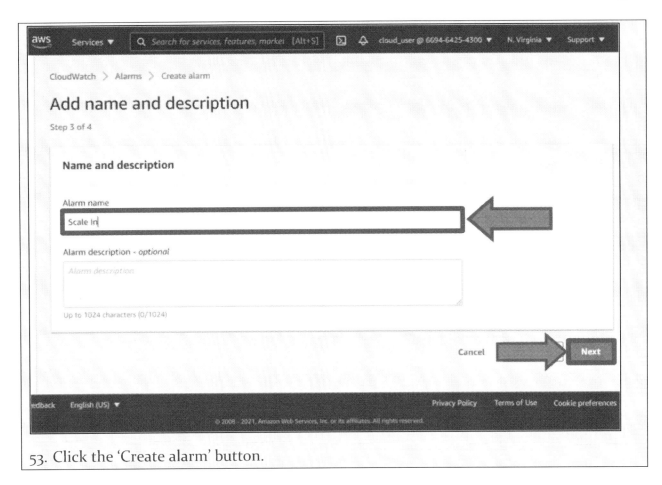

53. Click the 'Create alarm' button.

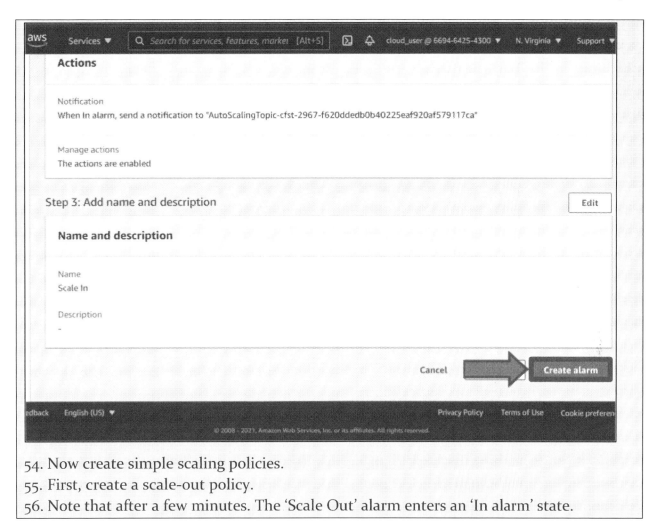

54. Now create simple scaling policies.

55. First, create a scale-out policy.

56. Note that after a few minutes. The 'Scale Out' alarm enters an 'In alarm' state.

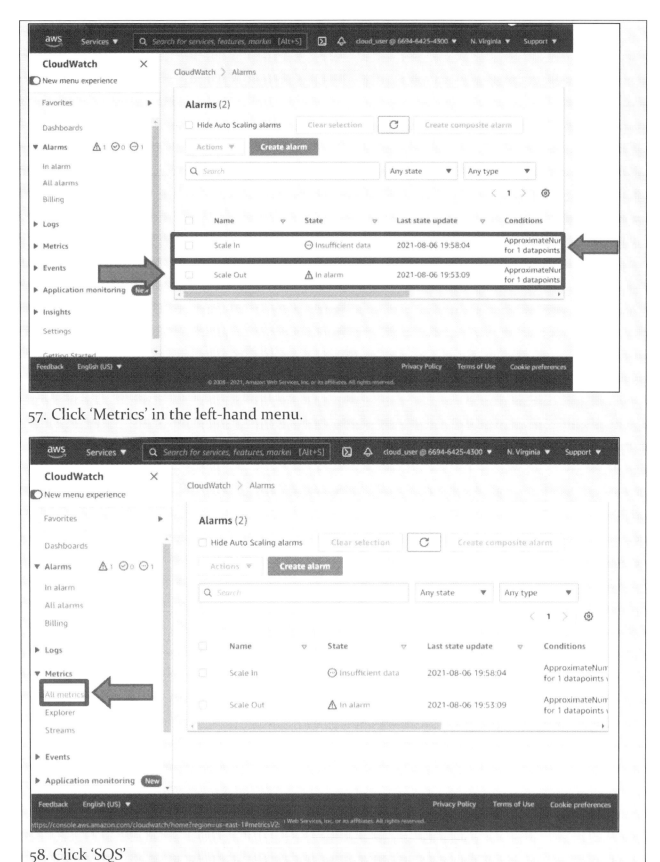

57. Click 'Metrics' in the left-hand menu.

58. Click 'SQS'

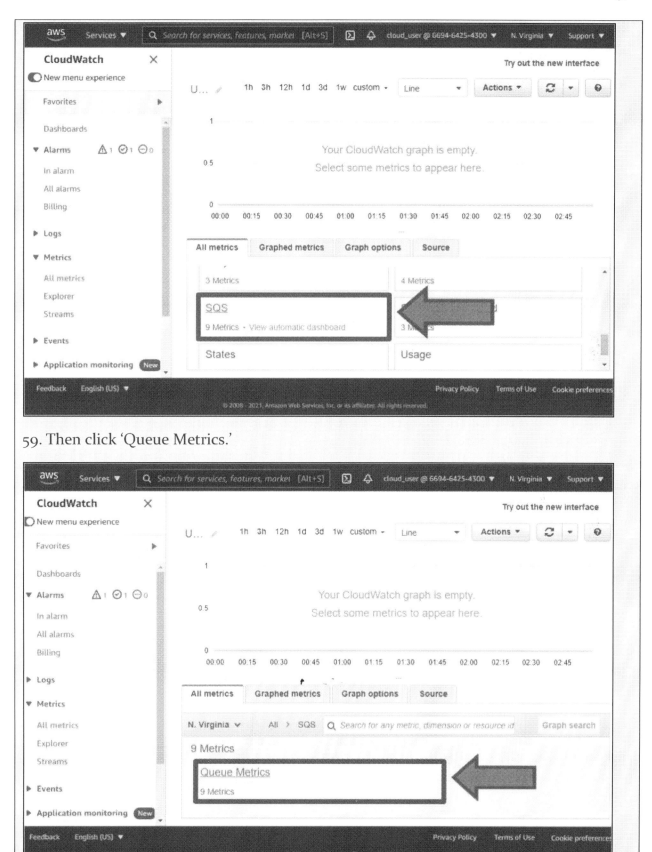

59. Then click 'Queue Metrics.'

60. Click the checkbox of the metric named 'ApproximateNumberOfMessagesVisible.'

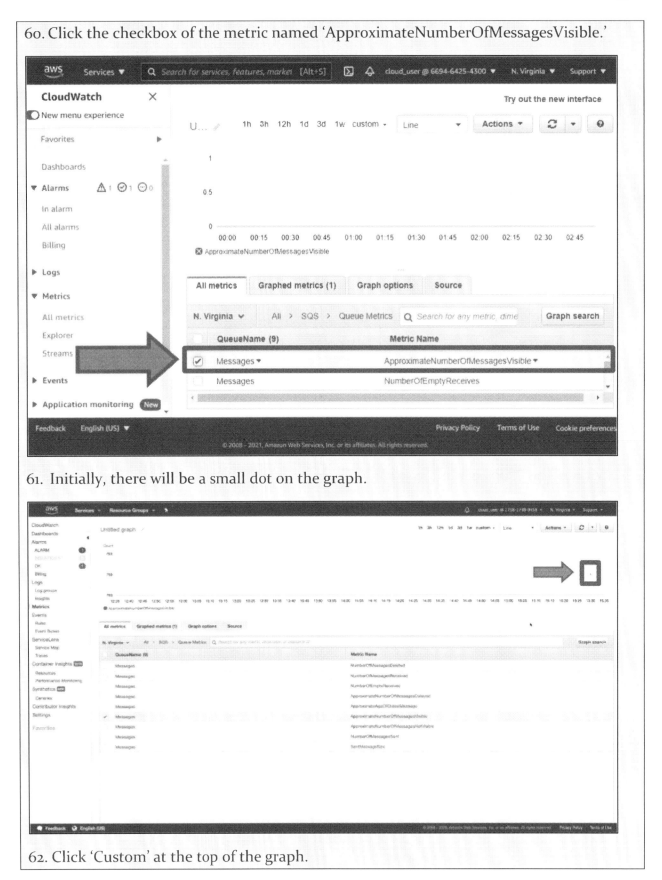

61. Initially, there will be a small dot on the graph.

62. Click 'Custom' at the top of the graph.

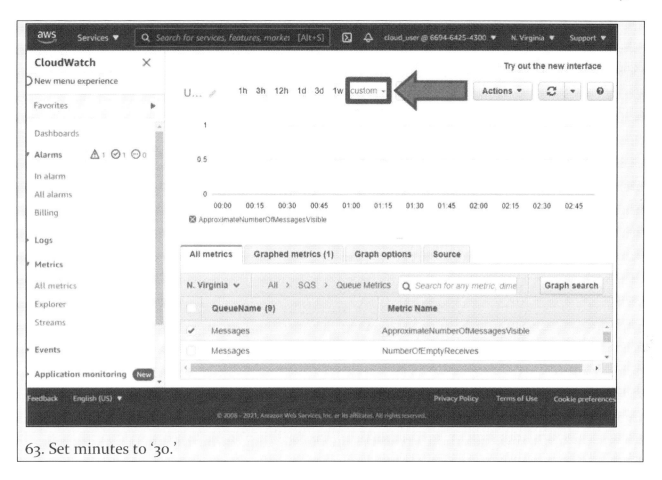

63. Set minutes to '30.'

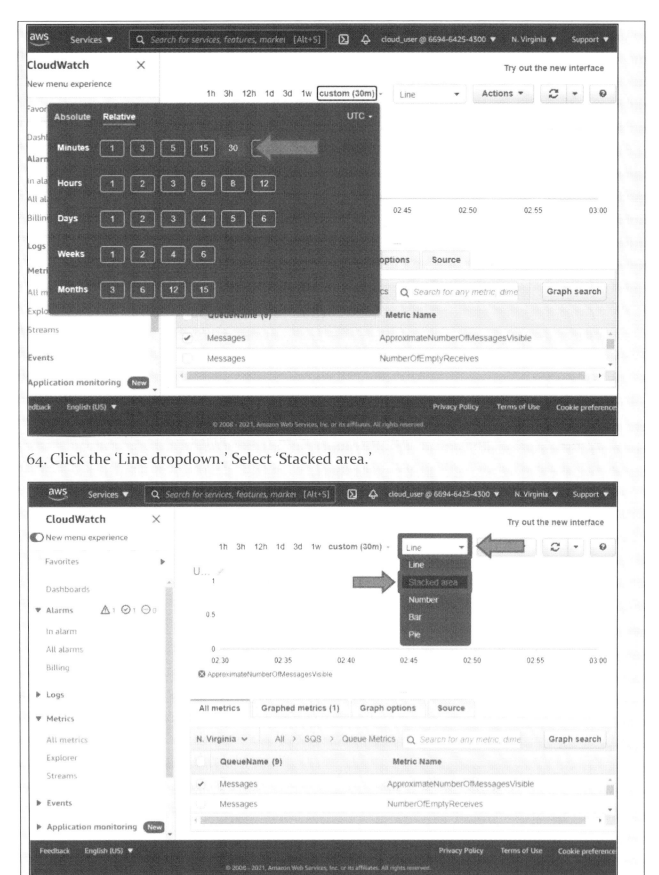

64. Click the 'Line dropdown.' Select 'Stacked area.'

65. Click the dropdown next to the refresh icon.
66. Select 'Auto-refresh.'
67. Set the refresh interval to '10 seconds'.

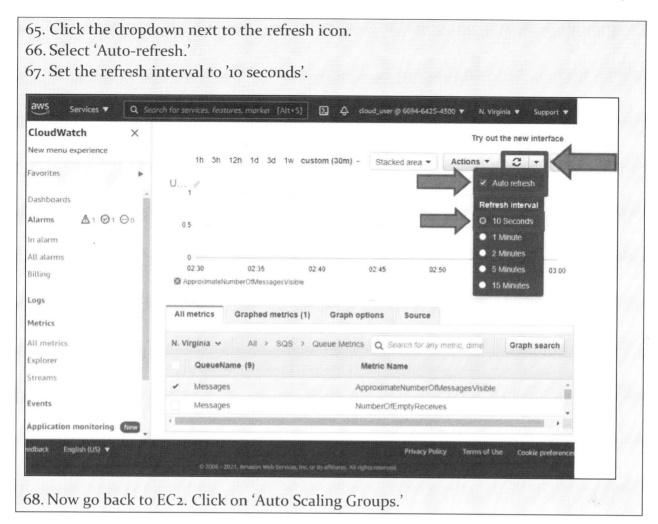

68. Now go back to EC2. Click on 'Auto Scaling Groups.'

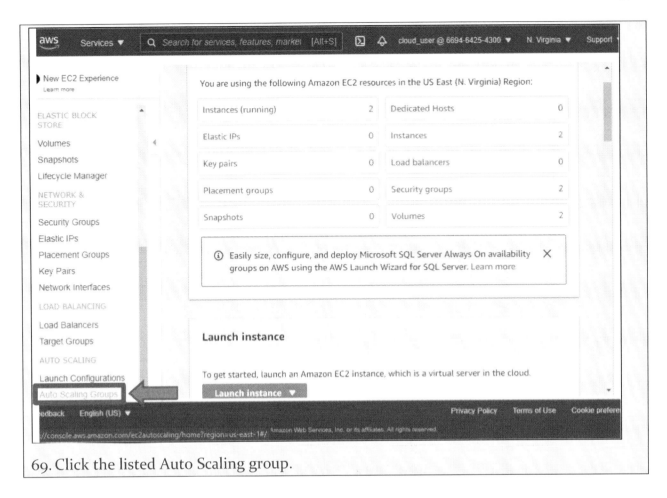

69. Click the listed Auto Scaling group.

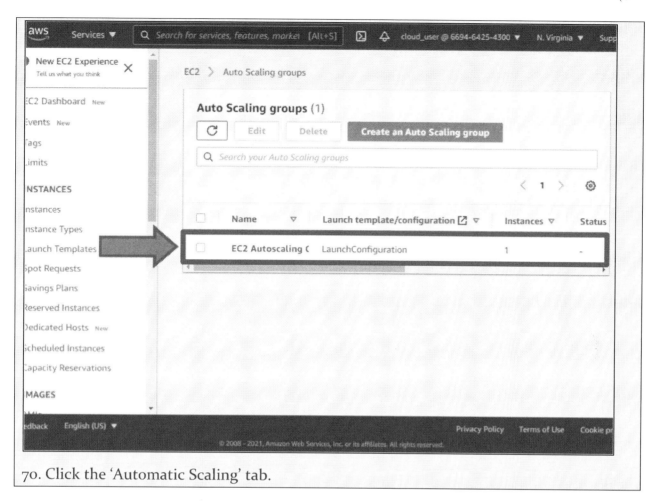

70. Click the 'Automatic Scaling' tab.

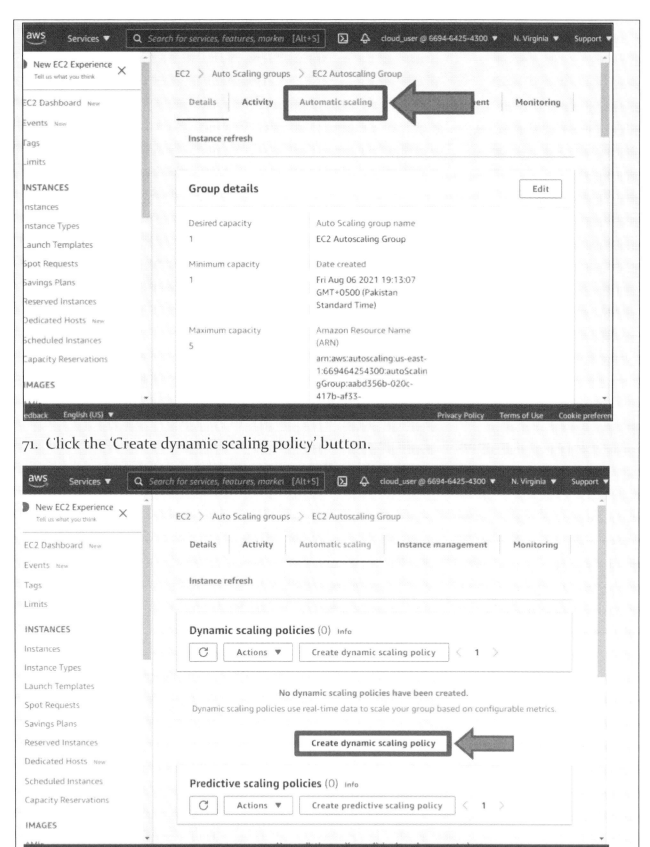

71. Click the 'Create dynamic scaling policy' button.

72. Set the following parameters.
73. Policy type 'Simple Scaling.'
74. Scaling policy name 'Scale Out.'
75. CloudWatch alarm 'Scale Out.'

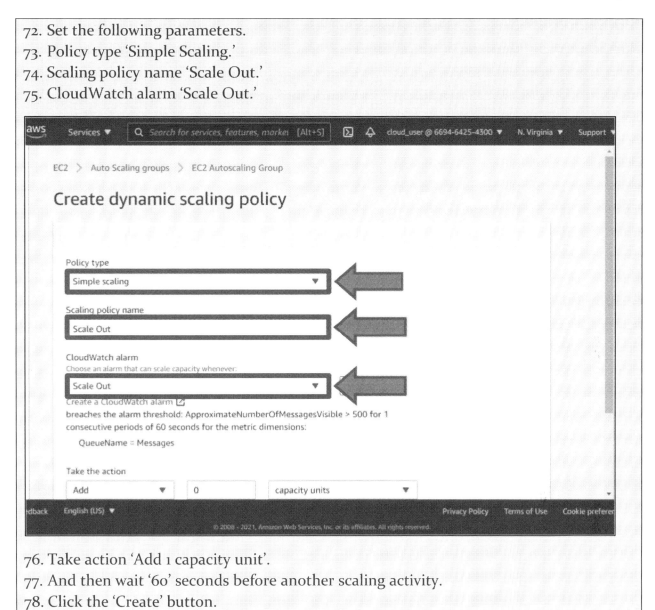

76. Take action 'Add 1 capacity unit'.
77. And then wait '60' seconds before another scaling activity.
78. Click the 'Create' button.

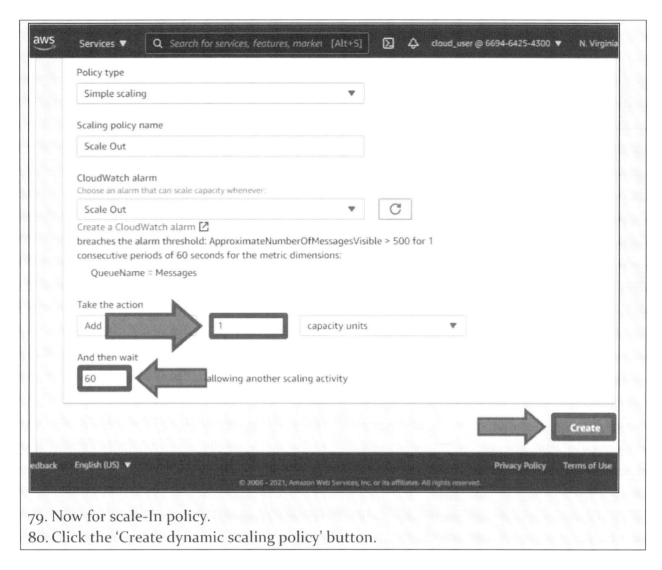

79. Now for scale-In policy.
80. Click the 'Create dynamic scaling policy' button.

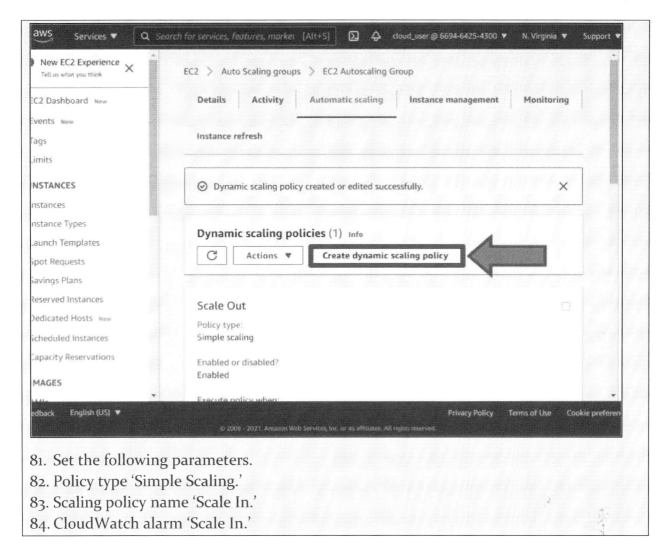

81. Set the following parameters.
82. Policy type 'Simple Scaling.'
83. Scaling policy name 'Scale In.'
84. CloudWatch alarm 'Scale In.'

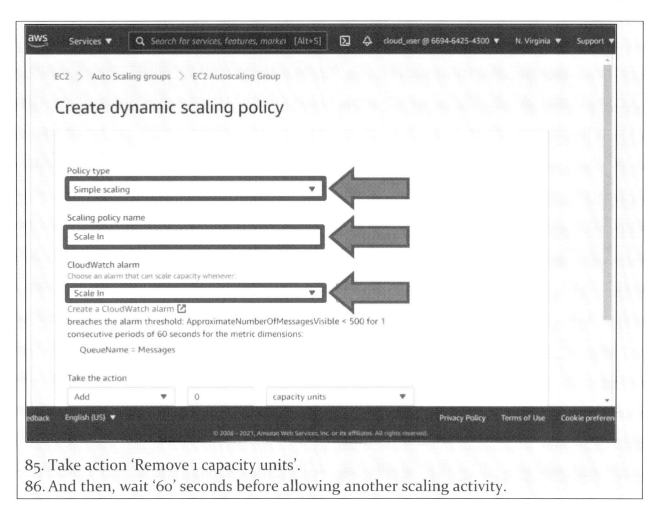

85. Take action 'Remove 1 capacity units'.

86. And then, wait '60' seconds before allowing another scaling activity.

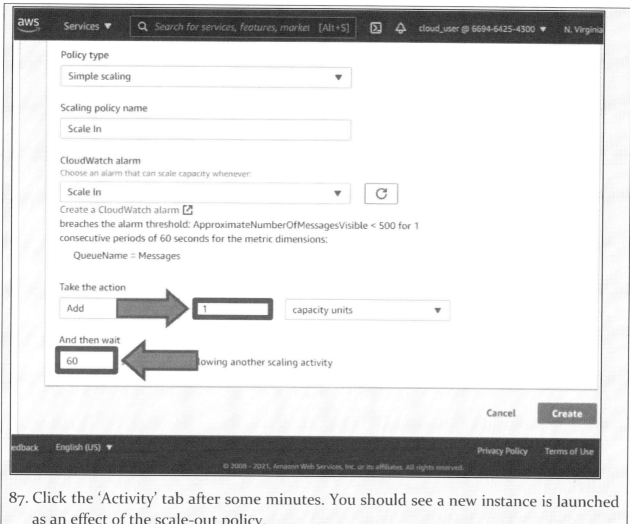

87. Click the 'Activity' tab after some minutes. You should see a new instance is launched as an effect of the scale-out policy.

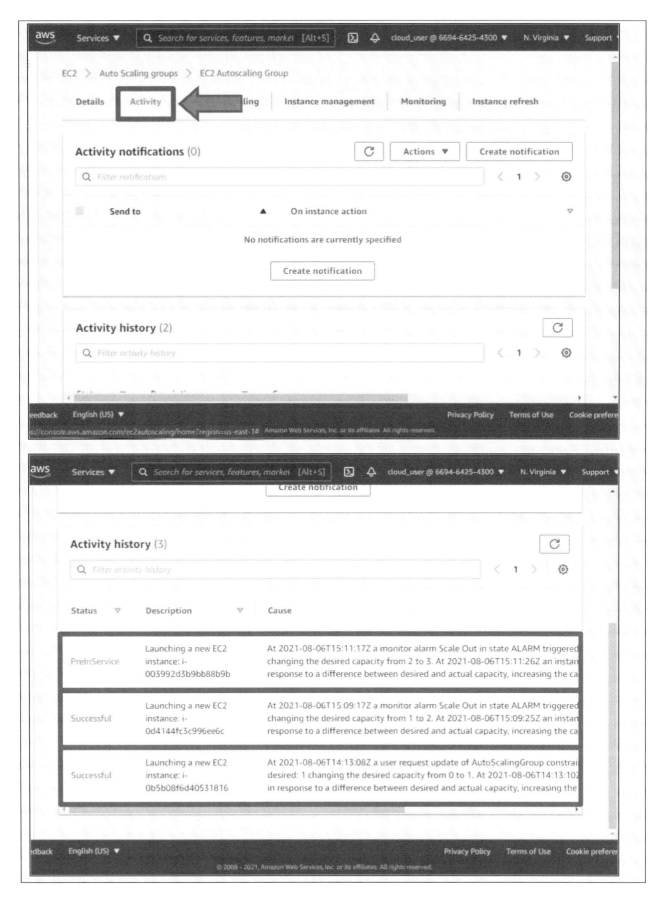

88. Click 'Instances' in the left-hand menu. You will see that a new 'AutoScaling Group' instance now exists.

Observe the Auto Scaling Groups Behavior in CloudWatch.

89. Go to 'CloudWatch.' Then go to 'Metrics.'

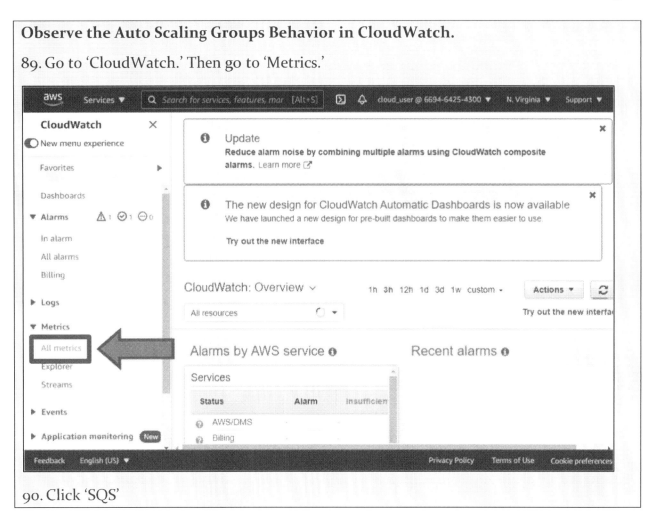

90. Click 'SQS'

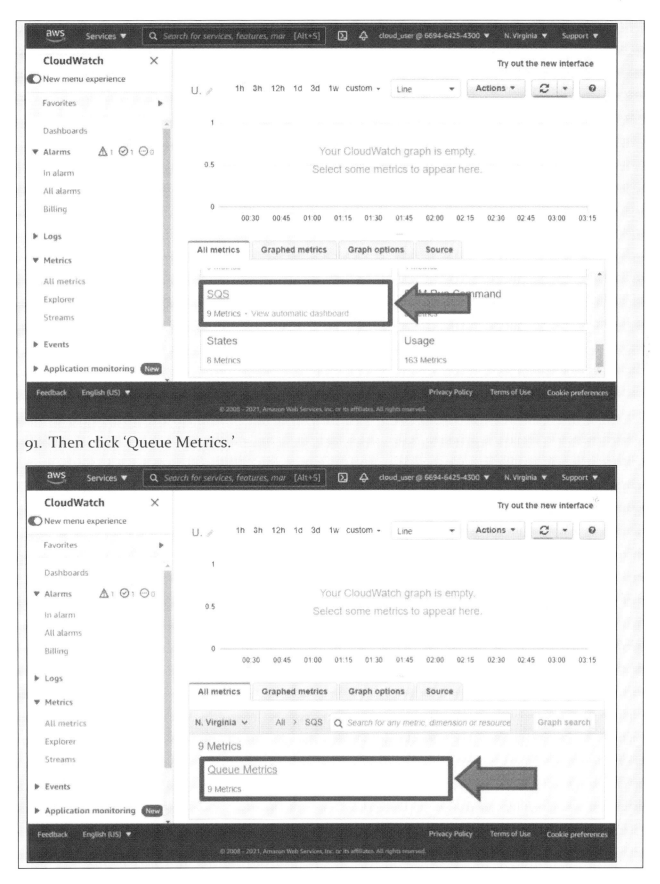

91. Then click 'Queue Metrics.'

92. Click the checkbox of the metric named 'ApproximateNumberOfMessagesVisible.'

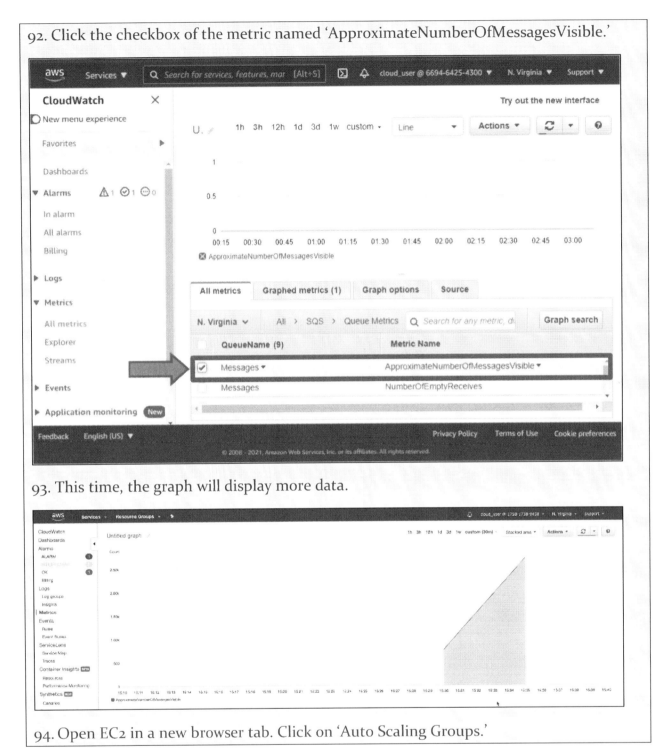

93. This time, the graph will display more data.

94. Open EC2 in a new browser tab. Click on 'Auto Scaling Groups.'

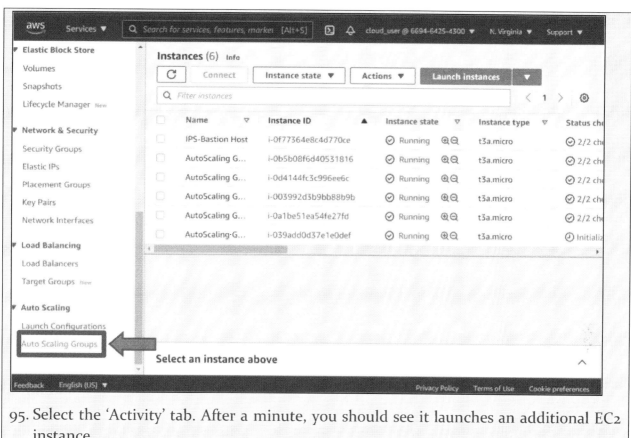

95. Select the 'Activity' tab. After a minute, you should see it launches an additional EC2 instance.

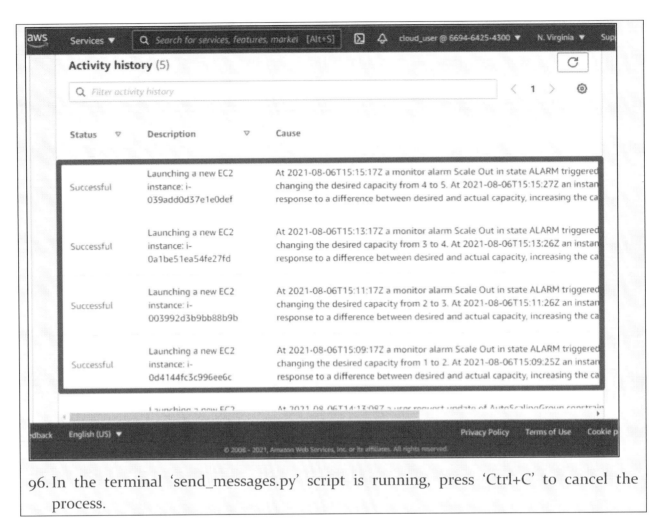

96. In the terminal 'send_messages.py' script is running, press 'Ctrl+C' to cancel the process.

```
[INFO] MessageId: de87bbde-09c0-472d-a617-1065ec5f03f2
[INFO] Sending message: 6f6fd0bc-27ec-4044-adc7-a4cf7cabcca1
[INFO] MessageId: 02f1bf6b-93d7-432b-a2a6-3d823739ff1d
[INFO] Sending message: 40cd6b0c-ab80-4188-8995-530412cfaf43
[INFO] MessageId: f387d799-17f1-4fbb-8d11-e050a56972ee
[INFO] Sending message: 3b29e480-ba75-4190-9df1-85c6db6bbd98
[INFO] MessageId: 521a59b7-dc6e-4d9c-9c82-5d6c2aa7f4fe
[INFO] Sending message: 71407cf5-b911-4260-a86e-ffcf69182957
[INFO] MessageId: acd195a6-9bde-44d9-83ab-0d8571d1ca07
[INFO] Sending message: a3317455-32b8-4f0d-91a3-20de6a3b2030
[INFO] MessageId: c859a6d9-4955-4392-b106-a1cb1d7ff824
[INFO] Sending message: 10f54e0d-58c3-42d3-9156-c53de4d591f4
[INFO] MessageId: c9da4853-54ba-4a93-bf62-837437c00c11
[INFO] Sending message: f2ae13f2-ff21-4fdb-b4aa-8f3ef60017aa
[INFO] MessageId: 11b2aca1-c7f3-4d95-9fcc-4c8ad5f6c79c
[INFO] Sending message: 2723ec0c-4fd3-4c72-bd85-99b5eaa4c92f
[INFO] MessageId: 5e0826b8-cfa3-4a98-a8b0-2ccaaee8b56b
[INFO] Sending message: be7b1d4f-9fd7-45f3-8d33-6e59b34bd22a
[INFO] MessageId: 2d64e6b5-7c24-488c-b421-b699c1ef62e6
[INFO] Sending message: 932bf353-1fe6-4662-bbb4-2c12f21dfdf9
[INFO] MessageId: c076f0fd-a163-40ad-803b-15355d9f3095
[INFO] Sending message: 7fb2d852-dcdc-48a8-9fee-a3bfdce464a5
[INFO] MessageId: a0a724fd-c791-41b3-91e4-f5447f92fd0b
[INFO] Sending message: 72b687d2-6e28-4722-a863-241a91f84d53
[INFO] MessageId: 87e9773b-a683-4532-8a9a-36365800ad4a
[INFO] Sending message: 9da71671-8a14-4543-9eb3-4c5d37298f74
[INFO] MessageId: 2f5ccfaf-ec33-4104-9241-bb2a8ea67fec
[INFO] Sending message: f6f1f92e-715b-4cdd-aa3b-eebc4e373d62

^CTraceback (most recent call last):
  File "./send_messages.py", line 43, in <module>
    sleep(args.interval)
KeyboardInterrupt
[cloud_user@ip-10-0-1-14 ~]$
```

97. Go back to the AWS console. View the CloudWatch metrics graph. After some minutes, you should see the graph start flatten out.

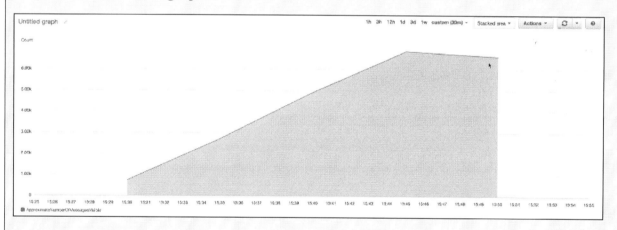

98. Wait some minutes more. You should see that the graph takes a downward turn as the messages are drained from the SQS queue.

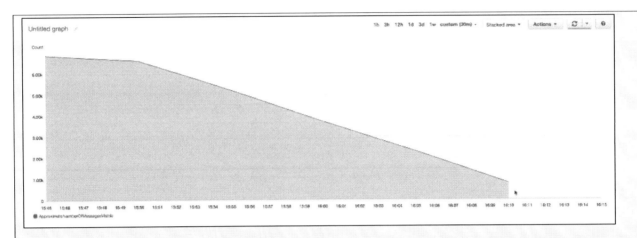

99. Go to the EC2 tab you should see instances are starting to be terminated since the 'Scale In' alarm has been triggered. It means the number of messages in the queue is below the threshold which you set. After some minutes, refresh the activity history to see that another instance is now being terminated.

Amazon MQ

It is a managed implementation of Apache ActiveMQ. An ActiveMQ is a message broker which takes messages, manages them, and allows other applications to access those messages via API. Its function is very similar to SQS, but it is a different implementation of a messaging queue. It is a fully managed service and highly available within a region. It supports ActiveMQ API, JMS, NMS, MQTT, and WebSocket. When you create a new application from scratch, then it is recommended to use SQS. If you are using the already existing application with a message broker, then use MQ in AWS.

AWS Lambda, Serverless Application Manager, and EventBridge

Lambda is a Function as a Service (FaaS) product, which means that you submit a function and AWS executes it. Server-less FaaS is a form of FaaS in which the vendor is in charge of providing provision-free scalability, and there are no virtual machines in the programming architecture. Node.js, Python, Java, Go, and C# are all supported by Lambda. It has a serverless architecture to it.

In this, unlike traditional compute, you are only billed for the number of milliseconds in which your code run. Lambda runs the code in an isolated environment and is also stateless, but you are responsible for persistence, as the environment where Lambda runs has default access to no information except incoming payload. Lambda does not maintain any result of data after the termination of a function, so it is your responsibility to put the result in a secure place.

Lambda functions can be triggered by events enabling you to build event-driven reactive systems. It can be triggered by other services or in response to advance from other services.

i)   S3 Bucket
ii) DynamoDB Tables
iii) Kinesis Streams
iv) SQS Notifications
v)   SNS

When there are several events to reply to, Lambda makes multiple copies of your function and runs them in parallel to scale the workload. Scaling a function has no inherent limitations. The Lambda function is used by architects to reduce capacity waste. Lambda functions can be used in any application because they will scale your code and provide high availability.

Lambda at Scale

Common architecture using Lambda at Scale is 'Fanout' architecture. In this type of architecture, when some information gets in, the Lambda function is used to launch multiple parallel Lambda functions. These parallel functions perform further activities.

AWS Serverless Application Model (SAM)

SAM is an open-source framework for developing serverless apps on Amazon Web Services. This framework was designed by AWS and shared on GitHub for anyone to use. SAM's configuration language is YAML. It has a CLI that allows different functions to create, deploy, or update your serverless applications using AWS services like Lambda, DynamoDB, and API Gateway. You can test or debug your serverless applications before pushing them to the Cloud.

It can be considered as the front-end of CloudFormation; it generates the CloudFormation templates in the background.

AWS Serverless Application Repository: AWS provided a repository having a number of pre-made serverless applications to guide the user.

AWS SAM vs. Serverless Framework

AWS SAM	Serverless Framework
YAML templates	YAML templates
Makes developing and deploying serverless applications efficient	Makes developing and deploying serverless applications efficient
Generates CloudFormation scripts	Generates CloudFormation scripts

Supports AWS	Support multiple cloud providers

Table 6-11: AWS SAM vs. Serverless Framework

Amazon EventBridge

It is a service that uses various event sources, applies some rules, and then launches further events like AWS Lambda function or SNS event. It is designed to link AWS with other 3rd party applications to use any event-based function.

Simple Workflow Service

Amazon Simple Workflow Service is a web service that makes it easy to coordinate work across distributed application components. Amazon SWF enables an application for a wide range of use cases, including media processing, web application back-ends, business process workflow, and analytics pipelines, to be designed as coordination of tasks.

Task represents the invocation of various processing steps in an application that can be performed by executable code, web service calls, human action, and scripts. Amazon SWF gives you a full authority on achieving and coordinating tasks without being concerned about basic complications such as tracking their progress and maintaining their state.

The worker and the decider can run on cloud infrastructure, such as Amazon EC2, or on machines behind firewalls. Amazon SWF breaks the interaction between workers and the decider. It allows the decider to get consistent views into the task process and initiate new tasks in an ongoing manner.

Workflows

You can use Amazon Simple Workflow Service (SWF) to create workflows from divided, asynchronous apps. Workflows are programmes that organize and sustain the execution of operations that may run asynchronously across numerous computer devices and include both sequential and parallel processing.

When designing a new application, AWS recommends looking at step function over SWF.

Analyze your application to discover its component tasks, which are represented in Amazon SWF as activities, while developing a workflow. The order in which actions are carried out is determined by the workflow's coordination logic.

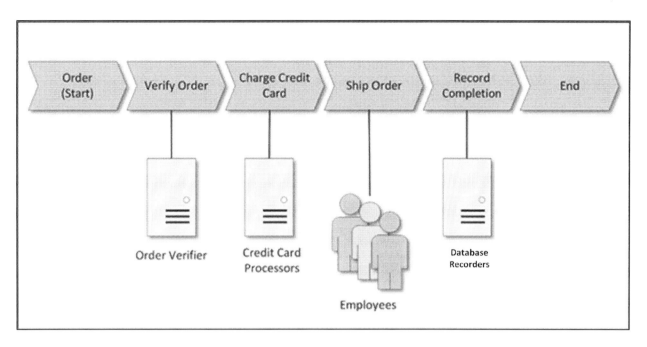

Figure 6-15: Workflow

SWF consists of two components:

Activity Worker

It is a user-defined program to assign any task, and it interact with SWS via SWS API.

Decider

It is a program that works on the task and makes a decision.

In the given architecture, the following are the steps:

1. Take an order which is "Activity Worker".
2. On-premises payment processing and after completion it updates SWF.
3. A decider task is triggered that decides from which warehouse the order is shipped.
4. Ship order worker is triggered.

Here, triggered is not exactly the worker getting notification but instead, they are continuously polling and checking that there is any task that they have to work for.

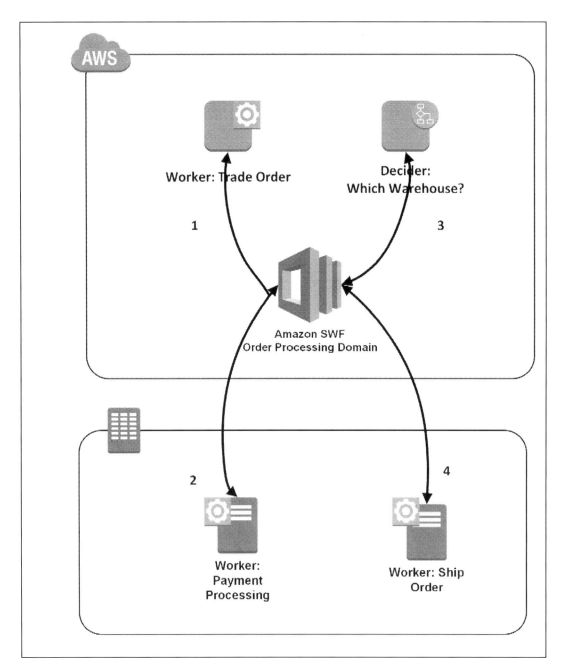

Figure 6-16: Workflow

Step Functions & Batch

AWS Step Functions is managed workflow and orchestration platform that is scalable and highly available. For modern applications, the AWS Step Functions provides serverless orchestration. It centrally manages a workflow, breaks it into several steps, adds flow logically, and tracks the inputs and outputs between the steps. Step Functions keeps track of the status of your apps as they run, tracks which process your app's workflow is in and retains an event data log that is transmitted across application components. When

networks fail, or components hang, your programme can pick up precisely where it left off. You must utilize JSON-based Amazon State Language to configure various phases.

You can easily update and edit workflows in one location without having to fight over multiple point-to-point integrations, control, and maintenance. Step Functions releases excess code for your functions and containers so that your applications are easier to write, resilient and maintain.

It is a web-based service that lets you visualize the components of your server-less applications. Step functions, as the name says, are the steps or jobs being carried out during the execution of a series of functions. When using AWS Step Functions, you are provided with a graphical console where you can arrange and visualize different AWS services as part of your server-less workflow. With the help of Step Functions, you can log and track large applications to analyze what went wrong and where. Applications can interact and update the stream by using Step Function API.

You can use AWS Step Function through the AWS management console; it lies under Application Integration.

AWS provides a "Task Timer" example of Step Function in its documentation. In this function, the function waits for a certain time stamp and then sends an SNS message.

```
{
  "topic": "arn:aws:sns:us-east-2:123456789012:StepFunctionsSample-TaskTimer-517b8680-e0ad-07cf-feee-65aa5fc63ac0-SNSTopic-96RHT77RAKTS",
  "message": "HelloWorld",
  "timer_seconds": 10
}
```

AWS Batch

AWS Batch is a management tool that helps in creating, managing and executing batch processing tasks by using EC2 instances. It includes the following steps:

- Creating a Compute Environment: Managed or unmanaged chooses from spot or on-demand instances, specify vCPUs
- Creating a Job Queue with priority and assigned to the Compute Environment
- Creating Job Definition: Script or JSON, you can include environment variables, mount points, IAM role, container image, etc.
- Scheduling the Job

Note:

- Step Functions should be used when you need out-of-the-box coordination of AWS service components - The use case is Order Processing Flow
- Simple Workflow Service is used when you need to support external processes or specialized execution logic - The use case is Loan Application Process with manual review steps. AWS recommends using Simple Workflow service instead of Step Function, when there is some manual interaction or any external source required
- Simple Queue Service is a messaging queue that is best for store and patterns - The use case is the Image Resize process
- AWS Batch is used where you have scheduled or reoccurring tasks without any heavy logic or decision - Use case is rotated logs daily on a Firewall appliance

Lab 6-02: Coordinating AI Services with Step Functions

Introduction

AWS Lambda

AWS Lambda allows you to run code without the need to create or manage servers. There is no charge when your code is not executing; you only pay for the compute time you use. You can run code for nearly any application or backend service with Lambda, and you do not have to worry about administration. Upload your code, and Lambda will handle everything necessary to run and grow it with high availability. You can establish your code to be triggered automatically by other AWS services, or you can access it directly from any computer or smartphone app.

AWS Simple Storage S3

Amazon S3 is a type of object storage that allows you to store and recover any quantity of data from any location. It is a low-cost storage solution with business resilience, reliability, efficiency, privacy, and infinite expansion.

Amazon S3 offers a simple web service interface for storing and retrieving any quantity of data at any time and from any location. You may quickly create projects that integrate cloud-native storage using this service. Because Amazon S3 is easily customizable and you only pay for what you use, you can start small and scale up as needed without sacrificing performance or dependability.

Amazon S3 is also built to be highly adaptable. It allows you to build a simple FTP system or a complex web application like the Amazon.com retail website; read the same piece of data a million times or only for emergency disaster recovery; store whatever type and amount of data you desire. Instead of finding out how to store their data, Amazon S3 allows developers to focus on innovation.

AWS Translate

Amazon Translate is a text translation service that uses Neural Machine Translation (MT) to translate text between supported languages. The service, powered by deep learning technologies, delivers high-quality, inexpensive, and configurable language translation, allowing developers to solve business and user-authored content and construct applications that require multilingual support. The service can be accessed using an API, which allows for real-time or batch Translation of the text from one language to another.

AWS Transcribe

Amazon Transcribe is an AWS service that makes converting speech to text simple for customers. Customers can use Amazon Transcribe for various business applications, including transcription of voice-based customer service calls, generation of subtitles on audio/video content. They conduct a (text-based) content analysis on audio/video content, using Automatic Speech Recognition (ASR) technology.

AWS Comprehend

Amazon Comprehend is a Natural Language Processing (NLP) service that searches for meaning and insights in text using machine learning. You can use Amazon Comprehend to extract key terms, places, people, brands, or events from a library of documents, understand sentiment about products or services, and identify the primary topics. This text could have come from various places, including online pages, social media feeds, emails, and newspapers. You can also input Amazon Comprehend, a collection of text documents, and it will pick subjects (or groups of words) that best reflect the data. Amazon Comprehends output can better analyze customer comments, provide a search experience through search filters, and organize documents using topics.

AWS Polly

Polly is an Amazon service that converts text into natural-sounding speech. Amazon Polly makes it possible for existing apps to talk as a first-class feature and for totally new categories of speech-enabled products, such as mobile apps and autos, as well as gadgets and appliances. Amazon Polly comes with dozens of lifelike voices and multilingual capabilities, allowing you to pick the perfect voice and distribute your speech-enabled apps across many locations. Amazon Polly is simple to use: transmit the text you want to be translated into speech to the Amazon Polly API. Amazon Polly will return the audio stream to your application, which you can play or save in a regular audio file format like MP3. You can change the speech pace, pitch, or volume using Amazon Polly because it supports Speech Synthesis Markup Language (SSML) tags like prosody. Amazon Polly is a safe service that provides these advantages at low latency and a large scale. Amazon Polly's generated speech can be cached and replayed at no extra charge. When you sign up for

Amazon Polly, you can convert millions of characters per month for free for the first year. Amazon Polly is a cost-effective solution to enable speech synthesis everywhere because of its pay-as-you-go pricing, low cost per request, and lack of constraints on storage and reuse of voice output. You can utilize Amazon Polly to provide high-quality spoken work for your app. This low-cost service provides quick response times and may be used for almost any application, with no constraints on storing and reusing created speech.

Scenario:

Assume you are a Machine Learning Developer in an organization like IPSpecialist, developing content on different cloud computing courses. The organization wants its content to be translated into the Spanish language. But there is an issue in translating the whole book by a content developer of 300 to 500 pages as the organization requires to complete the book in one week is impossible. So, as the Machine Learning Developer, you are asked to build a Natural Language Processing (NLP) model from scratch using Tensorflow or Pytorch framework. To do this, you require lots of data on the Spanish language and English language. You also need expensive hardware like GPU to train the model. To build the model from scratch can prove to be very time-consuming and expensive. Your task is to develop a Neural Machine Translation model within a lesser timeframe and lower cost. How can you automate this task?

Solution:

The solution is simple. You will need to design a Machine Learning pipeline using AWS Lambda functions in the background to run the logic of the channel. But you must also use AWS S3 for input and output of data, along with other Amazon helping services to automate this task. You will use AWS Translate, AWS Transcribe, AWS Comprehend, and AWS Polly, as shown in the figure below.

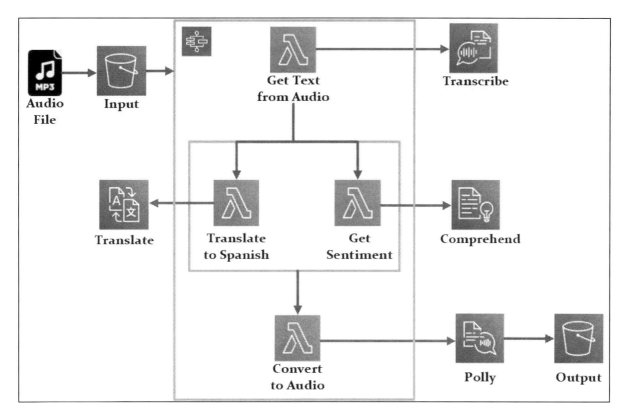

Figure 6-17: Coordinate AI Services with Step Functions

Follow the given steps to coordinate AI services with step functions.

Before deep-diving into the lab, create a Lambda Function, a Step Function, and an S3 Bucket, as discussed in the above lab sections.

1. Log in to the AWS Console.
2. Click on 'Services.'

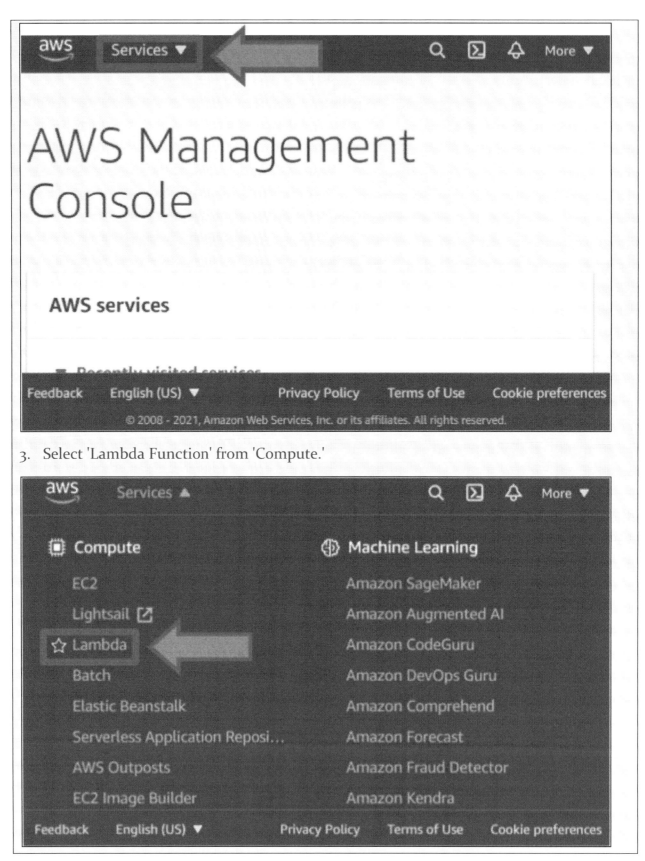

3. Select 'Lambda Function' from 'Compute.'

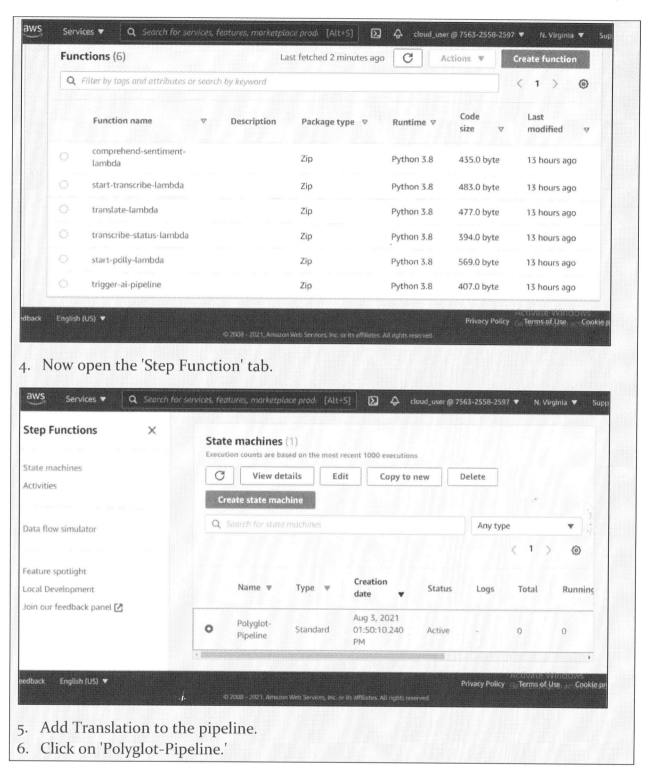

4. Now open the 'Step Function' tab.

5. Add Translation to the pipeline.
6. Click on 'Polyglot-Pipeline.'

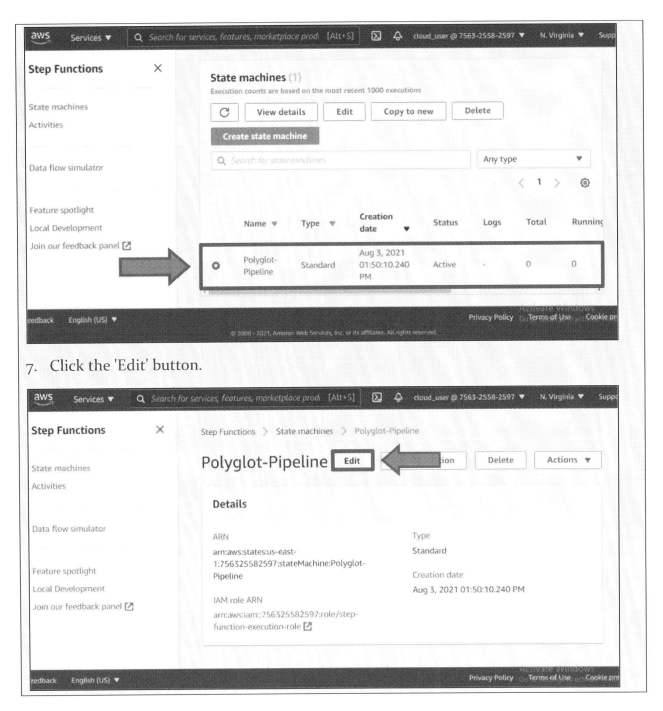

7. Click the 'Edit' button.

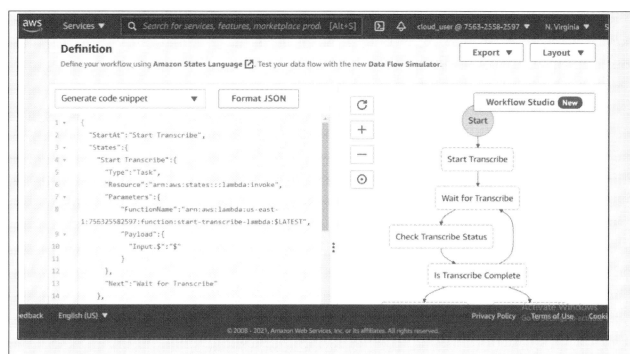

8. From 'Generate a code snipped,' select 'AWS Lambda : Invoke a function.'

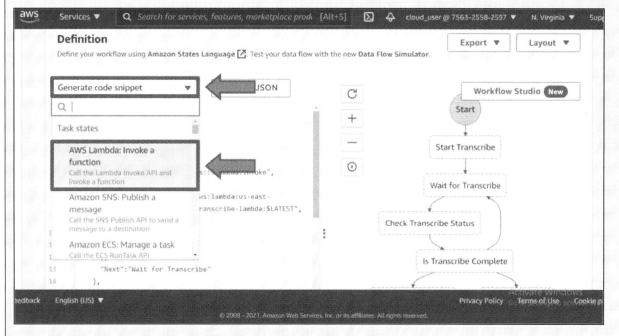

9. From the Lambda function dropdown menu, select a function from the list and then select the 'translate-lambda' function from the sub-menu.

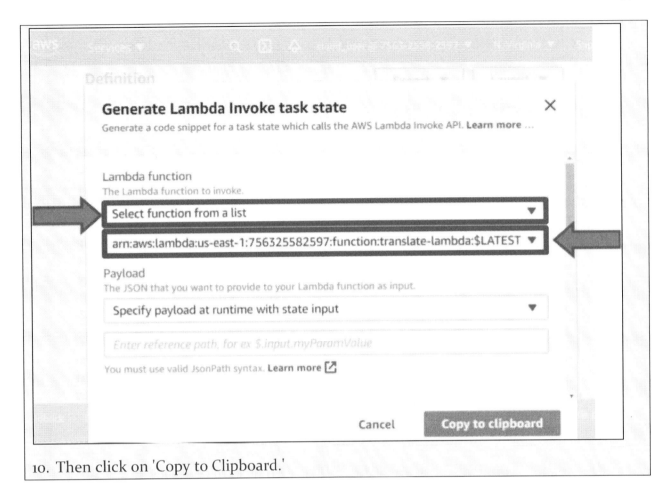

10. Then click on 'Copy to Clipboard.'

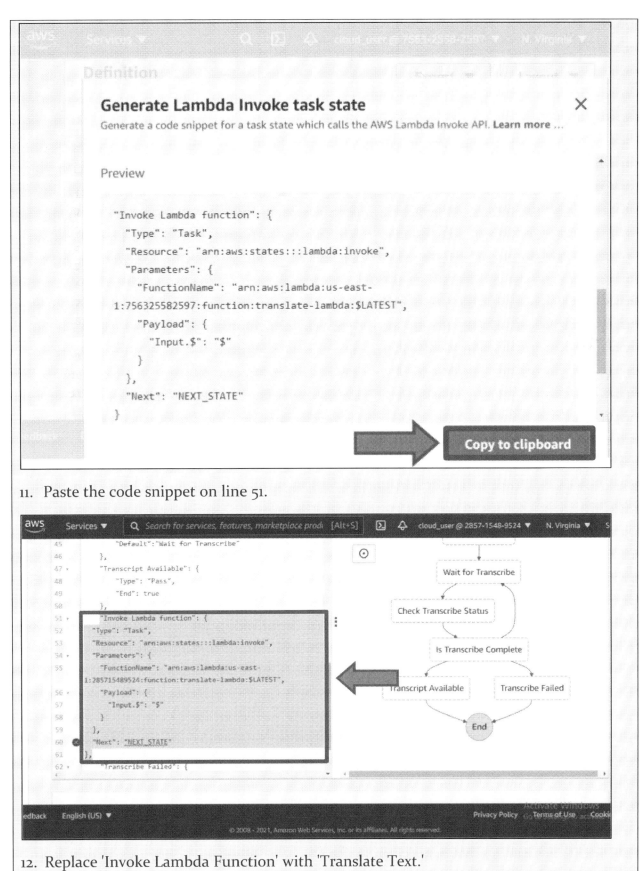

11. Paste the code snippet on line 51.

12. Replace 'Invoke Lambda Function' with 'Translate Text.'

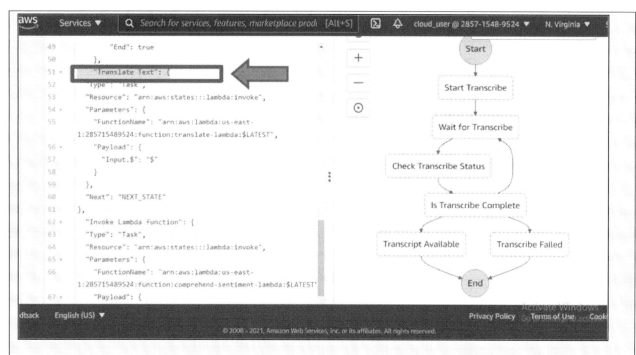

13. Now add 'Sentiment Analysis' to the pipeline.

14. In the 'Step Function' tab, from 'Generate a code snippet,' select 'AWS : Invoke a function.'

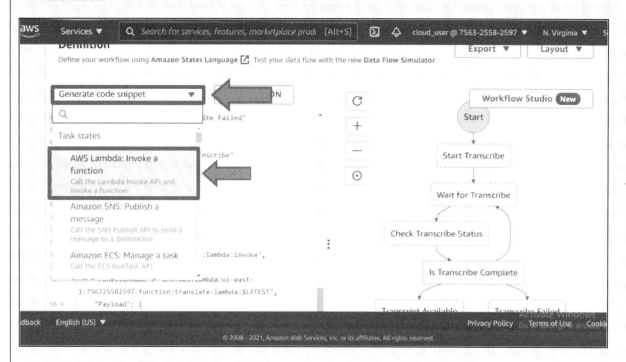

15. From the Lambda Function dropdown menu, select 'function from a list.'

16. Then select the 'Comprehend-Sentiment' function from the sub-menu.

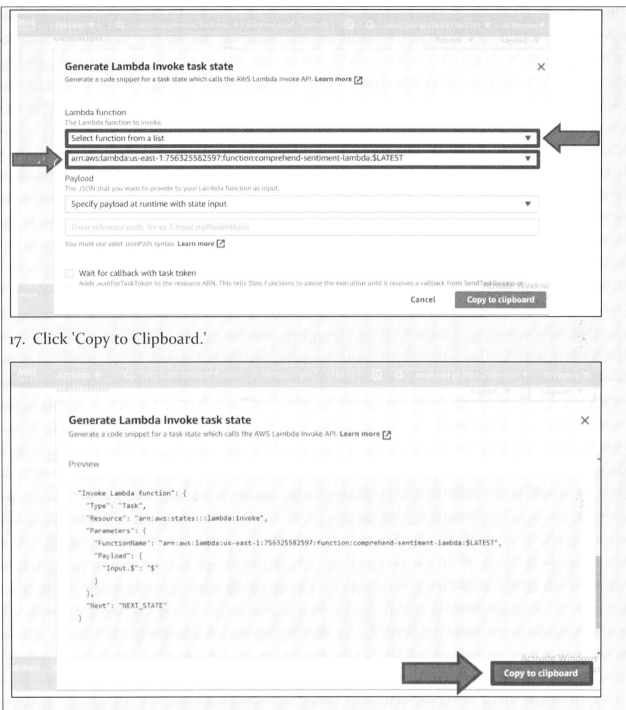

17. Click 'Copy to Clipboard.'

18. Paste the 'Comprehend-Sentiment' code snippet on line 62.
19. Replace 'Invoke Lambda Function' with 'Comprehend Sentiment.'

```
aws    Services ▼        Q  Search for services, features, marketplace prod

49              "End": true
50            },
51 ▾      "Translate Text": {
52        "Type": "Task",
53        "Resource": "arn:aws:states:::lambda:invoke",
54 ▾      "Parameters": {
55          "FunctionName": "arn:aws:lambda:us-east-
   1:285715489524:function:translate-lambda:$LATEST",
56 ▾        "Payload": {
57            "Input.$": "$"
58          }
59        },
60        "Next": "NEXT_STATE"
61      }
62 ▾    "Comprehend Sentiment": {  ⬅
63        "Type": "Task",
64        "Resource": "arn:aws:states:::lambda:invoke",
65 ▾      "Parameters": {
66          "FunctionName": "arn:aws:lambda:us-east-
   1:285715489524:function:comprehend-sentiment-lambda:$LATEST'
67 ▾        "Payload": {

dback   English (US) ▼

                              © 2008 - 2021, Amazon Web Service
```

20. Under 'Generate code snippet,' select 'Parallel State.'

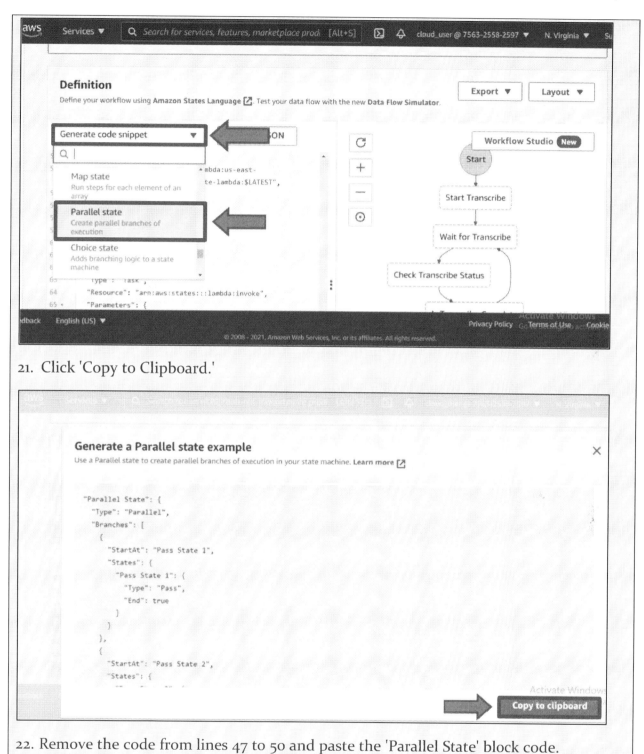

21. Click 'Copy to Clipboard.'

22. Remove the code from lines 47 to 50 and paste the 'Parallel State' block code.

```
aws    Services ▼    Q  Search for services, features, marketplace prod

38                          },
39 ▼                        {
40

       "Variable":"$.Payload.TranscriptionJobStatus",
41                      "StringEquals":"FAILED",
42                      "Next":"Transcribe Failed"
43                  }
44              ],
45          "Default":"Wait for Transcribe"
46      },
47 ▼      "Transcript Available": {
48          "Type": "Pass",
49          "End": true
50      },
51 ▼      "Translate Text": {
52      "Type": "Task",
53      "Resource": "arn:aws:states:::lambda:invoke",
54 ▼    "Parameters": {
55        "FunctionName": "arn:aws:lambda:us-east-
       1:285715489524:function:translate-lambda:$LATEST",
56 ▼      "Payload": {

dback    English (US) ▼

                                   © 2008 - 2021, Amazon Web Service
```

```
aws      Services ▼        Q   Search for services, features, marketplace prod

42                    "Next":"Transcribe Failed"
43                }
44            ],
45            "Default":"Wait for Transcribe"
46        },
47        "Parallel State": {
48        "Type": "Parallel",
49        "Branches": [
50          {
51            "StartAt": "Pass State 1",
52            "States": {
53              "Pass State 1": {
54                "Type": "Pass",
55                "End": true
56              }
57            }
58          },
59          {
60            "StartAt": "Pass State 2",
61            "States": {
62              "Pass State 2": {

dback    English (US) ▼
                                    © 2008 - 2021, Amazon Web Service
```

23. Replace 'Parallel State' with 'Transcript Available.'

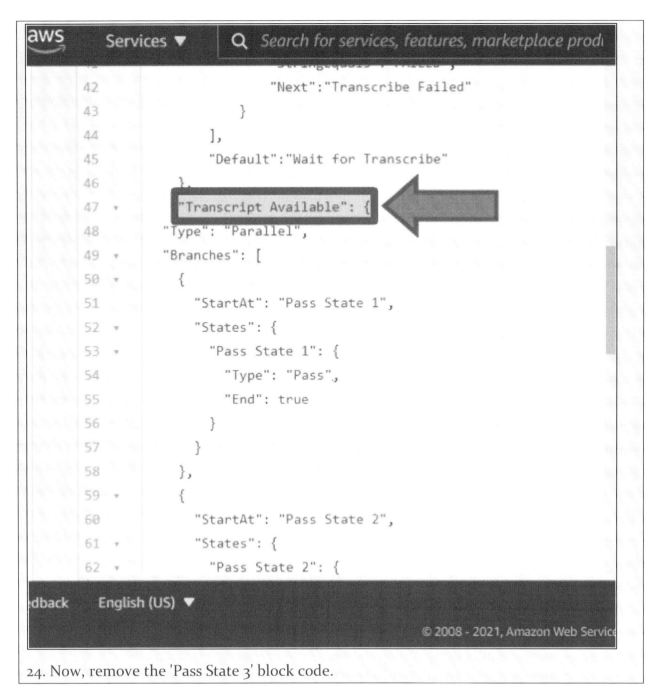

24. Now, remove the 'Pass State 3' block code.

```
aws      Services ▼        Q   Search for services, features, marketplace prod

58              "StartAt": "Pass State 2",
59  ▾          "States": {
60  ▾            "Pass State 2": {
61                 "Type": "Pass",
62                 "End": true
63               }
64             }
65
66
67           },
68  ▾        {
69             "StartAt": "Pass State 3",
70  ▾          "States": {
71  ▾            "Pass State 3": {
72                 "Type": "Pass",
73                 "End": true
74               }
75             }
76           }
77         ],
78         "Next": "NEXT_STATE"

edback    English (US) ▼
                                            © 2008 - 2021, Amazon Web Services
```

25. Copy the 'Translate Text' block code. Remove it from its current position.

```
aws    Services ▼        Q  Search for services, features, marketplace prod

64              }
65
66
67          }
68      ],
69      "Next": "NEXT_STATE"
70  }
71
72 ▾ ⊗    "Translate Text": {
73      "Type": "Task",
74      "Resource": "arn:aws:states:::lambda:invoke",
75 ▾    "Parameters": {
76        "FunctionName": "arn:aws:lambda:us-east-
        1:285715489524:function:translate-lambda:$LATEST",
77 ▾      "Payload": {
78          "Input.$": "$"
79        }
80      },
81      "Next": "NEXT_STATE"
82  },
83 ▾    "Comprehend Sentiment": {

dback    English (US) ▼

                                © 2008 - 2021, Amazon Web Service
```

26. Remove 'Pass state 1' from lines 53 to 56, paste the 'Translate Text' block code.

```
aws    Services ▼    Q  Search for services, features, marketplace prod  [Alt

44              ],
45              "Default":"Wait for Transcribe"
46            },
47 ▾      "Parallel State": {
48        "Type": "Parallel",
49 ▾      "Branches": [
50 ▾          {
51            "StartAt": "Pass State 1",
52 ▾          "States": {
53 ▾            "Pass State 1": {
54                "Type": "Pass",
55                "End": true
56              }
57            }
58          },
59 ▾          {
60            "StartAt": "Pass State 2",
61 ▾          "States": {
62 ▾            "Pass State 2": {
63                "Type": "Pass",
64                "End": true
```

eedback   English (US) ▼

27. For this block, replace 'StartAt' with 'Translate Text.'

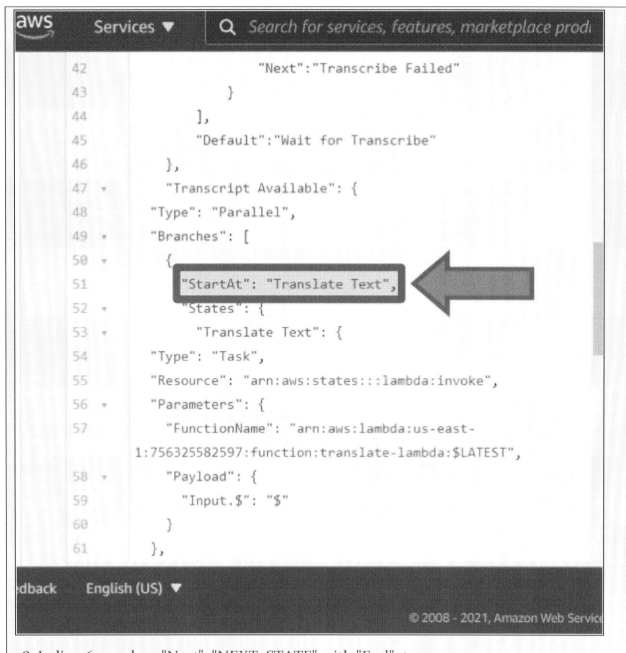

```
42              "Next":"Transcribe Failed"
43            }
44          ],
45          "Default":"Wait for Transcribe"
46        },
47        "Transcript Available": {
48      "Type": "Parallel",
49      "Branches": [
50        {
51          "StartAt": "Translate Text",
52          "States": {
53            "Translate Text": {
54      "Type": "Task",
55      "Resource": "arn:aws:states:::lambda:invoke",
56      "Parameters": {
57        "FunctionName": "arn:aws:lambda:us-east-
      1:756325582597:function:translate-lambda:$LATEST",
58        "Payload": {
59          "Input.$": "$"
60        }
61      },
```

28. In line 62, replace "Next": "NEXT_STATE" with "End": true.

```
aws        Services ▼        Q  Search for services, features, marketplace prodi

48          "Type": "Parallel",
49   ▾      "Branches": [
50   ▾        {
51              "StartAt": "Translate Text",
52   ▾          "States": {
53   ▾            "Translate Text": {
54        "Type": "Task",
55        "Resource": "arn:aws:states:::lambda:invoke",
56   ▾    "Parameters": {
57          "FunctionName": "arn:aws:lambda:us-east-
          1:756325582597:function:translate-lambda:$LATEST",
58   ▾      "Payload": {
59            "Input.$": "$"
60          }
61        },
62        "End": true
63        }
64            }
65          },
66   ▾      {
67            "StartAt": "Comprehend Text",
```

English (US) ▼

© 2008 - 2021, Amazon Web Service

29. Copy the 'Comprehend Sentiment' block code. Remove it from its current position.

30. Remove 'Pass State 2' from lines 69 to 72. Paste the 'Comprehend Sentiment' block code.

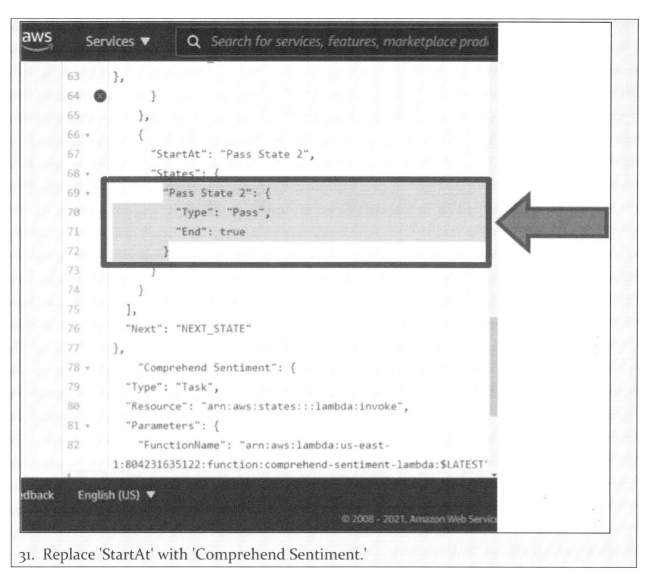

31. Replace 'StartAt' with 'Comprehend Sentiment.'

```
aws    Services ▼        Q  Search for services, features, marketplace prod

58  ▾            "Payload": {
59                 "Input.$": "$"
60              }
61            },
62          "End": true
63        }
64            }
65          },
66  ▾        {
67            "StartAt": "Comprehend Text",     ⬅
68  ▾          "States": {
69  ▾            "Comprehend Text": {
70          "Type": "Task",
71          "Resource": "arn:aws:states:::lambda:invoke",
72  ▾        "Parameters": {
73            "FunctionName": "arn:aws:lambda:us-east-
      1:756325582597:function:comprehend-sentiment-lambda:$LATEST
74  ▾          "Payload": {
75               "Input.$": "$"
76            }
77          },

dback   English (US) ▼
                                    © 2008 - 2021, Amazon Web Service
```

32. In line 78, replace "Next": "NEXT_STATE" with "End": true.

```
aws    Services ▼    Q  Search for services, features, marketplace prod

63        }
64            }
65          },
66  ▾      {
67            "StartAt": "Comprehend Text",
68  ▾        "States": {
69  ▾          "Comprehend Text": {
70      "Type": "Task",
71      "Resource": "arn:aws:states:::lambda:invoke",
72  ▾    "Parameters": {
73        "FunctionName": "arn:aws:lambda:us-east-
        1:756325582597:function:comprehend-sentiment-lambda:$LATEST
74  ▾      "Payload": {
75          "Input.$": "$"
76        }
77      }
78      "End": true          ⬅
79  }
80          }
81        }
82      ],

edback    English (US) ▼
                              © 2008 - 2021, Amazon Web Services
```

33. Now, convert the Translated Text to Audio.

34. In the 'Step Function' tab, from 'Generate a code snippet,' select 'AWS Lambda: Invoke a function.'

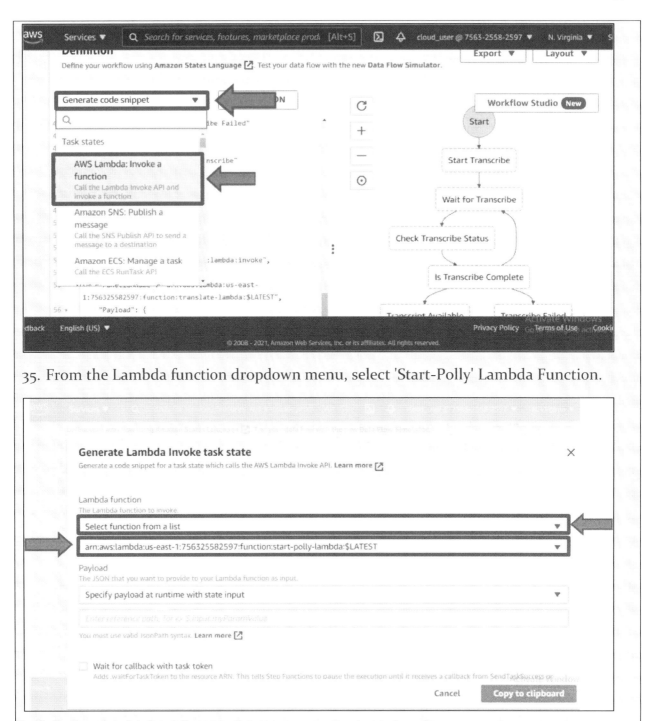

35. From the Lambda function dropdown menu, select 'Start-Polly' Lambda Function.

36. Click 'Copy to Clipboard.'

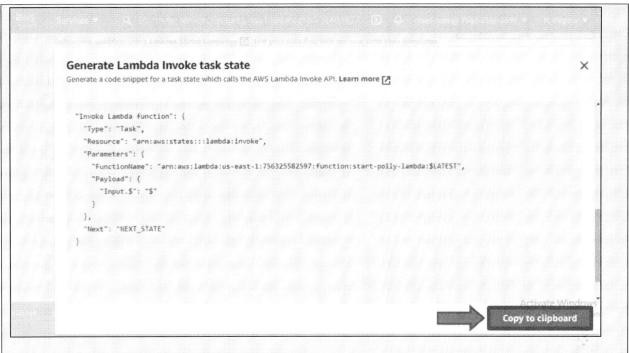

37. Paste the 'Start-Polly' code block on line 85.
38. Replace 'Invoke Lambda Function' with 'Convert Text to Speech.'

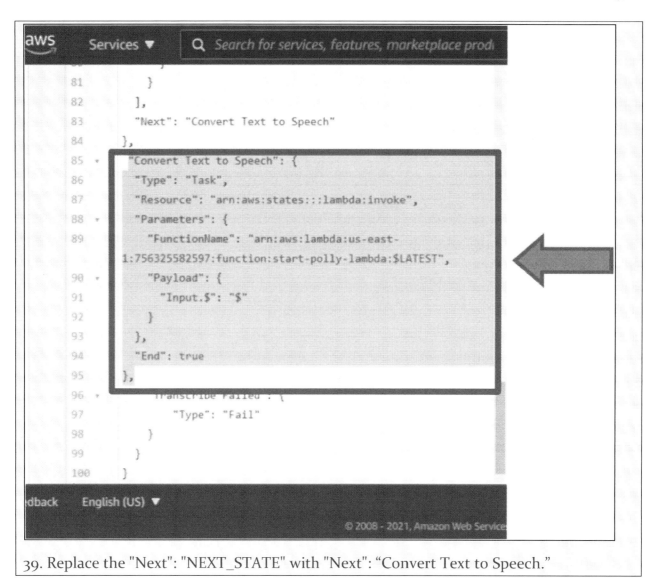

```
81          }
82        ],
83      "Next": "Convert Text to Speech"
84    },
85    "Convert Text to Speech": {
86      "Type": "Task",
87      "Resource": "arn:aws:states:::lambda:invoke",
88      "Parameters": {
89        "FunctionName": "arn:aws:lambda:us-east-
1:756325582597:function:start-polly-lambda:$LATEST",
90        "Payload": {
91          "Input.$": "$"
92        }
93      },
94      "End": true
95    },
96      "Transcribe Failed": {
97          "Type": "Fail"
98      }
99    }
100  }
```

39. Replace the "Next": "NEXT_STATE" with "Next": "Convert Text to Speech."

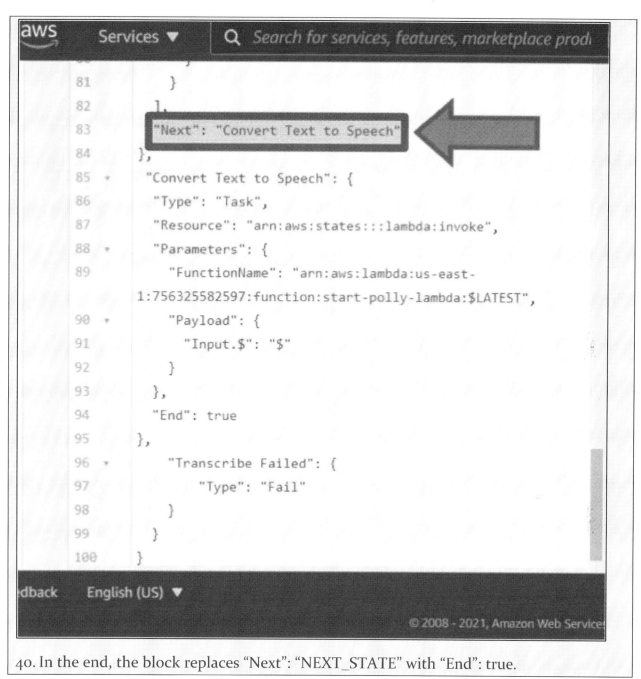

40. In the end, the block replaces "Next": "NEXT_STATE" with "End": true.

```
81          }
82        ],
83        "Next": "Convert Text to Speech"
84      },
85  ▾   "Convert Text to Speech": {
86        "Type": "Task",
87        "Resource": "arn:aws:states:::lambda:invoke",
88  ▾     "Parameters": {
89          "FunctionName": "arn:aws:lambda:us-east-
    1:756325582597:function:start-polly-lambda:$LATEST",
90  ▾       "Payload": {
91            "Input.$": "$"
92          }
93        },
94        "End": true
95      },
96  ▾   "Transcribe Failed": {
97          "Type": "Fail"
98        }
99      }
100   }
```

English (US) ▾

41. Click 'Format JSON.'

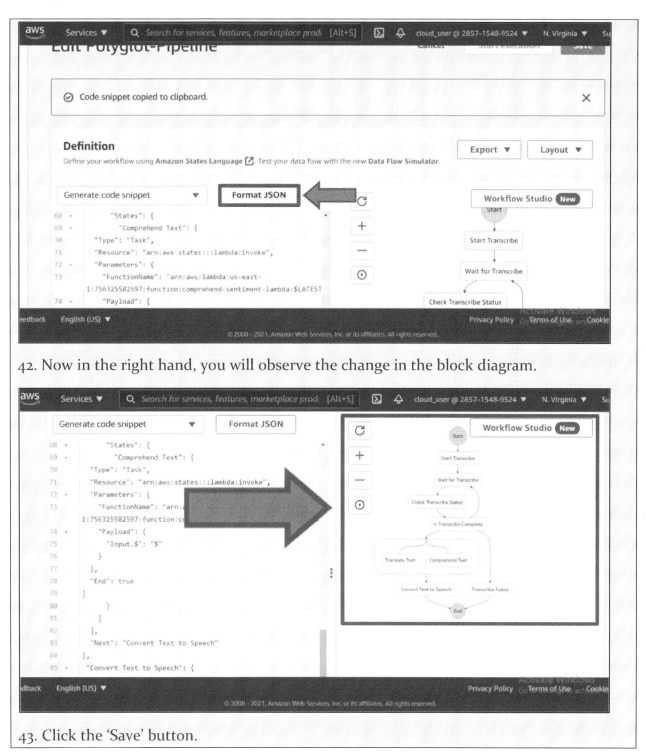

42. Now in the right hand, you will observe the change in the block diagram.

43. Click the 'Save' button.

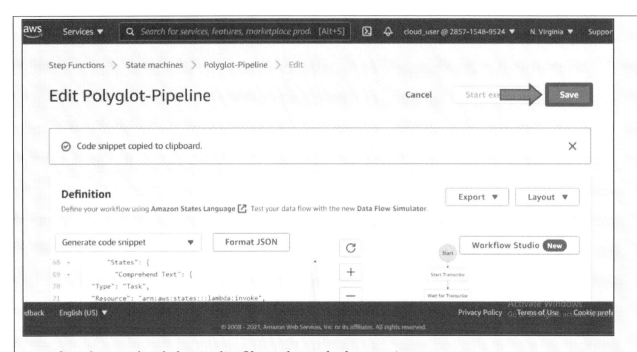

44. After that, upload the Audio file and watch the magic.

45. Go to the 'S3' tab.

46. Select the bucket whose name starts with 'input.'

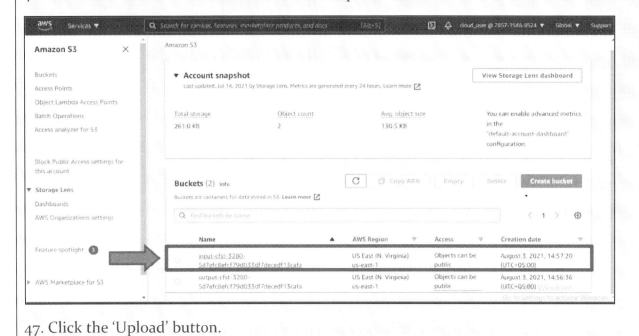

47. Click the 'Upload' button.

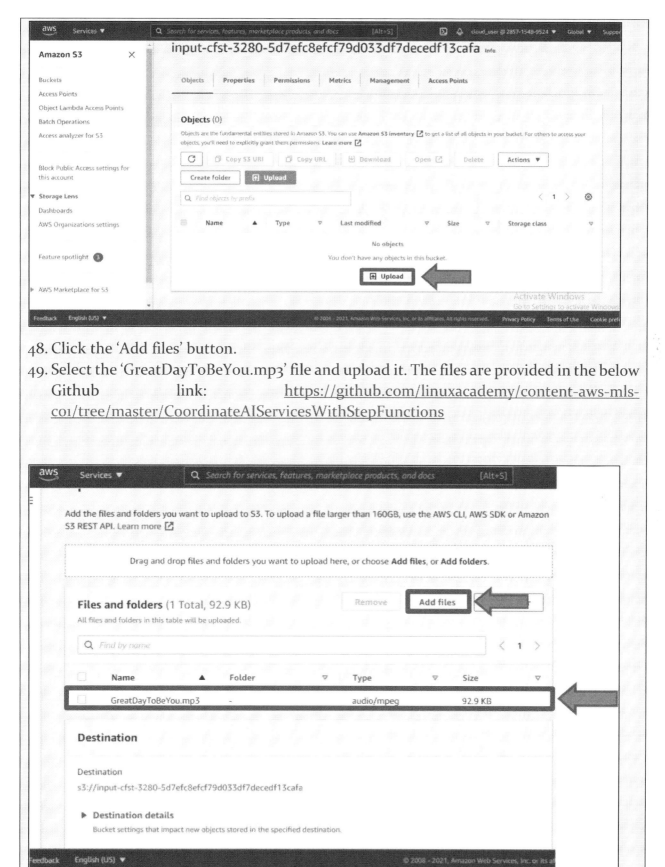

48. Click the 'Add files' button.

49. Select the 'GreatDayToBeYou.mp3' file and upload it. The files are provided in the below Github link: https://github.com/linuxacademy/content-aws-mls-c01/tree/master/CoordinateAIServicesWithStepFunctions

50. Click on the 'Upload' button.

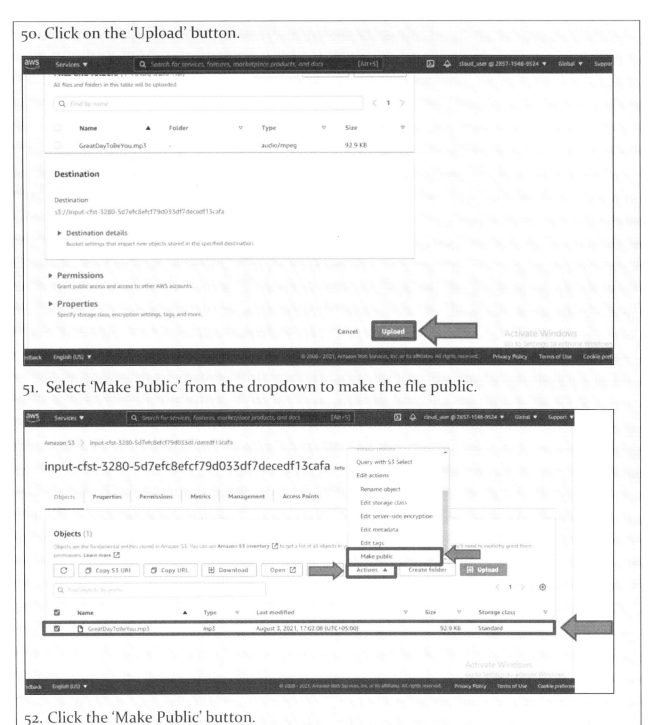

51. Select 'Make Public' from the dropdown to make the file public.

52. Click the 'Make Public' button.

53. Also, to listen to the file audio, click on the object URL.

54. Click the 'Ployglot- Pipeline' link at the top.

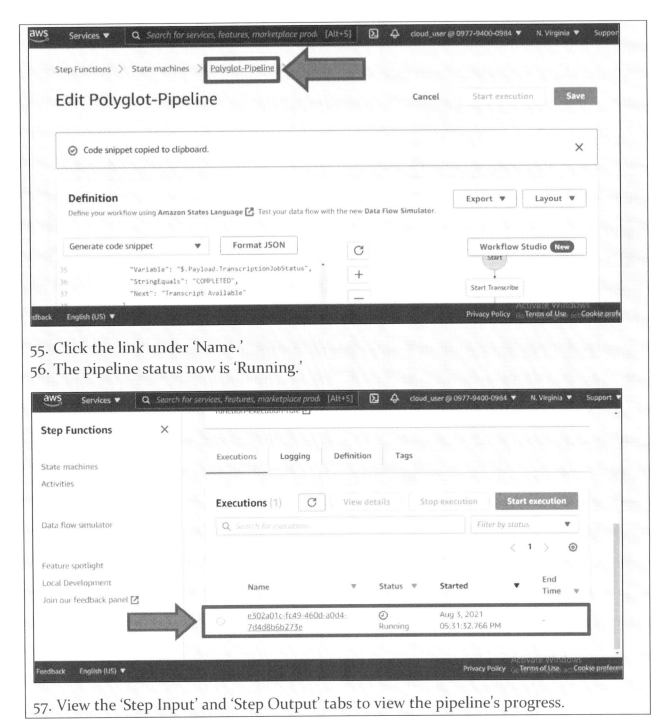

55. Click the link under 'Name.'

56. The pipeline status now is 'Running.'

57. View the 'Step Input' and 'Step Output' tabs to view the pipeline's progress.

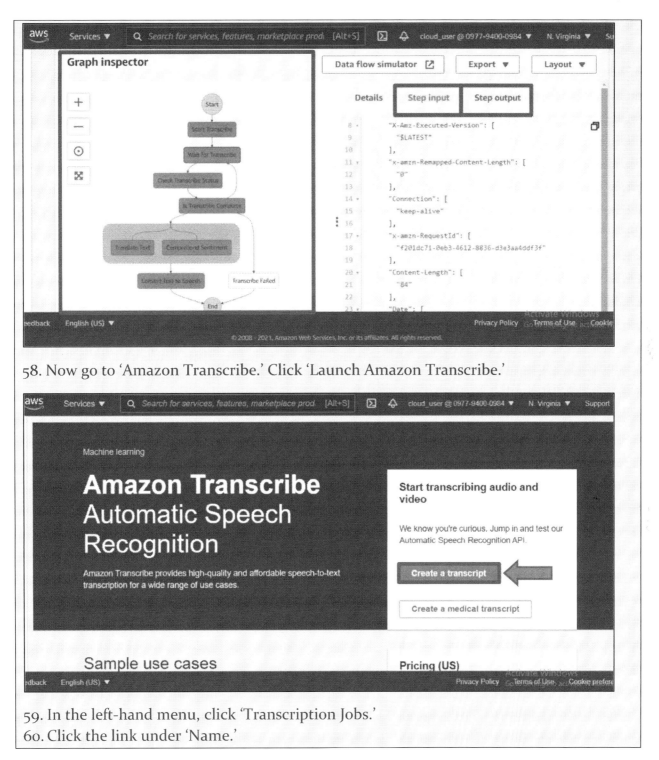

58. Now go to 'Amazon Transcribe.' Click 'Launch Amazon Transcribe.'

59. In the left-hand menu, click 'Transcription Jobs.'
60. Click the link under 'Name.'

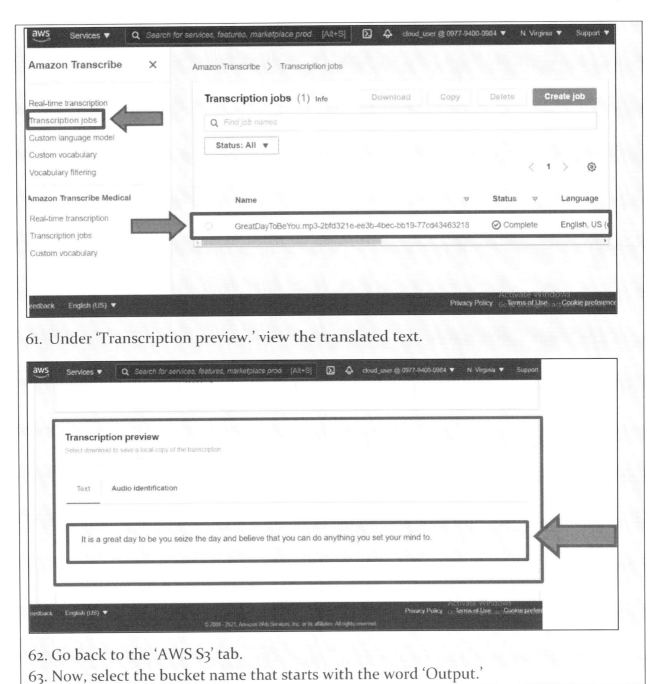

61. Under 'Transcription preview.' view the translated text.

62. Go back to the 'AWS S3' tab.

63. Now, select the bucket name that starts with the word 'Output.'

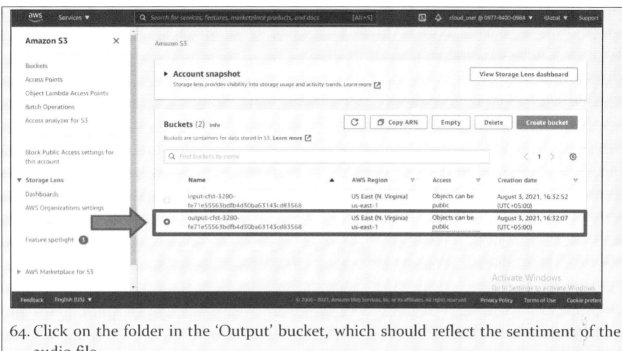

64. Click on the folder in the 'Output' bucket, which should reflect the sentiment of the audio file.

65. Click on 'Actions' to make the file public.

66. Click 'Make Public' to the public the object.

67. Click on the object URL to listen to the translated audio of the Spanish Language.

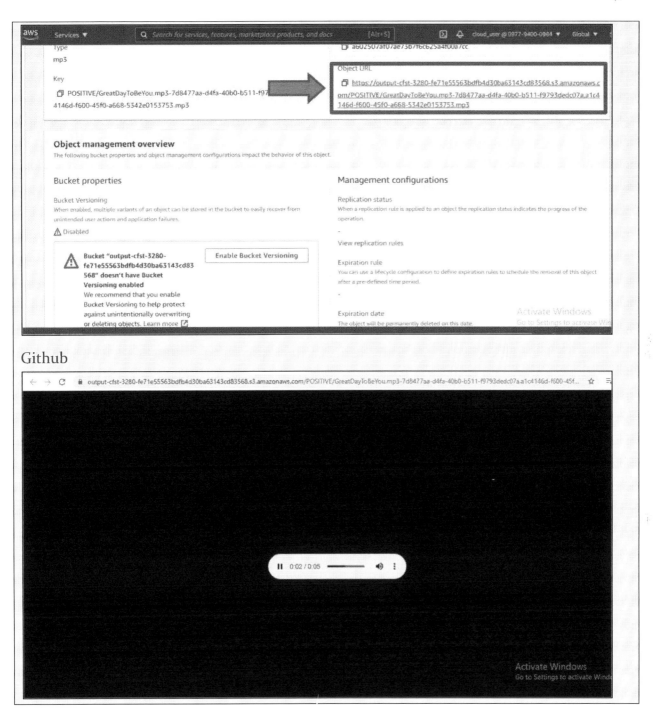

Github

Note: If there is trouble executing the code, you can also take help from the below-given code.

Code:

```
{
  "StartAt":"Start Transcribe",
  "States":{
    "Start Transcribe":{
      "Type":"Task",
      "Resource":"arn:aws:states:::lambda:invoke",
      "Parameters":{
          "FunctionName":"arn:aws:lambda:us-east-
1:756325582597:function:start-transcribe-lambda:$LATEST",
          "Payload":{
             "Input.$":"$"
          }
      },
      "Next":"Wait for Transcribe"
    },
    "Wait for Transcribe":{
        "Type":"Wait",
        "Seconds": 45,
        "Next":"Check Transcribe Status"
    },
    "Check Transcribe Status": {
      "Type":"Task",
      "Resource":"arn:aws:states:::lambda:invoke",
      "Parameters":{
          "FunctionName":"arn:aws:lambda:us-east-
1:756325582597:function:transcribe-status-lambda:$LATEST",
          "Payload":{
             "Input.$":"$"
          }
      },
        "Next": "Is Transcribe Complete"
    },
    "Is Transcribe Complete":{
        "Type":"Choice",
        "Choices":[
            {
                "Variable":"$.Payload.TranscriptionJobStatus",
```

```json
              "StringEquals":"COMPLETED",
              "Next":"Transcript Available"
            },
            {
              "Variable":"$.Payload.TranscriptionJobStatus",
              "StringEquals":"FAILED",
              "Next":"Transcribe Failed"
            }
          ],
        "Default":"Wait for Transcribe"
      },
    "Transcript Available": {
"Type": "Parallel",
"Branches": [
    {
      "StartAt": "Translate Text",
      "States": {
        "Translate Text": {
"Type": "Task",
"Resource": "arn:aws:states:::lambda:invoke",
"Parameters": {
  "FunctionName":                         "arn:aws:lambda:us-east-
1:756325582597:function:translate-lambda:$LATEST",
    "Payload": {
      "Input.$": "$"
    }
  },
  "End": true
}
        }
    },
    {
      "StartAt": "Comprehend Text",
      "States": {
        "Comprehend Text": {
"Type": "Task",
"Resource": "arn:aws:states:::lambda:invoke",
"Parameters": {
  "FunctionName":                         "arn:aws:lambda:us-east-
1:756325582597:function:comprehend-sentiment-lambda:$LATEST",
    "Payload": {
```

```
          "Input.$": "$"
        }
      },
    "End": true
}
         }
     }
   ],
  "Next": "Convert Text to Speech"
},
 "Convert Text to Speech": {
 "Type": "Task",
 "Resource": "arn:aws:states:::lambda:invoke",
 "Parameters": {
    "FunctionName":                    "arn:aws:lambda:us-east-
1:756325582597:function:start-polly-lambda:$LATEST",
    "Payload": {
      "Input.$": "$"
    }
  },
  "End": true
},
   "Transcribe Failed": {
       "Type": "Fail"
    }
  }
}
```

Amazon Elastic MapReduce (Amazon EMR)

AWS Elastic MapReduce is not a single product; it includes a number of open-source projects.

It includes the following products:

- Hadoop HDFS: Hadoop Distributed File System where data is stored
- Hadoop MapReduce: It is a framework to process the data
- ZooKeeper: It is the resource coordinator that makes sure all resources are properly working together
- Oozie: It is a workflow framework
- Pig: It is a scripting framework

- Hive: It is an SQL interface in a Hadoop landscape
- Mahout: It is a machine learning component
- HBase: It is a columnar Datastore to store Hadoop data
- Flume: It is used to ingest application and system logs
- Sqoop: It helps in importing data from different resources into Hadoop
- Ambari: It is a management and monitoring console

The main products of EMR are Hadoop MapReduce and HDFS. Other mentioned products can be considered as add-ons. There are other companies also that provide enterprise support, professional services and project contributions, for example, HOTONWORKS and Cloudera.

Amazon EMR is a fully managed service that provides a Hadoop framework to process a large amount of data fast. It is most commonly used in log analysis, financial analysis, and ETL activities. It also supports Apache Spark, HBase, Presto, and Flink.

A Step is a programmatic task for performing some process on the data (i.e., count words)

A cluster is a number of EC2 instances provisioned by EMR to run Steps.

You can also use another framework in EMR with interaction with Amazon S3 and Amazon Dynamo DB. It is easy and less costly to use and set up a Hadoop. Due to scaling with AWS, it can spin up the Hadoop cluster and start processing. It is reliable, and you have to pay less time for tuning and to monitor your cluster.

Components of EMR

It has a master node; then, there are core nodes with HDFS storage. You may also have the Task nodes (Worker nodes), which work on the Steps.

AWS EMR Process

In the EMR cluster, you may have multiple steps. Step 1 can be a Hive script; Step 2 may be a custom JAR that is created in Java, and Step 3 may be a PIG script. All of the process results are then transferred to an S3 bucket.

Lab 6-03: Auto-Scale Experiment

Scenario

A pharmaceutical company recently started using AWS. The employees run a series of calculations every night against data which is gathered by corresponding day research. The amount of data vary day to day; sometimes they have a lot of data gathered in a day, and sometimes it is not much. Recently, they came to know about the scalability feature of

AWS, and they want to know that whether it will work for them or not. They ask you to show any proof of scalability working. How can you do that?

Solution

You start to design and conduct an experiment to show the working of scaling in AWS in a cost-effective way.

1. Select "EC2" in the AWS console.

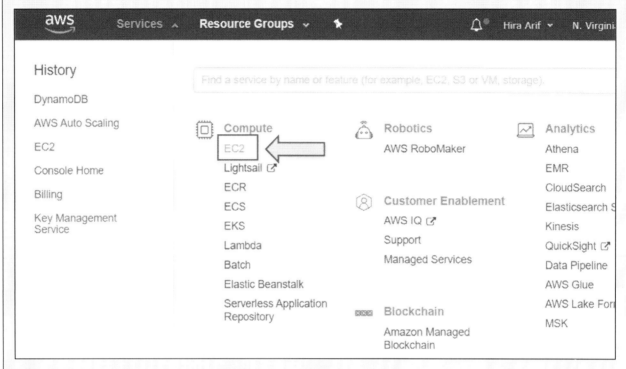

2. Click "Launch Configurations" in "AUTO SCALING".

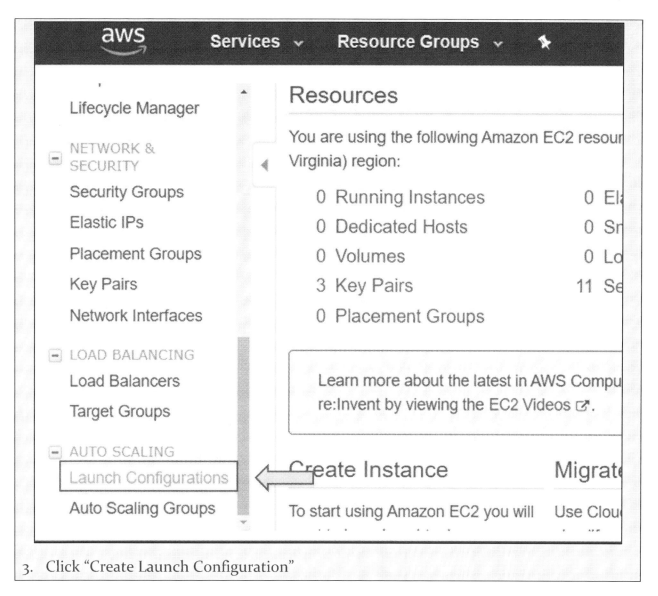

3. Click "Create Launch Configuration"

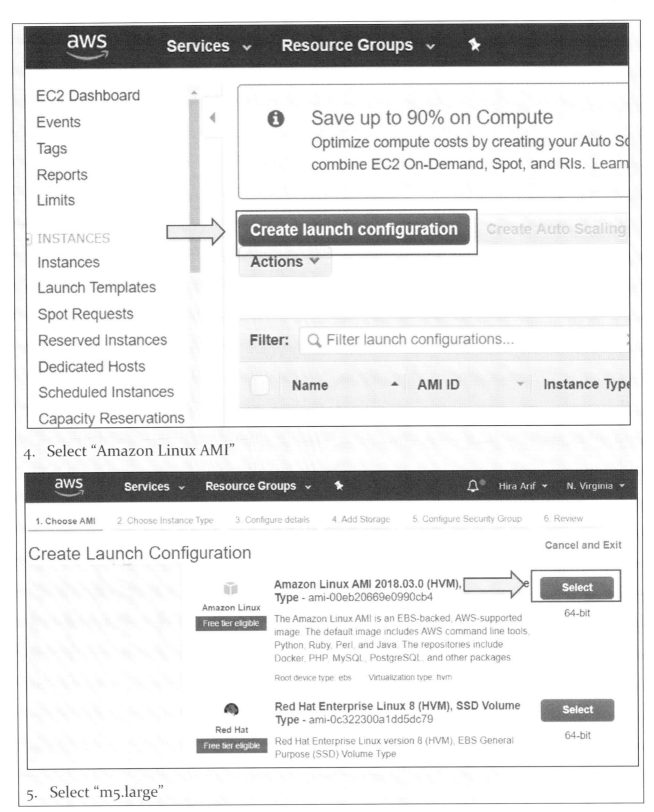

4. Select "Amazon Linux AMI"

5. Select "m5.large"

aws	Services ⌄	Resource Groups ⌄	📌	
1. Choose AMI	**2. Choose Instance Type**	3. Configure details	4. Add Storage	5

Create Launch Configuration

☐	Memory optimized	r5dn.16xlarge	64	512
☐	Memory optimized	r5n.24xlarge	96	768
☐	Memory optimized	r5dn.24xlarge	96	768
☑	General purpose	m5.large	⟵	8
☐	General purpose	m5.xlarge	4	16
☐	General purpose	m5.2xlarge	8	32

Cancel   P⟹   **Next: Configure details**

6. Give it a name and select "Request Spot Instances" for a cost-effective solution.

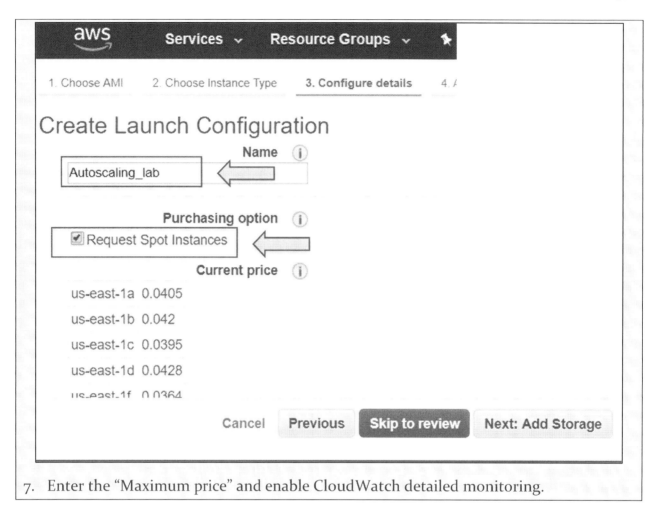

7. Enter the "Maximum price" and enable CloudWatch detailed monitoring.

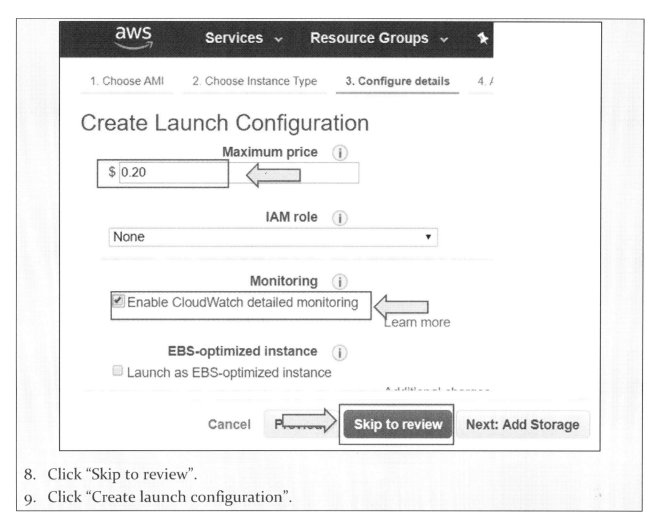

8. Click "Skip to review".
9. Click "Create launch configuration".

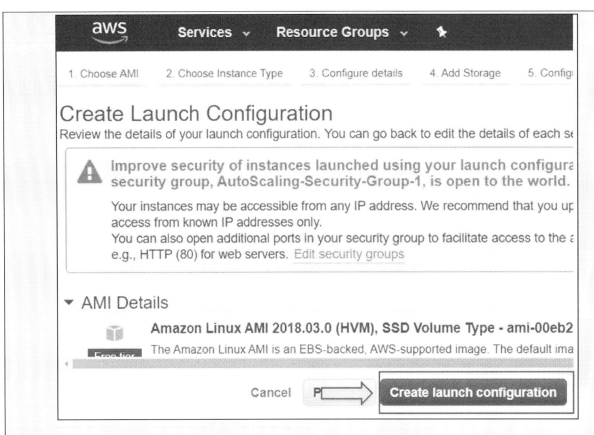

10. Choose any existing key pair or create a new one.
11. Click "Create launch configuration".

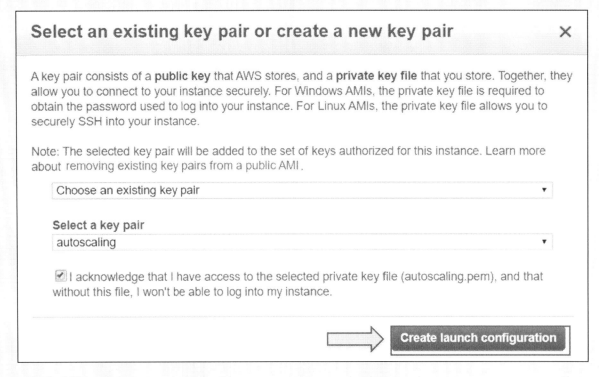

12. Click "Close".

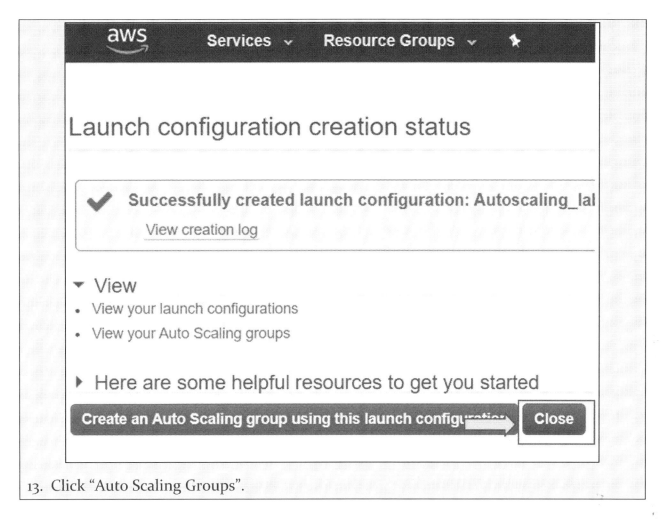

13. Click "Auto Scaling Groups".

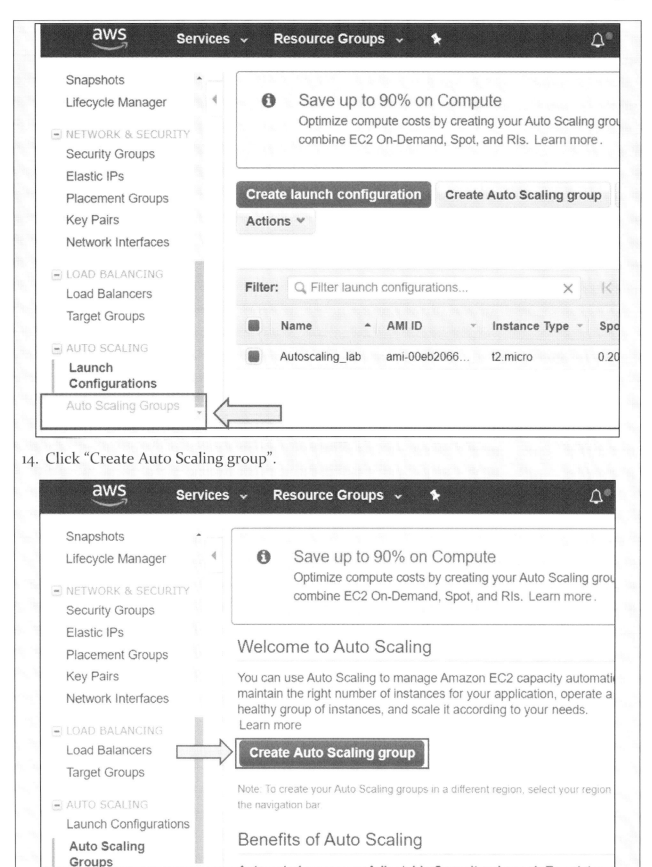

14. Click "Create Auto Scaling group".

15. Select the launch configuration and click "Next Step".

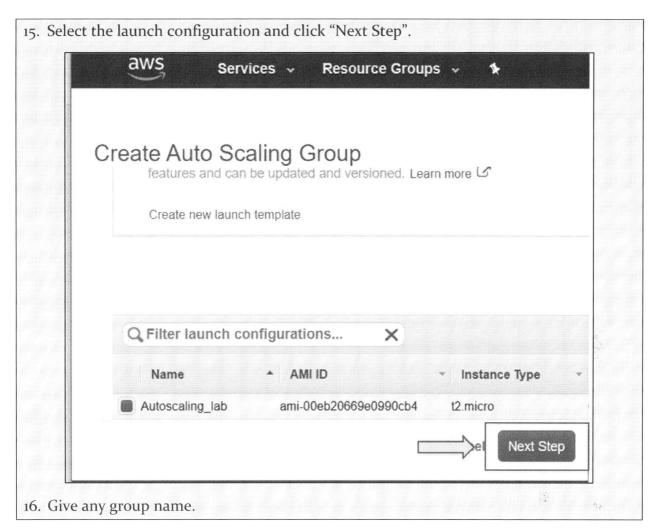

16. Give any group name.

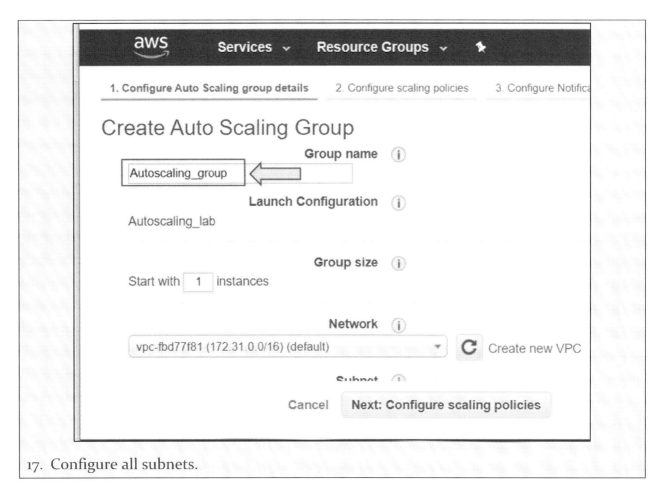

17. Configure all subnets.

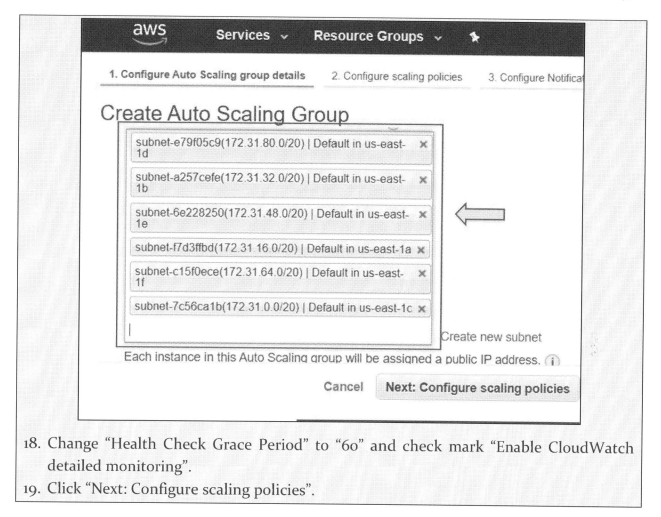

18. Change "Health Check Grace Period" to "60" and check mark "Enable CloudWatch detailed monitoring".

19. Click "Next: Configure scaling policies".

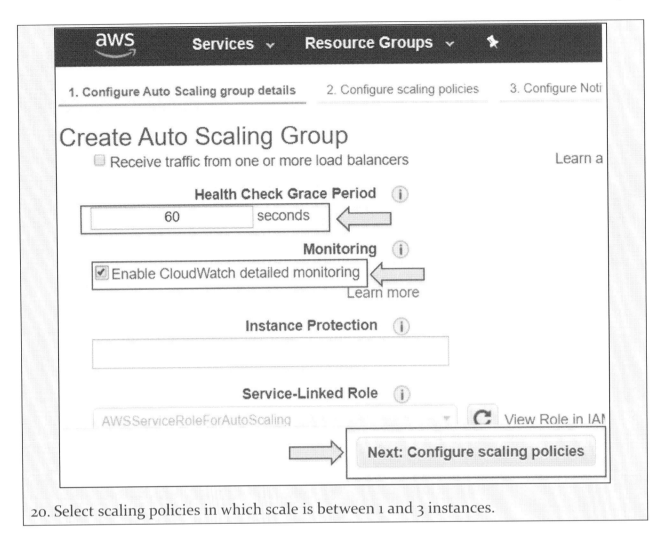

20. Select scaling policies in which scale is between 1 and 3 instances.

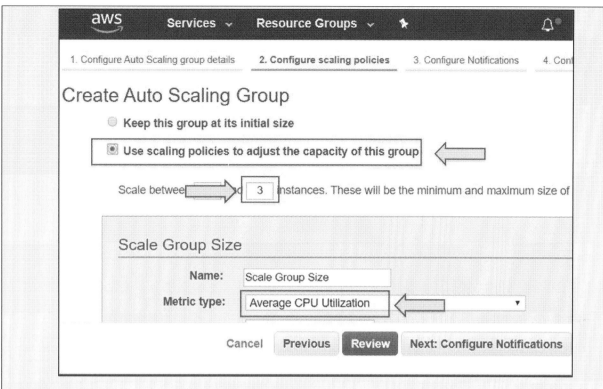

21. Enter 60 in "Target value" and warm up time then click "Review".

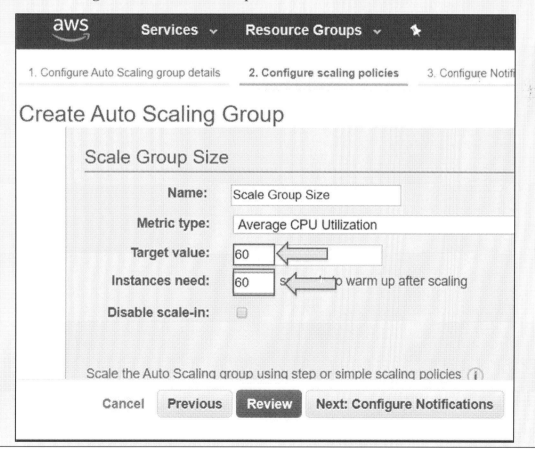

22. Click "Create Auto Scaling group".

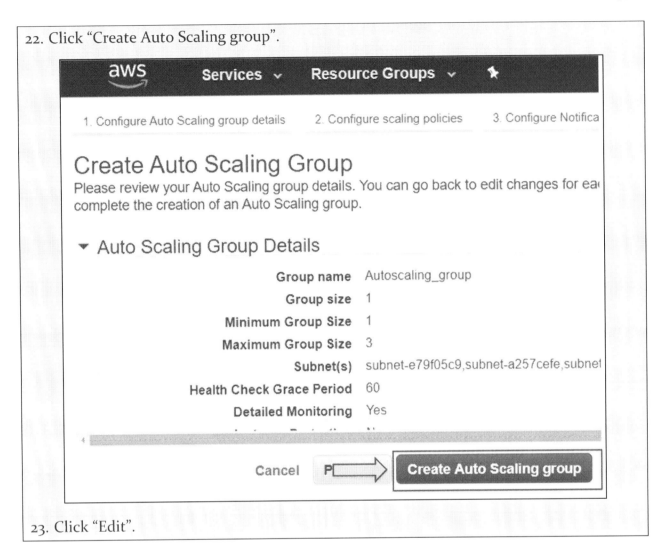

23. Click "Edit".

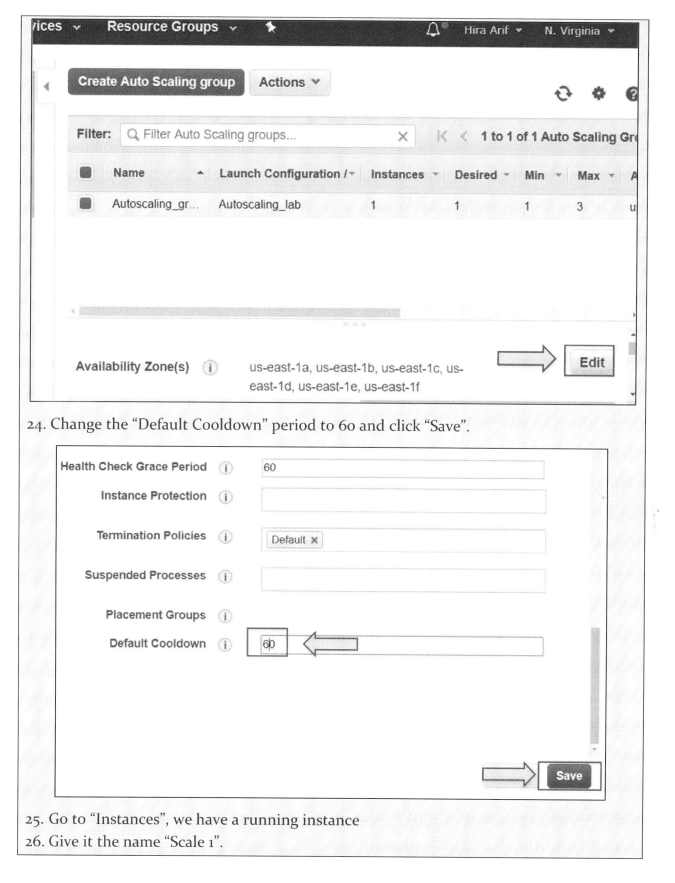

24. Change the "Default Cooldown" period to 60 and click "Save".

25. Go to "Instances", we have a running instance

26. Give it the name "Scale 1".

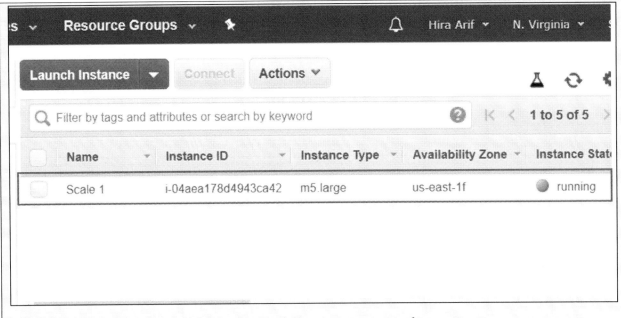

27. Login in to the instance and run the following commands:

"sudo yum update -y

sudo yum install stress -y

stress --cpu 64 --timeout 10m"

CPU utilization will start rising.

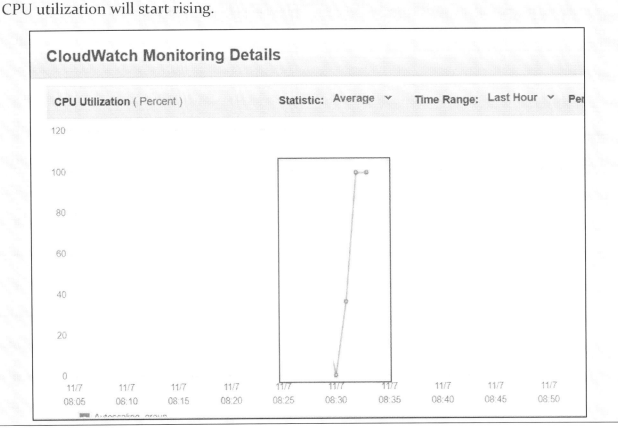

This changes the desired instances to "2".

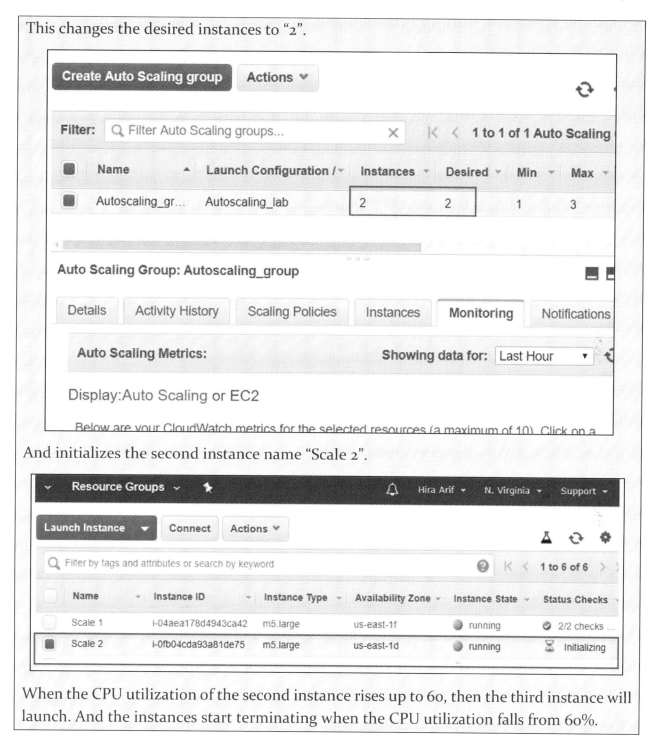

And initializes the second instance name "Scale 2".

When the CPU utilization of the second instance rises up to 60, then the third instance will launch. And the instances start terminating when the CPU utilization falls from 60%.

Challenge 1

A Mobile App company has assigned you as a consultant. They have designed an application, "SeeFood" which allows users to capture a high-resolution multi-megabyte

image of their food, and then it derives the nutritional value from that image. Their launching date is due within 5 days, and it should be ready to scale as the application is expected to be hit.

They got to know that the machine learning portion in the app is not perfect as required. They hired a large number of analysts to assist in analyzing the nutritional value and return the calculated value to the user.

How would you best architect to complete this challenge?

A. Configure the app to upload the image to S3. Using S3 Events, trigger a message to an SQS queue linking to the image. Provide analysts with a custom program to poll the queue and process the images

B. Use AWS SWF to receive the images from the mobile app. Use the weighted routing feature in SWF to forward the images equally across a pool of analysts to process the images

C. Use Kinesis Data Stream and Kinesis Firehose to take in the image and save them off to S3. Write a custom program that analysts can use to view the S3 images and process them

D. Use SNS to create a process that will email received images equally across a set of email accounts. Provide the analysts with a custom program to read those mailboxes and process the images

E. Create a pub/sub architecture, supplying the analysts with a custom program they can use to receive images pushed from SQS queues and process the images

Solution

Option A is the best option. The image is saved in S3, which has no such size limit. SQS will be used as a worker queue for that image.

Option B is invalid here because there is no such feature called weighted routing in SWF.

Option C is not applicable because Kinesis has a size limit of 1 MB, and we want the limit that can deal with multi-megabyte images.

Option D is not applicable because SNS has a size limitation of 236kB.

Option E is incorrect because SQS is a messaging platform and has no concern with the pub/sub architecture, and messages cannot be pushed from SQS; you have to pull the queues for the messages.

Challenge 2

A company has implemented EC2 Auto scaling for the web layer behind an ELB. Client traffic is quite unpredictable and can change rapidly; therefore, the company wants to rely on auto-scaling for providing the best customer experience and performance.

Every week, a third-party web analytics company sends your company a report that shows how your website is performing from the perspective of a user. Unfortunately, customer response is still slower than your target during high demand.

What do you think might be the issues and their corrections, remaining as cost-efficient as possible? (Select 2 options)

A. The default cool down time for scaling is too long. Create a scaling-specific cool down that overrides the default time

B. Your Internet Gateway has become saturated. Create a new VPC, ELB, and auto-scaling group with its own Internet Gateway and route traffic equally to either ELB

C. You do not have enough instances active during peak load times. Implement a scheduled scaling and increase the number of minimum instances during peak times

D. Customer demand is not stable enough to properly trigger scaling thresholds of your existing scaling policies. Implement a step scaling policy configured around CPU utilization.

E. Your launch configuration is set up to launch undersized instances. Edit your current launch configuration to launch larger instances to better absorb the load

F. You need more dynamic web capacity than your current configuration. Create a new launch configuration to launch smaller instances and implement a step scaling policy with a shorter cool down period

Solution

Option A is reasonable.

Option B is not valid because Internet Gateway has no concept of saturation, as it does not have any bandwidth limit.

Option C is incorrect because we cannot use scheduled instances, as our traffic is unpredictable.

Option D can also be a good suggestion.

Option E is incorrect because once a launch configuration is created, it cannot be edited.

Option F is invalid because the step scaling policy does not have any cool down period.

Mind Map

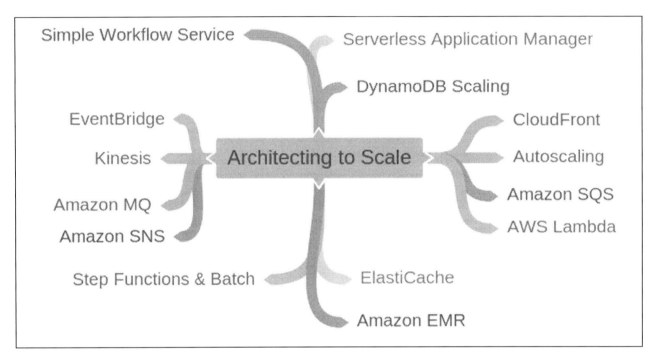

Figure 6-18: Mind Map

Practice Questions

1. Which AWS Service is used to distribute the content with a high transfer rate and low latency via the use of Edge Location?
   a. AWS CloudFormation
   b. AWS ElastiCache
   c. AWS CloudFront
   d. AWS RDS

2. AWS CloudFront can be used to Deliver Dynamic Content as well as static content. True or false?
   a. True
   b. False

3. AWS CloudFront Distribution types are _____. (Select 2)
   a. Horizontal
   b. Web
   c. RTMP

d. All of the above

4. To restrict any user belonging to a specific country from accessing the content, which feature of AWS CloudFront is used?
   a. CNAME
   b. Geo Restriction
   c. Zone Apex
   d. Invalidation

5. AWS CloudFront can work with the non-origin server as well. True or false?
   a. True
   b. False

6. Which features of AWS CloudFront can you use to remove malicious or harmful object before its expiration time from all edge locations?
   a. CNAME
   b. Zone Apex
   c. Invalidation
   d. Geo restriction

7. In AWS CloudFront, you can use SSL via default URL or Custom URL. For custom URL, you can use two types of configuration. Name them by selecting any 2 from the followings.
   a. Dedicated IP Custom SSL
   b. SNI Custom SSL
   c. Custom SSL using CloudFlare
   d. Custom SSL with Azure

8. For storage of simple data types, which cache engine is used?

   a. Redis
   b. MySQL
   c. No SQL

d. Memcached

9. Which cache engines are supported by Amazon ElastiCache? (Choose 2)
    a. My SQL
    b. Redis
    c. Couch base
    d. Memcached

10. _____ is used for backup and restoration of data in terms of caching.
    a. Membase
    b. Redis
    c. Memcached
    d. MySQL

11. Replication and Multi-AZ is one of the best approach for _____.
    a. Fast recovery
    b. Low latency
    c. Low availability
    d. Increasing effect of loss

12. When do you need to distribute your data over multiple nodes which the ElastiCache engine used?
    a. Membase
    b. Redis
    c. Memcached
    d. MySQL

13. Which ElastiCache engine is used for the persistence of key stores?
    a. Membase
    b. Redis
    c. Memcached
    d. MySQL

14. By using which of the following services, can you point to Zone Apex in CloudFront distribution?
    a. Route53
    b. AWS CodeCommit
    c. AWS CodePipeline
    d. AWS CloudFront

15. What are the HTTP methods that are not cached in CloudFront Edge Location?
    a. PUT, POST, PATCH, and DELETE
    b. PUT, POST, PATCH, and GET
    c. PUT, GET, OPTION, and DELETE
    d. HEAD, POST, PATCH, and GET

16. When you need to increase or decrease your system by scaling out, adding, and deletion of nodes, you can use_____.
    a. Membase
    b. Redis
    c. Memcached
    d. MySQL

17. For storage of complex data types like strings, which cache engine is used?
    a. Redis
    b. MySQL
    c. No SQL
    d. Memcached

18. Which AWS service is used when streaming a large amount of data is needed?
    a. AWS Kinesis
    b. AWS Redshift
    c. AWS CloudFront
    d. AWS ElastiCache

19. Kinesis is not good for persistence storage. True or false?
    a. True
    b. False

20. Data Producers put data in Kinesis Stream via _____ ways.
    a. 2
    b. 3
    c. 4
    d. 5

21. In single shard, you can support maximum _____ PUTS/sec.
    a. 2000
    b. 200
    c. 1000
    d. 100

22. The single shard in kinesis stream has throughput of _____.
    a. 10MB/sec
    b. 2MB/sec
    c. 1MB/sec
    d. 20MB/sec

23. To identify which data belongs to which shard, what type of record can you use?
    a. Sequence
    b. BLOB
    c. Partition key
    d. A and C

24. The function of data consumers is to _____.
    a. Input data
    b. Querying
    c. Processing
    d. B and C

25. Which Service of AWS can you use to push notifications on the custom application?
    a. AWS SQS

   b. AWS CloudFront

   c. AWS SNS

   d. AWS SWF

26. Choose the benefit of loosely coupled architectures for scalability.
   a. Permits more flexibility.
   b. More atomic functional units.
   c. Layers of abstraction are established.
   d. Greater resource utilization.
   e. Interchangeable components.

27. What are the main uses of Kinesis Data Streams? (Choose 2)
   a. They can undertake the loading of streamed data directly into data stores
   b. They can provide long term storage of data
   c. They can enable real-time reporting and analysis of streamed data
   d. They can accept data as soon as it has been produced, without the need for batching

28. In order to facilitate the processing of real estate contracts, we are developing an application. This process requires many manual and automated steps, which can take weeks to complete. Which service should we use choose to use in this case?
   a. Kinesis Data Streams
   b. Simple Notification Service
   c. Lambda
   d. Simple Queue Service
   e. Simple Workflow Service

29. We noted that we sometimes get traffic spikes on Monday mornings based on past reports of our web traffic. Which form of scaling should we use for this scenario that is the most cost-effective?
   a. Maintain
   b. Manual
   c. Scheduled
   d. Dynamic

30. What is the preferred method for reading data from a shard while creating an Amazon Kinesis Data Stream application?

a. KCL
b. KPL
c. SSH
d. API

Chapter 07: Business Continuity

Introduction

As per the updated blueprint of AWS Solution Architect Professional, Business Continuity and Disaster Recovery is essential for designing networks of complex organizations. It is necessary for implementing a new system or improving the existing environment. In this chapter, we will discuss in-depth about what AWS offers to maintain a certain level of availability and business continuity. Business continuity depends on a secure, continuous data flow across an enterprise – from operations to marketing to results. Even a small failure in continuity can mean thousands of lost sales opportunities, manufacturing disorders, and weakened consumer trust. This failure can range from natural disasters to mechanical failure or human errors.

Concepts

The main thing that you need to understand is that Business Continuity and Disaster Recovery (DR) are different terms. Business Continuity refers to the search of reducing the disruption when something unexpected happens in business activity. Disaster Recovery is an act of responding to an event that intimidates business continuity.

Secondly, you need to know the difference between High Availability and Fault Tolerance. High Availability (HA) is reducing the chance of service impact by designing the redundancies, while Fault Tolerance is the absorption of an issue without any effect on service. Fault tolerance might be sometimes expensive as it can tolerate the fault. In HA, you have some space for unexpected downtime.

We know that SLA is an agreement/commitment of the service that it gives a specific target or goal in terms of performance or availability or responsiveness. If a service provider is not able to meet SLA, then it faces some effects. In AWS, multiple services have their respected SLAs, and in case of SLA does not match, AWS offers some service credits to the customer. However, the customer has to prove the downtime and request service credit.

You also need to know about RTO and RPO. Recovery Time Objective (RTO) — is the time that it takes to recover from a disaster. It is measured from when the crash first occurred to when you have fully recovered to the service level. Recovery Point Objective (RPO) — is the amount of data your organization is prepared to lose in the event of a disaster.

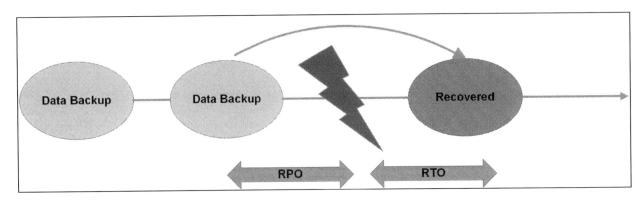

Figure 7-01: RTO and RPO

When the business continuity plan is designed, it defines the RTO and RPO, which need to be supported for this plan. The author of the Business Continuity plan has some assumptions of how long that downtime they could bear and how much data loss is acceptable. High Availability investment is made then justified by the RTO and RPO. RTO and RPO then also defines the process of DR because HA will try to mitigate the act of having a DR, but if DR is needed, then it delivers the required RTO and RPO.

There are different types of Disaster categories like Hardware Failure (Failure of power switch), Deployment Failure (Deploying patch that breaks the business process), Load Induced (DDoS attack), Data Produced, Credential Expiration (SSL/TLS certificate expired), Dependency Failure (S3 subsystem failure cause other services failure), Infrastructure Failure (cut in fiber) and Identifier Exhaustion (requesting of a service that is unavailable). Human error is also the main cause of disaster occurrence.

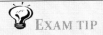

EXAM TIP

RTO is Recovery Time Objective is the duration of recovering from a disaster, and RPO is Recovery Point Objective is the acceptable amount of data loss during the disaster.

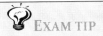

EXAM TIP

FMEA (Failure Mode and Effects Analysis) is used to study the problem which arises in the business. It is a systematic process to identify:

What could go wrong?

What impact might it have?

What is the likelihood of it occurring?

What is our ability to detect and react?

 EXAM TIP

To detect the risk priority, there is the formula:

Severity*Probability*(Ability of Detection) = Risk Priority Number

The higher the Risk Priority number is, the higher the potential of that risk. To apply all the redundancies and additional processes to avoid it from happening or reduce the RPN.

Disaster Recovery Architecture

You need a comprehensive cloud recovery strategy to keep the physical infrastructure up and running, which should be used in case of the unavailability of your infrastructure. AWS allows faster disaster recovery of its primary IT services without incurring second physical site infrastructure costs. There are different types of DR architecture in AWS; these types differ on the basis of the time required to recover from a disaster. The architecture that takes longer time costs less, while the recovery architecture that takes less time costs you more.

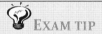 EXAM TIP

Disaster Recovery is a concept of recovery of your organization from any disaster, while Business Continuity is to limit the risk of any disruption in the continuity of operations in the business.

Backup and Restore

It is the common entry point in AWS. In this type, the data is backed to the tape and periodically sent to the off-site. In this, you need minimal configuration efforts and less risk presence. Amazon S3 is the data backup destination. We use Amazon Glacier for long-term data storage with the same durability as Amazon S3, but the difference is that its cost is lower than that of S3. The data can be backup from on-premises storage, AWS Storage Gateway, or VTL. It has less flexibility but needs downtime before restoration. It is similar to the off-site backup. In this method, the RPO value is huge.

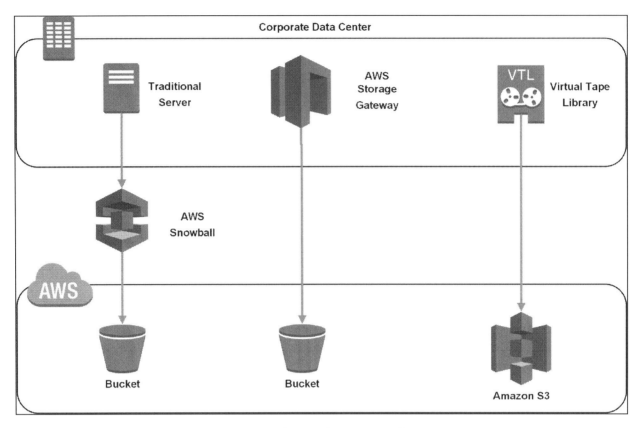

Figure 7-02: Backup and Restore Architecture

Pilot Light

The recovery time is less in contrast with the backup and recovery process in the Pilot Light system. The core component of the process, like a server, is already up to date in the Pilot Light framework on AWS. It is a cost-effective way of maintaining the hot-site concept.

> **Note:** A hot site is a business disaster recovery system that allows a company to continue computer and network operations if a device or equipment disaster occurs.

The RTO and RPO value is very low, so recovery takes only a few minutes. The disadvantage of this method is that it needs manual interference for failover. You also need to keep up to date with the AMI with an on-premises image. Also, spinning up the Cloud environment takes time, maybe minutes or hours.

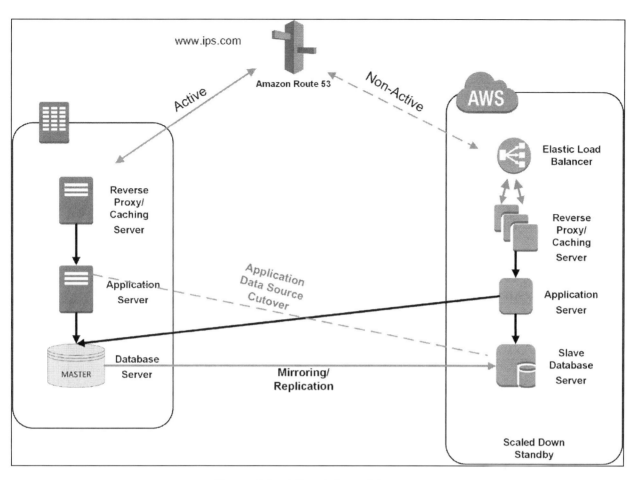

Figure 7-03: Pilot Light Architecture

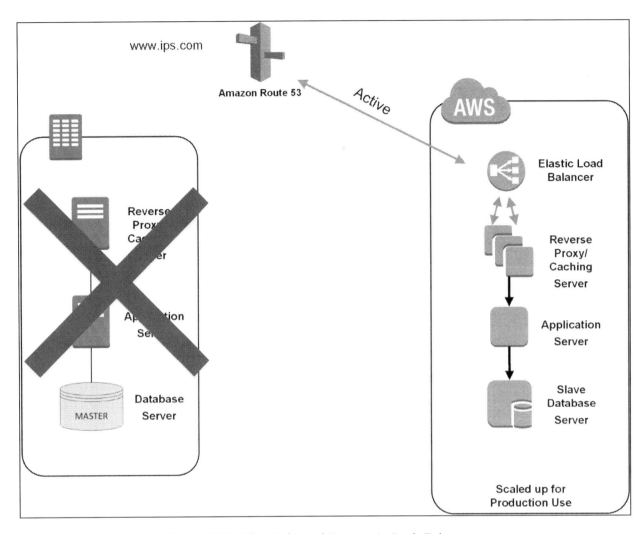

Figure 7-04: Pilot Light Architecture in Fault Tolerance

Warm Standby

It is an extended version of Pilot Light. It further decreases the recovery time, as part of the service is always running on warm standby. In this, all services are running and ready to accept a failover load quickly by taking up to minutes and seconds. Once the system fails, the standby network will be expanded to a production environment level at the time of recovery point, DNS records will be modified, and all the traffic will be diverted to a new AWS environment. You can use this new environment as a shadow environment for testing purposes.

As the new environment is always running, its cost is very high, but RTO and RPO are very low. The disadvantage of this method is that you need to scale the resources as per workload requirements and some adjustments in the environment with the script.

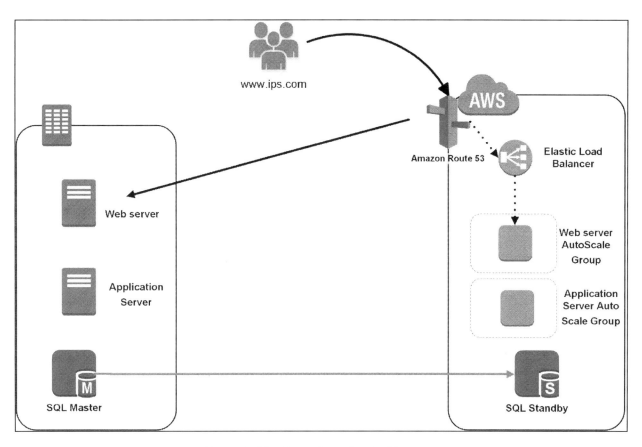

Figure 7-05: Warm Standby Architecture

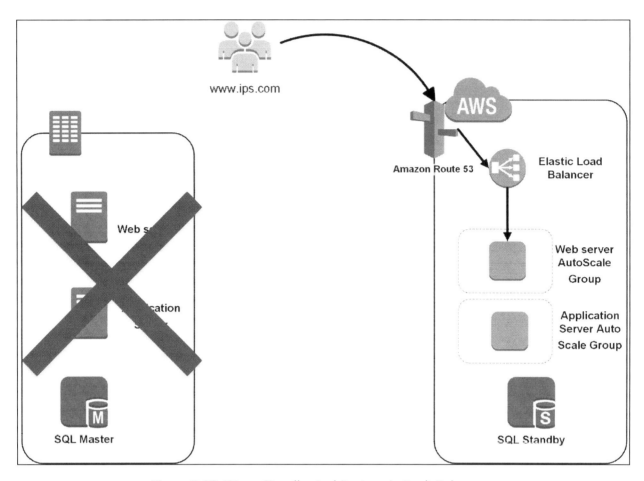

Figure 7-06: Warm Standby Architecture in Fault Tolerance

Multi-site

In the Multi-site method, the mirrored data center is running and ready to take a full load of the production environment in case of failure in the on-premises environment. Failover happens in seconds. It is one of the best ways for DR, but it is also the most expensive. The app works in both AWS and the existing infrastructure. The weighted routing is supported by the DNS system. The traffic will go to both the standby and the existing infrastructures.

The disadvantage of this method is that the resources are considered to be wasted, as they are waiting for the primary infrastructure to fail.

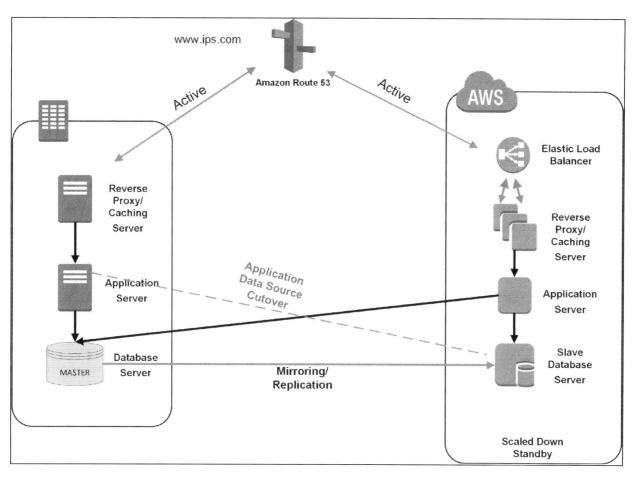

Figure 7-07: Multi-site Architecture

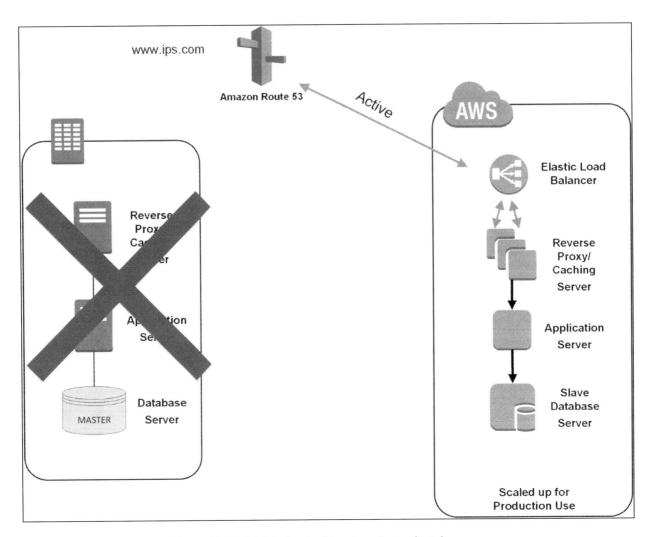

Figure 7-08: Multi-site Architecture in Fault Tolerance

 EXAM TIP

Before going to the exam, remember the four DR architectures with their trade-offs.

Storage HA

In this, we will discuss the different storage options that are available for High Availability.

EBS Volume - The annual failure rate of EBS is 0.2%, while the failure of commodity hardware is 4%. So, EBS volume is a better option as it also has 99.999% of availability. Each Amazon EBS volume is replicated automatically within its Availability Zone to protect you from the failure of a single component. You can attach a volume to one instance at a time but cannot attach one volume to many instances. Its easier to take a snapshot of the volume stored in S3, which is multi-AZ. Also, the snapshots can be copied to other regions. It supports RAID configuration as well.

There are multiple RAID configurations:

- RAID0- There is no redundancy but has high Read and Write capacity. It is also termed "Stripping."
- RAID1- There is one drive fail redundancy, which means it has two drives, so capacity is distributed and reduced to 50%
- RAID5- There are minimum of three drives, two drives for data storage and one for parity bits. This parity drive is used to recover the data in case of failure of any of the storage drives. As in RAID5, it calculates what is missing and recreates that. Capacity of RAID5 is (n-1)/n
- RAID6 – It is more advanced than RAID5, as it has two parity method drives, i.e., primary and secondary, as it has two drives failure redundancy. It requires a minimum of four drives. The capacity of RAID6 is (n-2)/n

In AWS EBS volume RAID5 and RAID6 are not recommended as it has parity bit, which takes a huge amount of volume because EBS volume is accessed over the internet. Let's see how the RAID level impacts the throughput and IOPS.

	No RAID	RAID1	RAID2
Volume Size	1000GB (1 drive)	500GB (2 drive)	500GB (2 drive)
Provisioned IOPS	4000	4000	4000
Total IOPS	4000	8000	4000
Usable Space	1000GB	1000GB	500GB
Throughput	500MB/s	1000MB/s	500MB/s

Table 7-01: Different RAID Configurations

S3 Storage- There are many different options available in S3. Its durability is eleven 9's (99.999999999%). It is used as a backup storage service for EBS snapshots and many other services.

- Availability of Standard Storage Class is 99.99% (52.6 minutes/year, unavailable)
- Availability of Standard Infrequent Access is 99.9% (8.76 hours/year)
- Availability of One-Zone Infrequent Access is 99.5% (1.83 days/year)

The durability of Standard and Standard IA is Multi-AZ, while One-zone has single AZ durability.

Amazon EFS - is an implementation of the NFS system. It is robust, through which you can achieve Multi-AZ redundancy for a file share. Its Mount target is highly Available, and

it is a file system as opposed to Block storage or Object storage. You can concurrently access the files from multiple AZs.

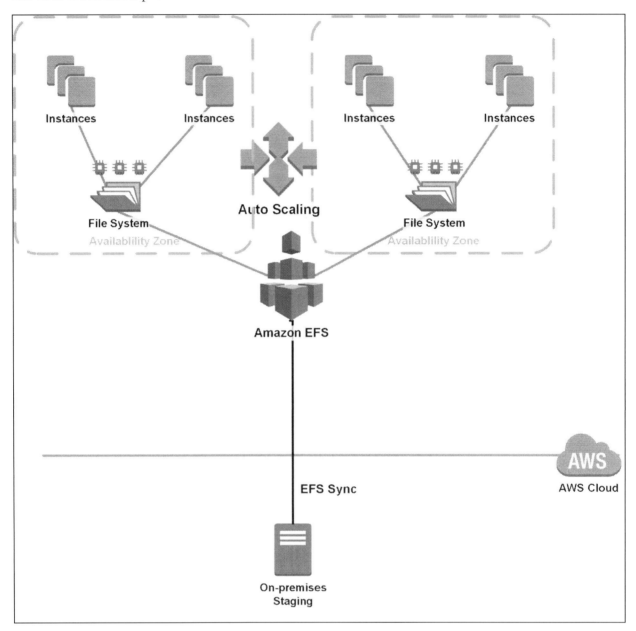

Figure 7-09: EFS Architecture

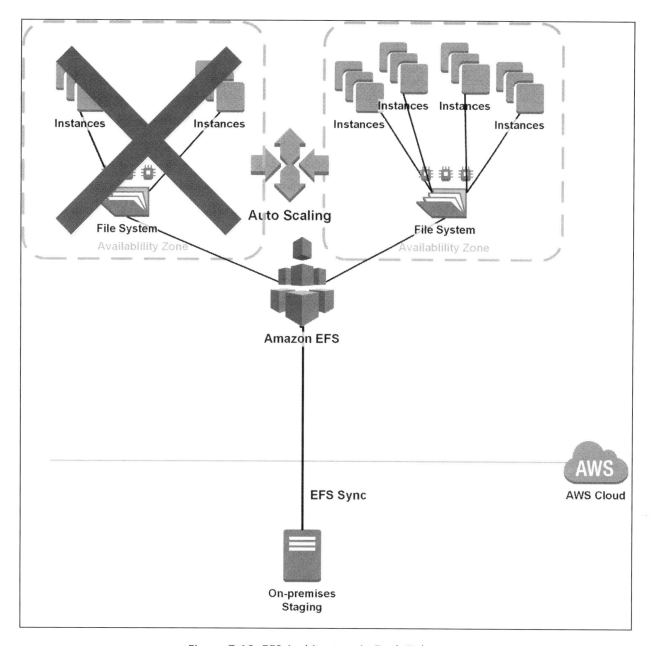

Figure 7-10: EFS Architecture in Fault Tolerance

Storage Gateway - It is suitable for off-site backup of on-premises data to AWS with synchronization when needed. In backup and restore the DR model, we can use Storage Gateway.

Snowball - It is suitable for migrating a huge amount of data to AWS, but only for batch transfer of data.

Glacier - It is for long-term archival and safe off-site archive storage.

Compute HA

For HA, there are some compute options available, but the first thing you need to keep in mind is that the AMI is required to be up to date. It is the critical component for failover. Also, make sure that you do not have an outdated AMI in AWS. For DR staging and keeping it safe, copy the AMI to other regions. For HA, Horizontal scaling is preferred, as the risk can be spread to multiple small machines as compared to one big machine. If you want that instance to be available when needed, then use Reserved Instance. With Auto scaling and Elastic Load Balancing, you can get a resilient design for providing an automated recovery by maintaining a minimum number of instances.

For HA, you can use Route53 health, which can provide "self-healing" redirection of traffic without doing anything. Consider an example; we have an infrastructure for web on AWS and on-premises. If Route 53 health check fails for on-premises infrastructure, then the customer is instantly routed towards AWS infrastructure.

> EXAM TIP: In Compute, horizontal scaling is used to spread the risk to multiple small machines.

Database HA

Some considerations of Databases for HA:

- Choose DynamoDB over RDS because DynamoDB has built-in redundancy and failover
- If you want to use RDS and you cannot use DynamoDB, then use Aurora because it has failover and redundancy capability
- If you cannot use Aurora, then use Multi-AZ RDS
- For protecting the data against failure or interruption, you need to take frequent snapshots of RDS. The snapshot does not affect performance, as it takes snapshots from the standby database
- You can also use Read Replica, but it is not strongly consistent, which means it is not updated with a master
- If you use EC2 for the database, then you need to design HA by yourself

Consider an example, you have an RDS with Multi-AZ deployment and Read Replicas. The databases in Multi-AZ are synchronized, while in Read Replica it is synchronized. The replicas are eventually consistent replicas. In case of failure of Master DB, then RDS is promoted to Standby DB, and replication continues.

If the whole Region in which Multi-AZ deployment has been done goes down, promote to Replica and make one of the replicas as the master node, and then create another one in the same region for Multi-AZ. But promoting Read replica to the master node can be a difficult task. So instead of using a script, use an automated method for this.

HA for Redshift - In Redshift, Multi-AZ deployment is not supported, so for HA, we use the Multi-node cluster option. This option supports replication and node recovery. In a single-node cluster, there is no replication and in case of disk failure, use snapshots from S3 to restore.

HA for ElastiCache - In Memcached, you need to use multiple nodes in each shard to avoid data loss in node failure because it does not support replication. If one node fails, its data is lost. For avoiding AZ failure, launch multiple nodes in different AZs.

In Redis, there are multiple nodes in each shard that are distributed across multiple AZs. For automatic failover in case of failure of primary nodes, enable Multi-AZ on replication group, and schedule the backup for Redis Cluster.

Network HA

The network option which is available for HA can be done via creating subnets in multi-AZ and placing the systems in those AZs. In this way, you create a Multi-AZ presence for VPC.

Also, you are recommended to have two VPN tunnels from a corporate network to Virtual Private Gateway. As we know, DirectConnect has no high availability option by default. So you need to create another DirectConnect connection or VPN for HA.

Route 53 has health checks that provide a basic level of redirecting DNS resolution. For HA, you can also use Elastic IPs that give the flexibility to change the backend without repointing the DNS entries. If you want Multi-AZ redundancy for NAT gateways, then create it in multiple AZs and also define a route in a private subnet to use local gateways.

Challenge 1

A banking firm has support for all transactions out of its global datacenter. The Point of Sales (POS) system is comprised of a store client application and a central 2-tier processing engine. The sales transactions are uploaded from the stores to the datacenter. This transaction can be processed by any of the three app servers and inserted into the 2TB MySQL database. SAN space is used to store transaction files as an encrypted text file for 5 years. Currently, 10TB of archived files are stored in SAN.

There is a cron job defined by the bank to purge out the files that are older than 5 years on a monthly basis. POS clients can run offline mode for 4 hours only, so RTO must be less than 4 hours. POS clients cache the data locally for the past 12 hours, so the RPO is less than 12 hours.

From the following options, which is the best to meet given the requirement of RTO/RPO in the most cost-effective way?

A. Use Snowball to pre-load the SAN data into the AWS S3 bucket, then schedule the daily snowball deliveries to batch sync SAN data. Provision of a Single AZ Amazon Aurora instance and setup replication between Aurora and on-premises MySQL database. Import images of the app server into EC2 as AMIs.

B. Use Snowball to pre-load the SAN data into the AWS S3 bucket, then set up the Storage Gateway File Gateway to keep SAN in sync. Provision a Single AZ RDS instance and set up replication between MySQL RDS and on-premises MySQL database. Import images of the app server into EC2 as AMIs.

C. Create a RAID5 array using EBS and EC2, then use rsync to keep the data sync with the AWS version. Perform regular backups to tape using VTL. Create CloudFormation scripts to provision the MySQL and App servers, restoring them from VTL as needed.

D. Setup a cron job that uses rsync to replicate the SAN data to EFS volumes mounted on an EC2 instance. Configure lifecycle rules on EFS to purge anything over 5 years. Provision an RDS MySQL ReadReplica and set up mirroring to the on-premises database. Import images of App servers into EC2 as AMIs.

Solution

As per the given requirements of RTO and RPO of less than 4 hours and 12 hours, respectively, preparation steps are required in cost-effective way. **Option B** is the best cost-effective solution. As in this, Snowball is used to pre-load data into S3 bucket. Use Storage Gateway to keep sync SAN data with S3. Also, provision a single AZ RDS instance to setup replication between MySQL RDS and on-premises MySQL database.

Then, import the images to EC2 as AMIs. This solution uses very minimal instances to keep in sync, and we also have AMIs that we can use to up the instance in case of any issue.

Option A is invalid as it uses snowball to pre-load data; it is reasonable but uses it as a daily batch to keep in sync. In Amazon Aurora is by default Multi-AZ, so a single AZ instance is suspected.

Option C is not valid, as we know that AWS doesn't recommend RAID5 and RAID6 configurations because parity bits slow the IOPS, as they consume 1/4th or 1/5th of IOPS. The use of EBS volume is also an expensive solution than S3. In this option, VTL is also used to recover, which takes several hours and exceeds our given RTO.

Option D is also not valid because EFS is not a cost-effective solution for storing the data; it is actually 15 times more expensive than S3. We also need EC2 running up to perform the sync.

Challenge 2

An organization has multiple business processes, which are running on the ERP system of the organization, and they can only be able to face 10 minutes of unpredictable down time with no data loss. You, as Solution Architect Professional, are asked to look into the DR plan, and you observe that after 10 minutes, there is an extreme financial and commercial impact.

When you look into the architecture landscape, it consists of a fleet of app servers behind an ELB and multi-AZ MySQL RDS. All of these are placed in three AZs within the region. Read replica of the RDS is created into another region.

If you are doing an audit, then which of the following would be the concern in DR documentation?

A. The app servers are defined in an auto-scaling group to keep a minimum of six instances equally distributed across multiple AZs.
B. The app servers are configured for RAID0 to provide both performance and redundancy for local data.
C. A minimum of 2 reserved instances has been purchased in each of three AZs to be used by app servers.
D. In the case of an AZ failure, the database will auto failover to one of the read replicas.

E. The ELB has cross zone load balancing enabled, so traffic is distributed equally across all app servers.

F. Use Route 53 health checks to detect and remove routes to unhealthy app servers in under a minute.

G. To provide the best read performance, chose to use the MyISAM storage engine for our MySQL database.

Solution

Most of the company has a third party to audit and review the DR strategy in order to make sure that they do not miss anything. So from the options given in the question, the wrong assumptions are:

Option A is not valid because it is perfectly best to define a minimum number of the resource in an Auto-scaling.

Option B is valid because it is an invalid assumption of using RAID0 for providing redundancy, as in real, it is not.

Option C is also invalid, as it is the best solution when you need the resource to be available 100%; buying the reserved instances means that you have to access those resources frequently.

Option D is valid, as we know that Aurora will automatic failover to replicas but here MySQL RDS is used, and it cannot perform an automatic failover to one of the read replicas.

Option E is also not valid, as we know that cross zone load balancing is one of the best solutions for equally using all instances independent of which AZ it is in. If cross zone load balancing is not enabled, then each ELB endpoint has only access to the resource within that AZ.

Option F is also valid, as we are using ELB, and there is no need to use Route 53 for update routes to specific app servers. We must allow ELB to do health checks for us.

Option G is also not appropriate, as in the question, they already have read replica, and it is supported only in MySQL DB engine. So, using the MyISAM storage engine is not preferred.

Mind Map

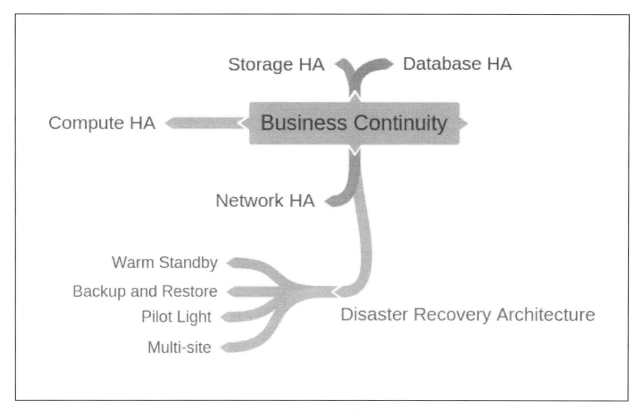

Figure 7-11: MindMap

Practice Question

1. Which of the following gives the highest performance for Write?
a) RAID0
b) RAID1
c) RAID5
d) RAID6

2. Redshift, by default, supports a multi-node cluster by deploying on Multi-AZ. True or False?
a) True
b) False

3. By using Spread Placement Group, you can reduce the risk of hardware failure in AWS. True or False?
a) True

b) False

4. From the following, which option is suitable for in-memory cache and is able to handle AZ failure?
a) Memcached
b) DynamoDB
c) Redis
d) Athena

5. You need RAID fault-tolerance for 1TB of data for a new EC2 file server. What is the choice you must select?
a) RAID5 with two EBS volumes of not less than 1 TB each
b) RAID1 with two EBS volumes of not less than 1 TB each
c) RAID0 with two EBS volumes of not less than 500 GB each
d) RAID0 with two EBS volumes of not less than 1 TB each

6. What is the relationship between RPO and BC?
a) RPO informs what business processes should be prioritized for recovery after a disaster
b) RPO defines the time of a potential outage for creating contingency plans
c) RPO justifies the amount of investment in HA to counter the potential risk
d) RPO provides an expectation of potential manual data re-entry for recovery plans

7. For a 2 GB server, your customer described an RPO and RTO of 24 hours. Which general approach do you recommend for the most cost-effective implementation of these requirements?
a) Backup and Restore
b) Pilot light
c) Multi-site
d) Pilot light

8. A sun flare removes an Electromagnetic Pulse (EMP) from the electric grid. What kind of disaster is it?
a) Load Induced
b) Hardware Failure

c) Infrastructure

d) Data induced

9. In what type of architecture, the replica environment is not active?

a) Backup and Restore

b) Pilot light

c) Multi-site

d) None of the above

10. If you want the RDS that has fault tolerance and HA capability, then which service can you use?

a) DynamoDB

b) MongoDB

c) Aurora

d) MySQL

Chapter 08: Deployment and Operation Management

Introduction

In this chapter, we will discuss deployment management, deployment strategies, operational excellence and deployment of existing solutions. We will also discuss CI/CD. Then, we will explore all the services that are used for building and deploying the highly available, scalable and fault-tolerant infrastructure on AWS.

Types of Deployment

There are multiple software deployment types which we break into three general groups:

- BigBang - means all tasks are performed at once. Its trade-off is that it is risky but takes the shortest time in implementation
- Phased Roll-Out – it works gradually over time. Its trade-off is that it is less risky but takes time during implementation
- Parallel Adoption - means we have both new and old environments. It takes the most time, but it does not have the least amount of risk as in that it has to maintain the two systems, which is one of the most challenging tasks. You have to keep the running data in sync when implementing parallel adoption.

Rolling Deployment

In this type of deployment, the update is not done on all fleets of targets at once. The group of targets is divided into x-number of targets so that when updating is done on this x-number of targets, the remaining is running with the old version. Once the updating process is completed on the x-number of targets, updating in other x-number of targets is started. Hence, in this process, there are two versions of the software.

For updating the version of target instances, you need to create a new launching configuration with an updated AMI version.

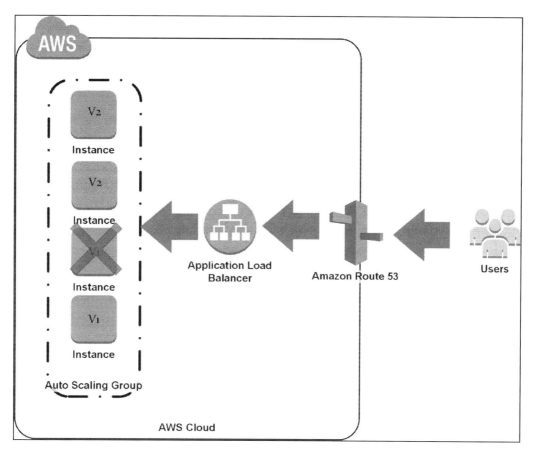

Figure 8-01: Rolling Deployment

AB Testing

AB testing is similar to Blue/Green Deployment, but the only difference is that in AB testing, both environments are running, while in Blue/Green Deployment, only one is running at a time, and the other one is idle. In AB testing, you can test your code performance and usability. In this, you can route the traffic with 50% each on both environments to check which environment works best. In this deployment, you can shift a small subset of users to test the environment, and if you get bad feedback from the user regarding the environment, you can roll back to the previous environment, or if the feedback is good, then you can shift completely (100%) to this new feature. This way, you have a different version of the code with different reliability.

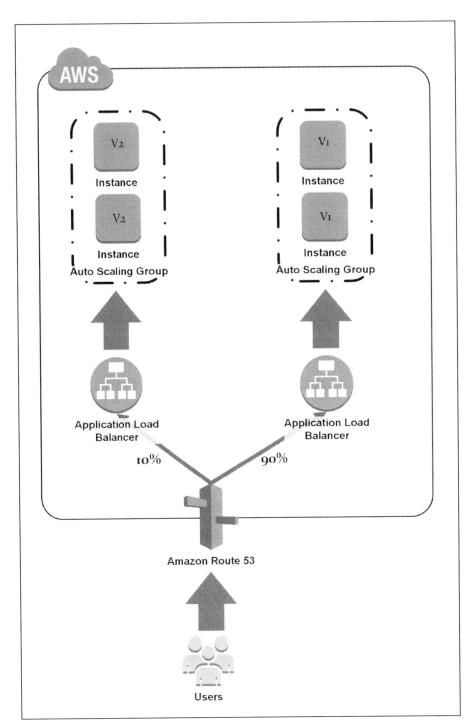

Figure 8-02: AB Testing

Canary Release

In Canary Release, we reduce the bad impact of the new version by continuously modifying it. If any problem is detected in this new release, then we roll back to the older one. In that

type of deployment, instead of pointing to any one of the environments, DNS points to both environments. In canary deployment, the new version is slowly released for more and more users. In the beginning, the split is 99% to the old and 1% to new, which gradually increases to 50% on both. Once you are satisfied with the new environment performance, then you can redirect 100% traffic towards the new release. In AWS, you can do this using Route 53- weighted round-robin where you define how much traffic goes to each app deployment.

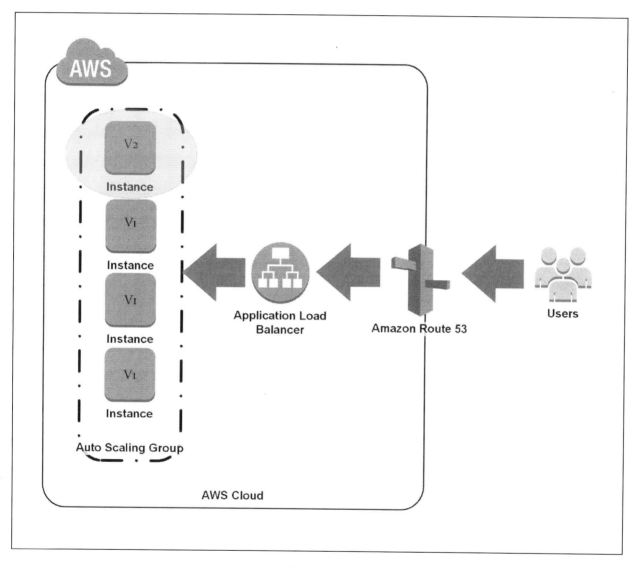

Figure 8-03: Canary Release

Blue/Green Deployment

In this technique, there are two environments; one is running with an older version, and another with the new version. For both environments, we have separate Load Balancers

because this deployment uses DNS for application deployment. At some point, you may decide to switch to the new environment at Route 53 level. If you face any issue in a new environment, then you can switch back to the older one. The main purpose of using Blue/Green Deployment is to achieve immutable infrastructure. If you do not want to make changes in your application after deploying, you can do redeploying. To perform Blue/Green Deployment, there are various methods available such as:

- Updating DNS with Route 53 to point to new ELB or instances
- Swap Auto Scaling Group of new version behind ELB
- Change launch configuration of Auto Scaling Group with the new AMI version and delete the old one
- Use Elastic Beanstalk for Swapping the environmental URL of the stack that has a new version
- You can also clone stack via OpsWorks and then update DNS

There are some scenarios where Blue/Green Deployment is not recommended for deploying, those in which rollback is difficult, like:

- When your code is tightly coupled with Datastore Schema because for Blue/Green Deployment, your deployment code needs to be independent of the data layer and handy. If your Schema changing has the capability for going back and forth, then you can use this deployment model
- During deployment, when you need to upgrade for specific upgrade routines
- Off-the-shelf products that are not Blue/Green Deployment friendly

> **EXAM TIP:** The difference between blue-green deployments and A/B testing is, A/B testing is for measuring the application's functionality while Blue/Green Deployment is for releasing new software safely and rolling back predictably.

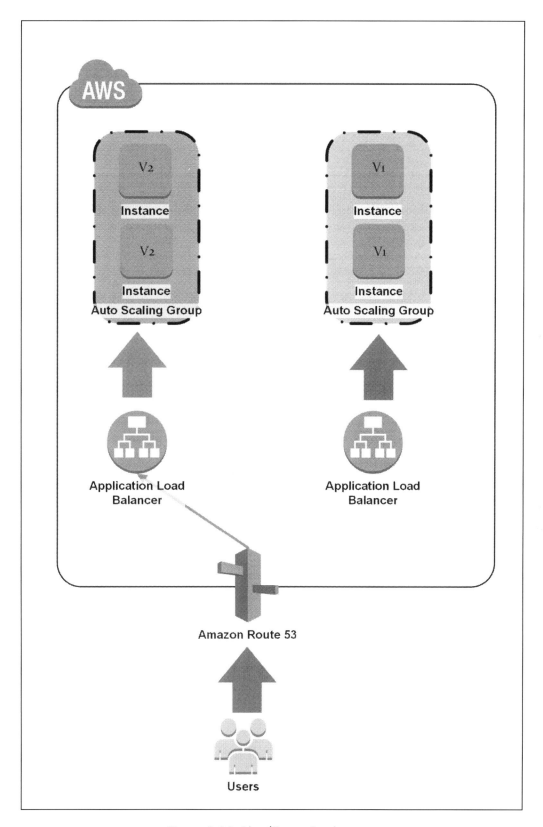

Figure 8-04: Blue/Green Deployment

Continuous Integration and Deployment

CI and CD are the software development best practices, and both of them are at the core of software development. CI/CD refers to Continuous Integration and Continuous Delivery/Deployment. CD terms are often used interchangeably, although there is a difference in the meaning of these two.

Continuous Integration (CI) means merging of the changes in the code to the main branch as soon as possible, with automated testing. This approach helps in finding and resolving bugs sooner. It is mostly referred to as the *build* stage of the software release process.

Continuous Delivery (CD) means you have an automated releasing process of the software, which includes building, testing, and staging updates. Then you can deploy it to the live environment with a click.

Continuous Deployment is the process in which we automate the entire deployment. Any specific change in code which passes all stages of release will be released to the production environment without any requirement of human interruption.

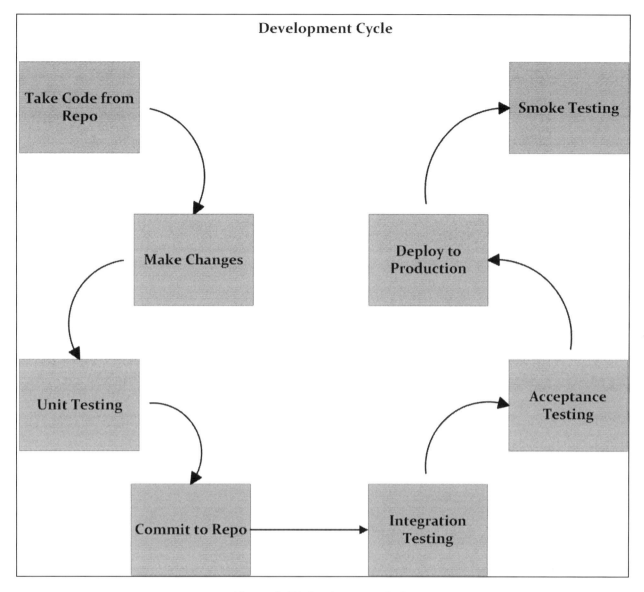

Figure 8-05: Deployment Cycle

In the above figure, smoke testing means testing of production environment after complete deployment. Many of the software do the unit testing, integration testing, acceptance testing, deployment to production, and smoke testing manually. If we implement the test automation in this, then the process becomes streamlined, and we take out the human element from this process.

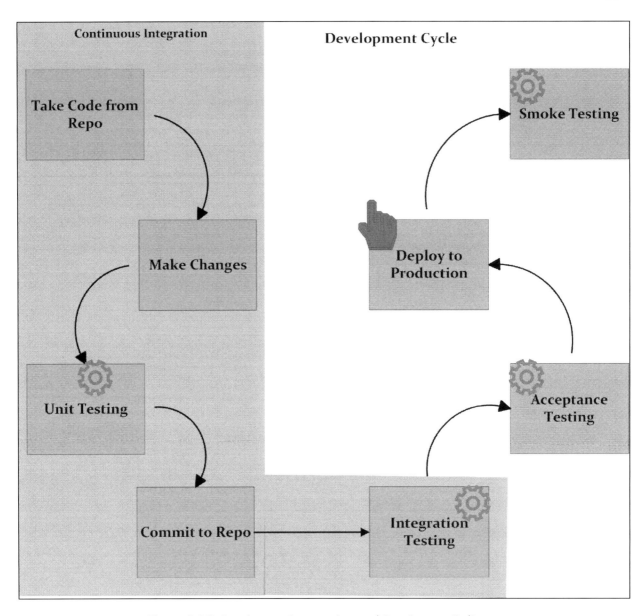

Figure 8-06: Continuous Integration and Continuous Delivery

As we see in the above diagram that from getting updates, perform changes until the integration testing is part of Continuous Integration. This thing happened several times a day as the code changes. For Continuous Delivery, we push that button of manual deployment of the software in the production once a day. While if automation is not applied, we will be able to push the button for production deployment once a month, as everything is manual, so testing takes a lot of time.

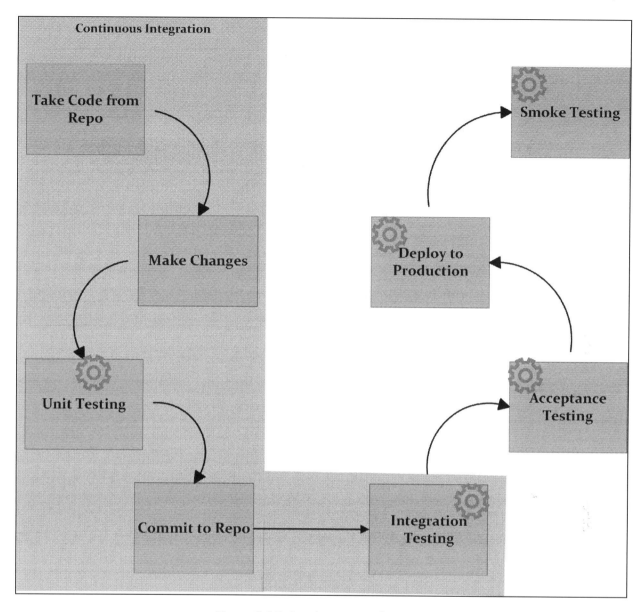

Figure 8-07: Continuous Deployment

In the above figure, the entire deployment to the production is automated. The deployment is triggered once all the tests are passed.

CI/CD Consideration

- Create a small discrete package that gets implemented very regularly rather than increased complex changes
- Lowest deployment risk when you deploy chunks of code, and if the negative happens, then it will be isolated
- Test automation needs to be very strong

- If the feature is not ready for deployment at production, then maybe you create a branch and merge later, or you can use feature Toggle. Toggle pattern is that wrapping of the new feature in some logical condition, like switch off or on
- Microservices architecture is suitable for CI/CD practices

In AWS, there are various tools for deployment like:

- **CodeCommit**- CodeCommit is a fully managed service that is used to host secure and highly scalable Git repositories
- **CodeBuild**- AWS CodeBuild is a fully managed service that compiles your source code, performs unit tests, and produces artifacts that are ready to deploy
- **CodeDeploy**- AWS CodeDeploy is a fully managed service that automates the whole software deployment process. It eliminates manual processes and makes it easy to implement CI/CD practices. It performs deployment on EC2 instances, Lambda, Elastic Beanstalk, or ECS. It also deploys on the on-premises system as well
- **CodePipeline**- It is a workstation mechanism that helps to do all things together. With this service, you can model, visualize and automate the steps of the software release process
- **AWS X-Ray**- For Debugging of distributed applications or on serverless applications, you can use AWS X-Ray
- **AWS CodeStar**- You can quickly develop, build and deploy AWS applications with AWS CodeStar

AWS Elastic Beanstalk

AWS Elastic Beanstalk is an orchestration solution that makes deploying scalable web landscapes as simple as pressing a button. The quickest and most straightforward way to get an application up and running on AWS is with AWS Elastic Beanstalk. It's one of the best services for developers who want to deploy their code without having to worry about the infrastructure. After the application is deployed, AWS Elastic Beanstalk manages all aspects of capacity provisioning and monitoring. Within the app, it enables numerous environments (DEV, PRO, QA, etc.). It is adequate for deployment, but it's not ideal if you need a lot of control and flexibility. Elastic Beanstalk is made up of several layers; the bottom layer is the management layer, also called as the application layer. Multiple environments, including instances, load balancers, Auto scaling groups, and monitoring, exist within the application layer. There are programme versions on top of these layers, and you can have as many as you want.

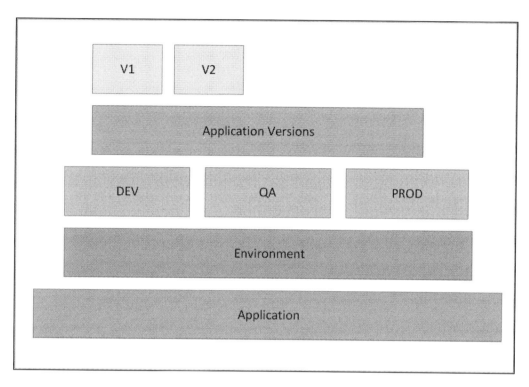

Figure 8-08: Elastic Beanstalk Layers

Features

Management complexity is also reduced via AWS Elastic Beanstalk. Elastic Beanstalk uses Auto scaling and Elastic Load Balancing to support highly variable amounts of traffic quickly. This is a helpful service for those who do not know much about the cloud yet need their environment up and running. Elastic Beanstalk does not support CloudFormation templates, but CloudFormation supports Elastic Beanstalk services. CloudFormation is a way of scripting AWS for people to know the different aspects of AWS, while Elastic Beanstalk is for those who do not know about AWS. Although both are provisioning services, it is better to choose CloudFormation over Elastic Beanstalk.

In Elastic Beanstalk, you can access CloudWatch for monitoring purposes, and you can be notified of specific events or health. You can also access log files without logging in to the application server. With the help of Elastic Beanstalk, you can modify the setting of the application server.

- With the help of Elastic Beanstalk, you can scale your application up or down; it is the easiest way to deploy the application
- You can choose EC2 instance of your choice

- You can control the resources by yourself because either you have full access or Elastic Beanstalk can do it on your behalf
- Monitoring and managing health
- For performance data and metrics, you can integrate it with CloudWatch
- It has a managed and updated platform, which automatically updates OS, Node.js, etc.

Supported Languages and Application Server

- Packer Builder
- Single Container Docker
- Multicontainer Docker
- Preconfigured Docker
- Go
- Java SE
- Java with Tomcat
- .NET on Windows Server with IIS
- Node.js
- PHP
- Python
- Ruby
- Apache Tomcat for Java application (Java 6,7 & 8)
- Apache HTTP server for PHP and Python applications
- Nginx or Apache HTTP server for Node.js applications

Architectural Concept

To deploy a web application, you must first construct an environment. You must choose a platform, environment tier, and environment type when creating a new environment.

The levels of the environment are separated into two categories:

- The web server environment is where web applications are hosted, and HTTP(S) requests are handled.
- Web applications are hosted in the working environment, which also performs long-running or scheduled background processing tasks.

Creating a Web Application Source Bundle

To deploy a web application or to change the version of the existing application in Elastic Beanstalk; you need to create a source bundle of source code. The source bundle must contain these features:

1. A ZIP or WAR file
2. The maximum size of the file is 512 MB
3. You can make a ZIP file of multiple WAR files
4. Does not contain a parent directory

> **EXAM TIP:** In Elastic Beanstalk, you can also run other application components like memory caching service side-by-side in Amazon EC2.

> **EXAM TIP:** In Elastic Beanstalk, you can upload the code in a WAR file or push Git Repository, and then the rest of the work will be done for you. With the help of AWS Toolkit for Eclipse and Visual Studio, you can deploy the app in Elastic Beanstalk and manage it without leaving IDE (Integrated Development Environment).

Working

When you upload an application file, Elastic Beanstalk stores these files and server log files to S3. If you are using Git, Management Console, or Toolkit to upload a file, an S3 bucket is created in the account, and uploaded files are copied to Amazon S3. For server log files, you must edit the settings of environment configuration in Elastic Beanstalk to copy the server log files every hour in the S3 bucket. In S3 bucket, you can also store your application data like images by adding AWS SDK along with the application deploying file, e.g., in the WAR file.

> **EXAM TIP:** Elastic Beanstalk has the capability to provision RDS DB instances. With the help of environment variables, the connectivity to that DB instance is disclosed to the application.

In Elastic Beanstalk, fault tolerance is not configured for multiple regions, but it will be configured in a single region for multiple AZs. Elastic Beanstalk supports IAM fully. Through integrating it with AWS VPC, you can restrict the IP in white-listed IP address in Security Group or Network Access Control list that who can access the app, because, by default, your app is publicly available at "myapp.elasticbeanstalk.com".

Elastic Beanstalk Deployment Options

When you push updates from Git, it only transmits modified files to Elastic Beanstalk. In Elastic Beanstalk, multiple environments are supported, and the configuration of each environment is independent of each other. Resources that run are also separate. In Elastic Beanstalk, tracking and storing of versions are also available, so you can quickly return to the previous version from an existing one or create a new version of the environment. When we have multiple versions in the application version layer, and we want to deploy these versions, then you have multiple deployment versions.

- **All at once**- In this deployment method, old version instances are terminated, and new version instances are launched. This deployment method requires downtime, but it is the fastest method. Its rollback process is manual
- **Rolling**- In this method, the old version instances are terminated one by one and are replaced with new ones. It requires more time than all-at-once but with no downtime. The rollback is also manual
- **Rolling out with additional batch**- In this, we launch the first new set of instances before taking the older one out of the service. It requires more time than Rolling but with no downtime. The rollback is also manual
- **Immutable**- In this, we launch a separate Auto scaling group with the new version and only cutover when health checks pass. It takes a longer time, but the rollback option merely is terminating the old instances
- **Blue/Green Deployment**- This is the exclusive option in Elastic Beanstalk to swap the environmental URLs and points to the new version. It takes time similar to immutable, but rollback can be done by swapping the environmental URL to the old version

> **EXAM TIP:** Elastic Beanstalk allows multiple environments to support version control. You can also return to changes, but only the changes from the Git repository are replicated.

AWS Cloud Formation

IaaS is a method of supplying and managing cloud services using a human-readable and machine-readable template file. AWS CloudFormation is the built-in Infrastructure as a Service option for AWS cloud development. AWS CloudFormation is a service that aids in the modelling and configuration of AWS resources. You can spend less time managing those resources and more time working on your AWS-based applications by using AWS CloudFormation. You will need to create a template that outlines all of the AWS resources you will need, and AWS CloudFormation will provision and configure them for you. You do not need to individually configure and create AWS resources and figure out what is

dependent on what. AWS CloudFormation handles all of that. With AWS CloudFormation, you can do automatic deployment and rollbacks as well. You can also nest different components for reusability.

AWS CloudFormation offers a common language for you to provision and describes all the infrastructure resources in your cloud environment. CloudFormation permits you to use a simple text file to model and provision all the resources required for your applications across all accounts and regions in a secure and automated manner. For your cloud environment, this file acts as a single source of truth. You can also use AWS CloudFormation to construct custom resources using SNS or Lambda services.

You do not have to pay anything extra for AWS CloudFormation, and you simply pay for the AWS resources you need to run your apps.

One of the most powerful parts of AWS, CloudFormation, permits you to take what was once old-style hardware infrastructure and convert it into a code. CloudFormation provides developers and system administrators with an easy way to manage and create a collection of related AWS resources, provisioning and updating them in a predictable and orderly fashion.

You do not require figuring out the order for provisioning AWS or the subtleties of making those dependencies work. CloudFormation takes care of this for you.

When the AWS resources are deployed, you can update and modify them in a predictable and controlled way, in effect applying version control to your AWS infrastructure the same way you do with your software.

EXAM TIP: A template in CloudFormation is a document that defines the resources or services for the application through which CloudFormation makes a stack.

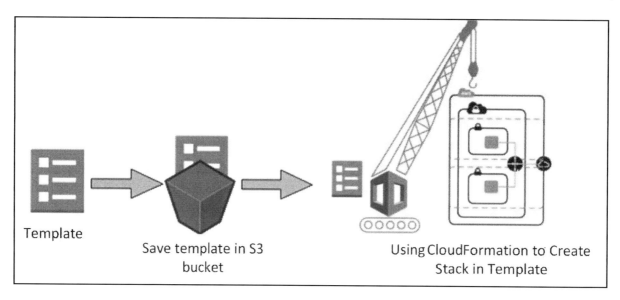

Figure 8-09: Creation of Simple Stack

Features

CloudFormation supports bootstrap script, Chef, and Puppet configuration. In Chef and puppet configuration, you can deploy and configure on the application layer. In the bootstrap script, you can define the files, services, and installation packages on an EC2 instance by setting them in the template. When you create a stack, "automatic Rollback on error" is enabled in the creation of stack by default. This means when the error occurred at a particular point, all the AWS resources that are created successfully before that point are deleted. If an error occurs, you must charge for the resources that are provisioned. Although CloudFormation itself is free, you need to pay for the resources that you have created through CloudFormation.

EXAM TIP: Automatic Rollback an error is enabled by default, but you pay for errors although CloudFormation, itself is free.

In AWS CloudFormation, there is the property of waiting for application in a stack, which means you have a "Wait" condition for resources that behave as obstruction or blockage in creating other resources up till it receives a signal of completion from external resources, like form application or management system. In CloudFormation, you can also specify deletion policy for resources in the template, or you can define the creation of Snapshots of volumes and database instances before deletion. You can also specify that if the stack is deleted, the particular resource will not be removed. This property will be helpful in those cases where you have data in a bucket, and you want to preserve that bucket even after the stack has been deleted.

> **EXAM TIP:** You can delete the stack with the deletion of all resources. Alternatively, by using the deletion policies, you can retain some of the resources, which you do not want to delete. If any resource is not removed, then it will remain in the stack until the stack is deleted successfully.

You can use CloudFormation to create roles and allow EC2 instances to access the roles. It also helps to create or modify the VPC and all the things that are inside VPC like Route Tables, Subnets, and Network ACLs, and it creates resources like EC2 Instances, Auto scaling group, Security group, ELB, etc.

> **EXAM TIP:** With CloudFormation, you can create IAM roles and assign them.

In CloudFormation templates, you can also define specific IP address ranges for specific instances in both terms; individual IP addresses and CIDR ranges, or you can define previous Elastic IPs like in properties of an EC2 instance in the template, you can define IP address.

With the help of CloudFormation, you can enable VPC peering, or you can build multiple VPCs in a single template. CloudFormation supports Route53 means that with the help of templates, you can build a new hosted zone or modify hosted zone that already exists; the modification includes the addition and changing of Aliases, A Records, and CNAMEs.

> **EXAM TIP:** In CloudFormation, multiple VPCs are created in one template, it also enables VPC peering. CloudFormation supports Puppet and Chef Integration and a bootstrap script as well.

Supported AWS Services

AWS CloudFormation supports the following AWS and features through the listed resources.

- Analytics
- Application Services
- Compute
- Customer Engagement
- Database
- Developer Tools
- Enterprise Applications
- Game Development
- Internet of Things
- Machine Learning
- Management Tools
- Mobile Services
- Networking
- Security and Identity
- Storage and Content Delivery
- Additional Software and Services

EXAM TIP: Before going for the exam, you must remember all the supported services of CloudFormation.

AWS CloudFormation Concepts

When you use AWS CloudFormation, you work with stacks and templates. CloudFormation template is an architectural diagram, while CloudFormation Stack is the result of that diagram. You can create templates to define your AWS resources and their properties. Whenever you create a stack, AWS CloudFormation provisions the resources that are described in your template. The stack is considered to be a single unit that you can create, update or delete. Change Stack is the component of AWS CloudFormation, where the changes in the stack are proposed, and then you will be able to see what is its impact on the resources before implementation.

By adding, updating, and deleting a stack, you can add, update and delete resources through AWS CloudFormation Templates. The format of the Template is JSON or YAML. In CloudFormation, when you create a template, you do not need to be careful about resource provisions or the working of dependencies because all these things will be taken care for you. According to your demand, you can update the stack's resources in the existing stack. There is no need to delete or create a new stack. To modify a stack, create a change set by entering an updated version of the stack's template. AWS CloudFormation compares

an updated version with the original version and creates a list of changes. After checking these changes, you can execute the changes to your stack.

EXAM TIP: When you use AWS CloudFormation, you can reuse your template to set up your resources consistently and repeatedly. Just describe your resources once, and then provide the same resources repeatedly in multiple regions.

Elements of Template

There are two main elements of the template.

- Mandatory Element
- Optional Element

Mandatory Element

When you provision resources in CloudFormation, you need to define the list of resources along with the configuration value, which you provision. If you do not define resources in the template, then CloudFormation does not provide any resources. So defining a list of resources is mandatory.

Optional Element

In the template, the optional element is the template format and its version. The template parameter is also optional, which includes input value and output value. Input values are provided at the creation time of the stack, and output values are the values like IP address and ELB address that are needed after the complete creation of the stack. The limit of both the input value and the output value is 60. List of data tables are also optional, and these are used to find static configuration values.

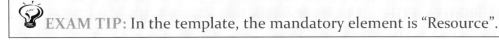

EXAM TIP: In the template, the mandatory element is "Resource".

In both given template formats, Cloud Formation creates S3 buckets with a default setting named as MyIPSBucket. Hence, you can see here, S3 is a mandatory element, which means defining of resource and bucket name is an output parameter.

JSON

```
{
    "Resources" : {
        "MyIPSBucket" : {
            "Type" : "AWS::S3::Bucket"
        }
```

```
   }

}
```

YAML

```
Resources:

 HelloBucket:

  Type: AWS::S3::Bucket
```

For outputting the data, you can use "Fn:GetAtt".

```
{ "Fn::GetAtt" : [ "logicalNameOfResource", "attributeName" ] }

Example:

{ "Fn::GetAtt" : [ "Myip", "IPv4 Public IP" ] }
```

Stack Policy

All upgrade activities on all resources are allowed when you build a stack. By default, anyone with stack updates can update all stack resources. The Stack Policy is used to design a policy for protecting the resources in a stack from any accidental deletion or modification. In the process of upgrading, some resources can require interruption or be replaced entirely to produce new physical identifications or new storage. A stack policy is a JSON file that specifies the updates on specified resources. Stack Policy can be added via Console or CLI during the creation of the stack. Once the stack is created, you can attach the stack policy only via CLI. After attaching the stack policy, it cannot be removed but can be modified.

The below-given policy is allowing all the resources to perform any action because when you set a stack policy, it by default protects all resources. Then we add an action that the database is not allowed for any updates from any resource, by explicitly defining the Deny policy for that database.

```
{

 "Statement" : [

  {

   "Effect" : "Allow",

   "Action" : "Update:*",

   "Principal": "*",

   "Resource" : "*"
```

```
    },
    {
      "Effect" : "Deny",
      "Action" : "Update:*",
      "Principal": "*",
      "Resource" : "LogicalResourceId/ProductionDatabase"
    }
  ]
}
```

Best Practices

There are some best practices that AWS supports for CloudFormation.

- It provides a Python script also termed as "Helper Script" to install the software and start services on EC2 instances. It is useful for building installation software or download patches when AMI is built with the CloudFormation template
- You can use CloudFormation to make changes in Stack rather than the resource directly
- Use Change Sets before updating the stack to check for issues in the updates
- Use some stack policies that explicitly protect your critical resources
- Use a version control system for tracking the changes in the template, such as CodeCommit or GitHub

Lab 8-01: Understanding CloudFormation Template Anatomy

Introduction

AWS CloudFormation is a tool that makes it simple for developers and organizations to construct a collection of linked AWS and third-party resources and then provision and manage them logically and reasonably.

Developers may use a simple, declarative approach to deploy and change compute, database, and many other resources, abstracting away the complexities of individual resource APIs. AWS CloudFormation is meant to make resource lifecycle management repeatable, predictable, and safe, with features such as automatic rollbacks, automated state management, and resource management across accounts and regions. Multiple ways to generate resources have recently been added, including leveraging AWS CDK for writing in higher-level languages, importing existing resources, and detecting configuration drift.

It is a new registry that simplifies the creation of custom types that inherit several of CloudFormation's fundamental features.

Scenario:

Assume you are a DevOps engineer in a company. Your task is to continue innovating with technology and platform improvements to create an excellent experience for customers. For this, you need a tool that will automate all of your manual work, such as launching and configuring EC2 instances or creating S3 storage buckets. How can you automate this work?

Solution:

The solution is simple. You use the AWS CloudFormation service to automate all the work. In CloudFormation, you run a template of JSON or YAML to deploy the entire frontend and backend stack into the AWS environment.

```
{

"AWSTemplateFormatVersio
n" : "version date",

 "Description"     :    "JSON
string",

 "Metadata" : {
   template metadata
 },

 "Parameters" : {
   set of parameters
 },

 "Mappings" : {
   set of mappings
 },

 "Conditions" : {
   set of conditions
 },

 "Transform" : {
   set of transforms
 },

 "Resources" : {
   set of resources
 },

 "Outputs" : {
   set of outputs
 }
}
```

```
---
AWSTemplateFormatVer
sion: "version date"

Description:
  String

Metadata:
  template metadata

Parameters:
  set of parameters

Mappings:
  set of mappings

Conditions:
  set of conditions

Transform:
  set of transforms

Resources:
  set of resources

Outputs:
  set of outputs
```

Figure 8-10: Understanding CloudFormation Template Anatomy

Follow the given steps to understand the CloudFormation Template Anatomy.

Before deep-diving into the lab, create VPC and subnets.

1. Login into the 'AWS Console.'
2. Click on 'Services.'

aws | Services ▼   Q ⊠ ⬡   IPSpecialist @ ipscloud-aws ▼   N. Virginia ▼   Support ▼

AWS Management Console

AWS services

▼ **Recently visited services**

    ▣ EC2   ▣ CloudWatch

    ▣ CloudFormation   ▦ Simple Queue Service

    ⬡ VPC   ⓘ IAM

▶ All services

edback   English (US) ▼   Privacy Policy   Terms of Use   Cookie preferenc

© 2008 - 2021, Amazon Web Services, Inc. or its affiliates. All rights reserved.

3. Select 'CloudFormation' from 'Management & Governance.'

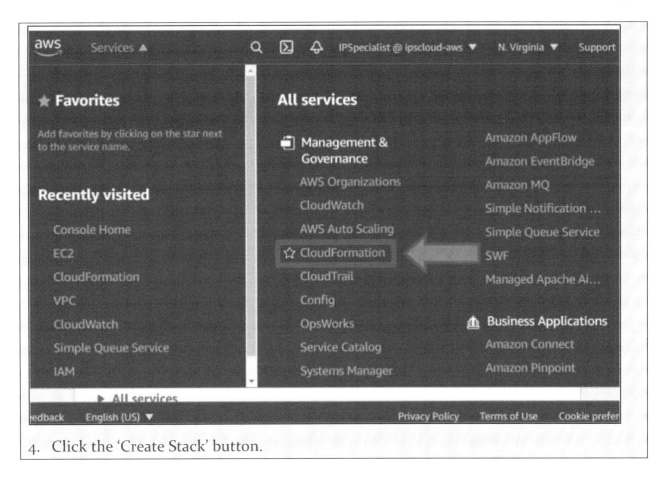

4. Click the 'Create Stack' button.

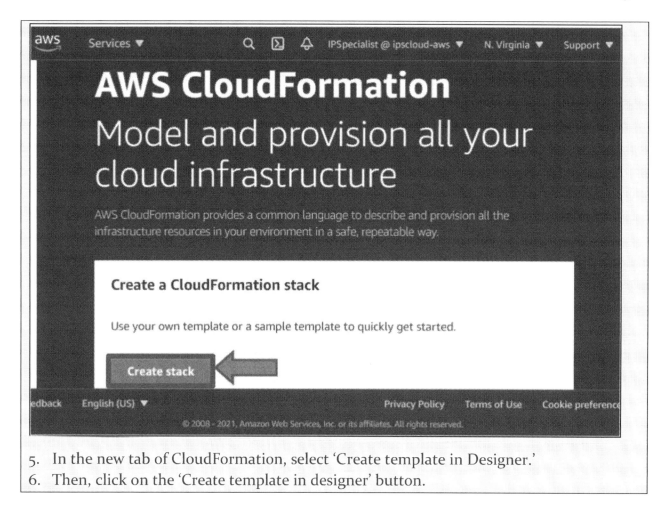

5. In the new tab of CloudFormation, select 'Create template in Designer.'
6. Then, click on the 'Create template in designer' button.

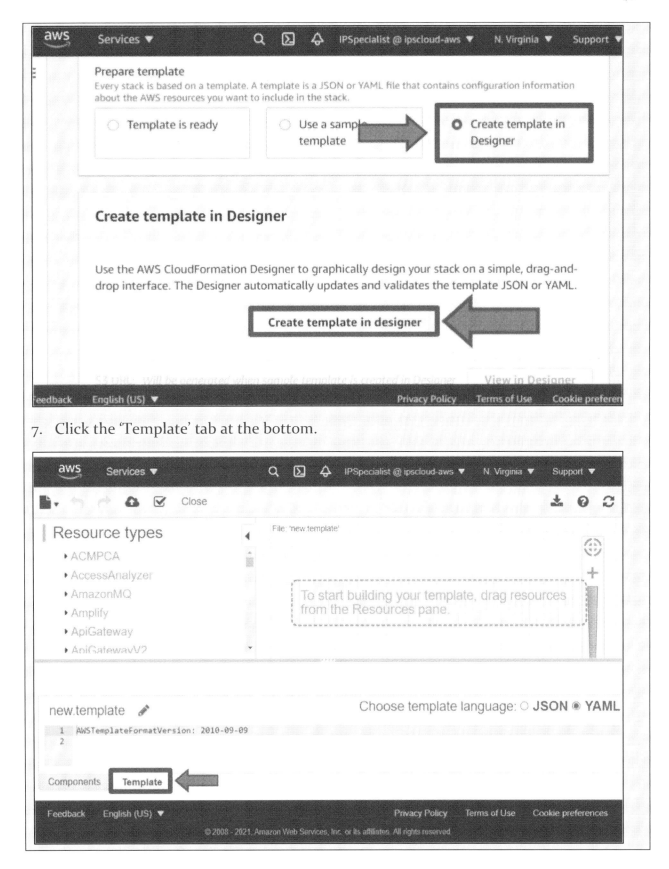

7. Click the 'Template' tab at the bottom.

8. Copy everything in the 'Template_Anatomy2.yaml' file. The files link is provided in the Github link:

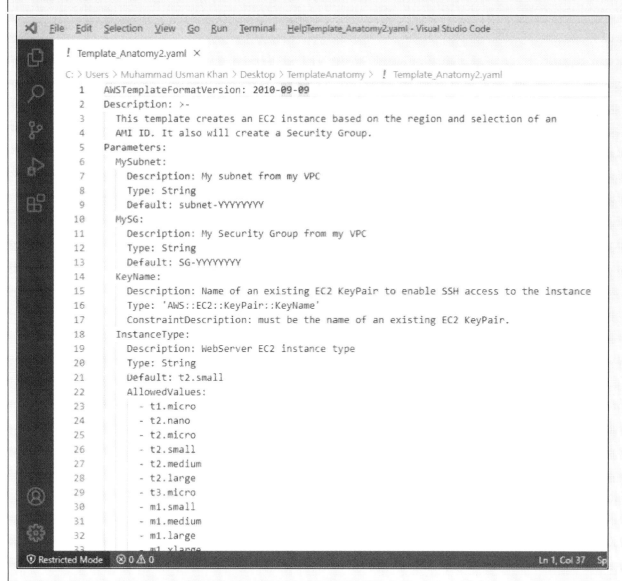

9. Paste the code in the 'new.template' tab.

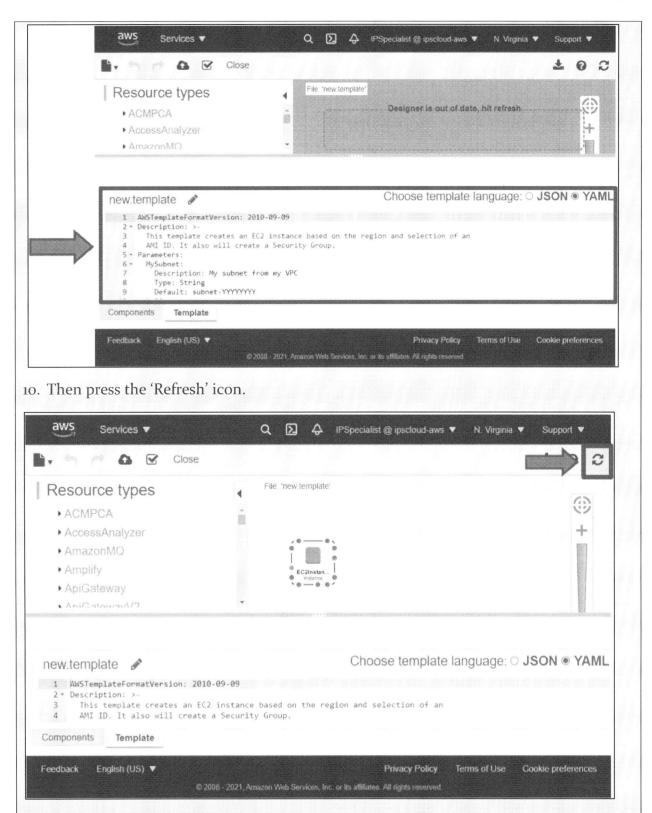

10. Then press the 'Refresh' icon.

11. Open the EC2 in a new browser tab. Then on the left-hand menu, click on 'Key Pairs.'

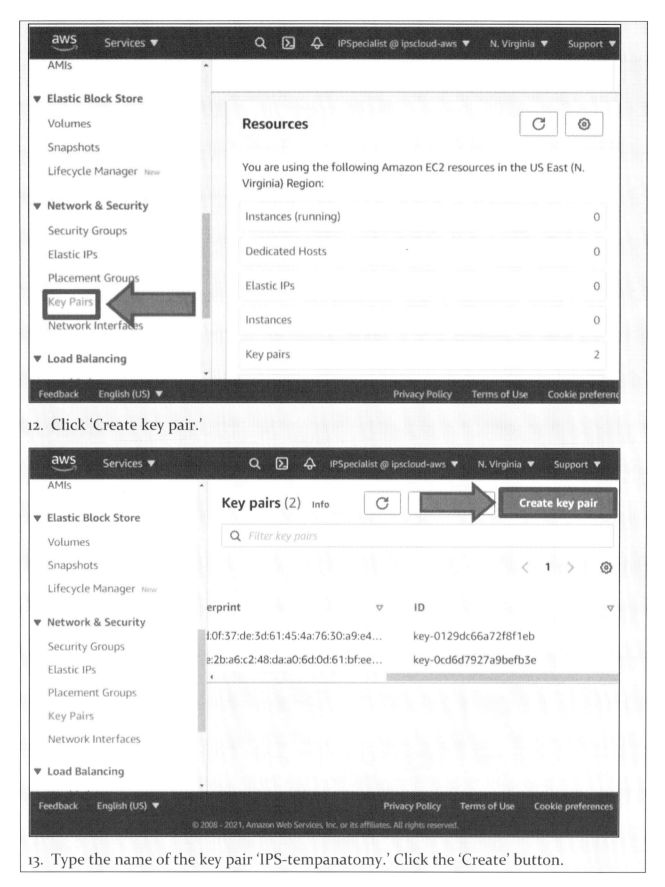

12. Click 'Create key pair.'

13. Type the name of the key pair 'IPS-tempanatomy.' Click the 'Create' button.

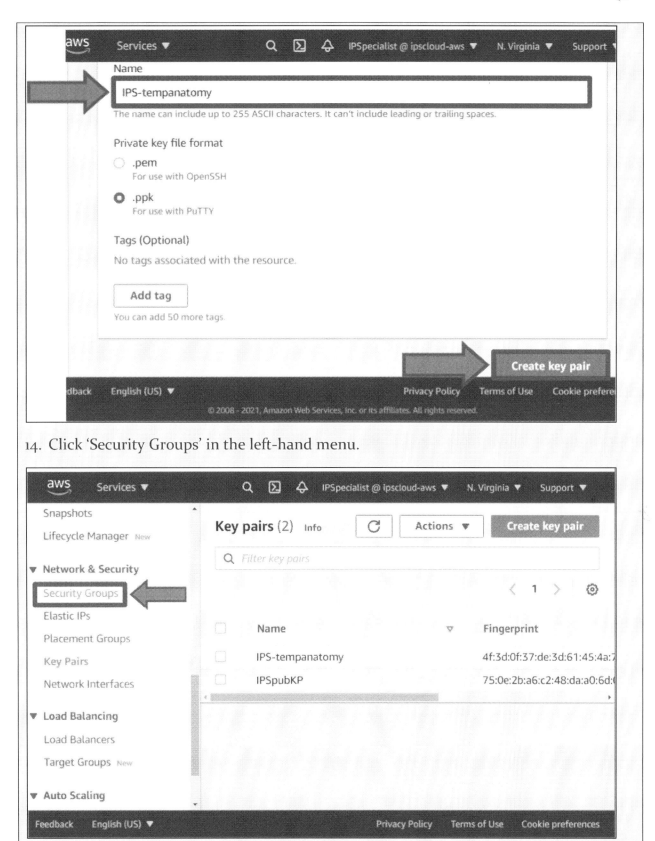

14. Click 'Security Groups' in the left-hand menu.

15. Copy the security group ID. Paste it into a text file since you will need it in a minute.

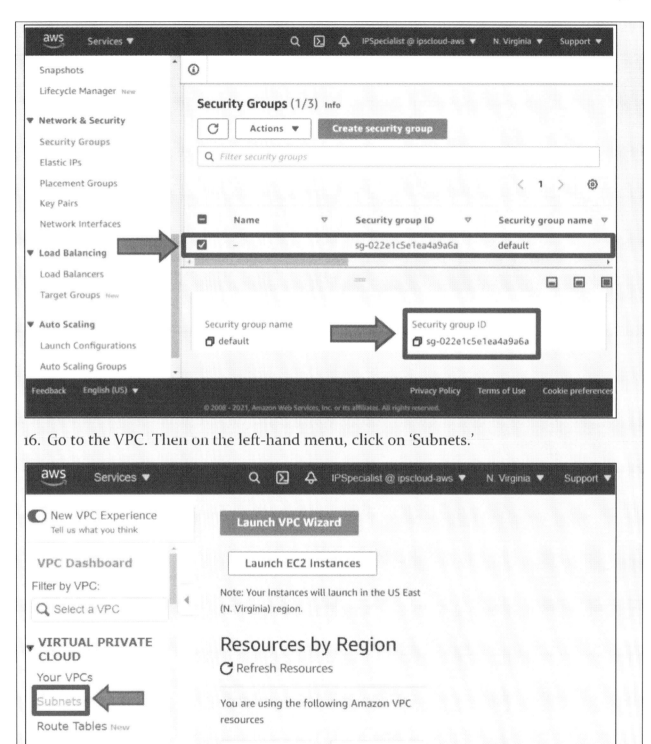

16. Go to the VPC. Then on the left-hand menu, click on 'Subnets.'

17. Select the 'IPS-Subnet-01' and copy its subnet ID. Paste it into a text file since you will need it later.

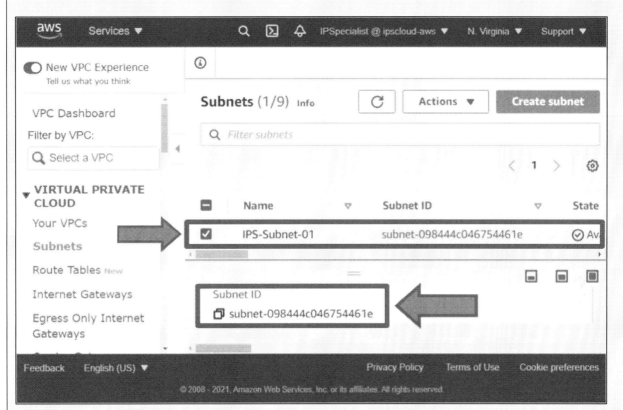

18. Go back to the 'CloudFormation' template. Click the 'Checkbox' at the top to validate the template.

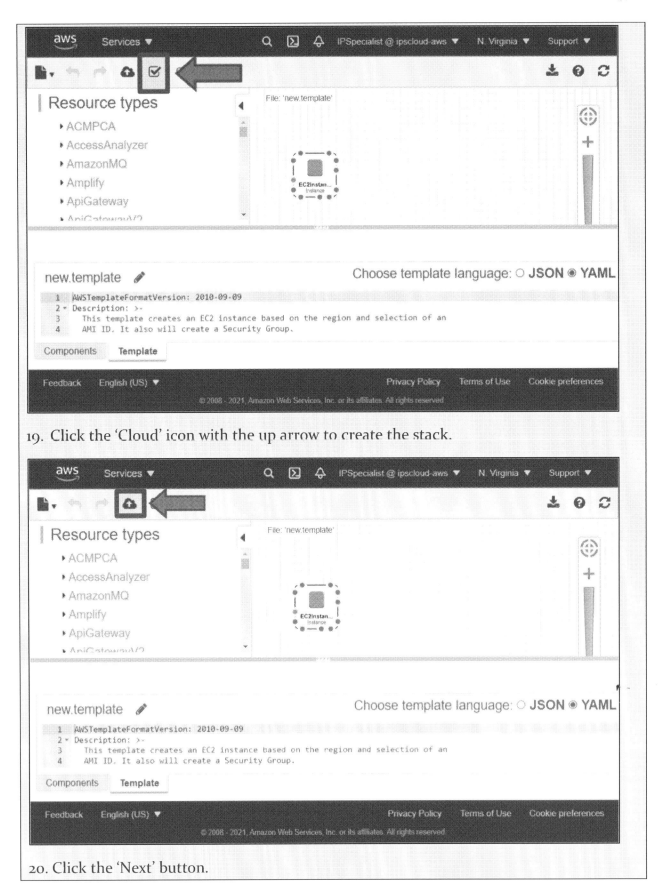

19. Click the 'Cloud' icon with the up arrow to create the stack.

20. Click the 'Next' button.

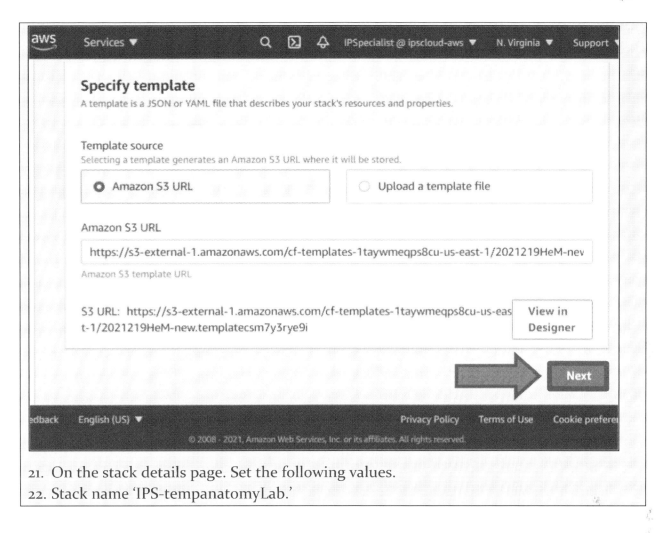

21. On the stack details page. Set the following values.
22. Stack name 'IPS-tempanatomyLab.'

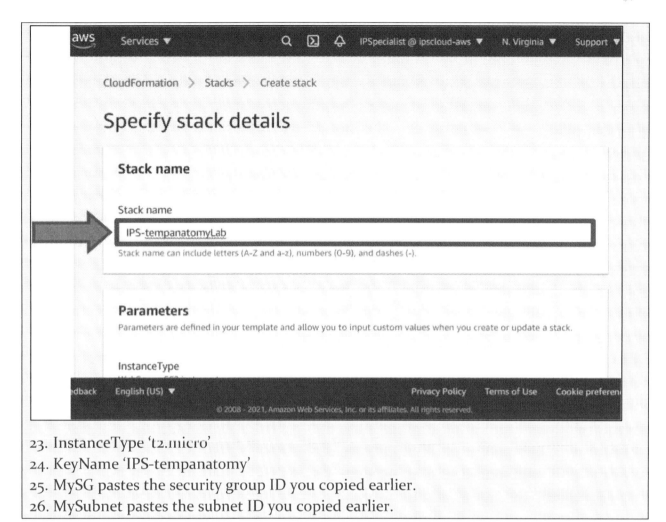

23. InstanceType 't2.micro'
24. KeyName 'IPS-tempanatomy'
25. MySG pastes the security group ID you copied earlier.
26. MySubnet pastes the subnet ID you copied earlier.

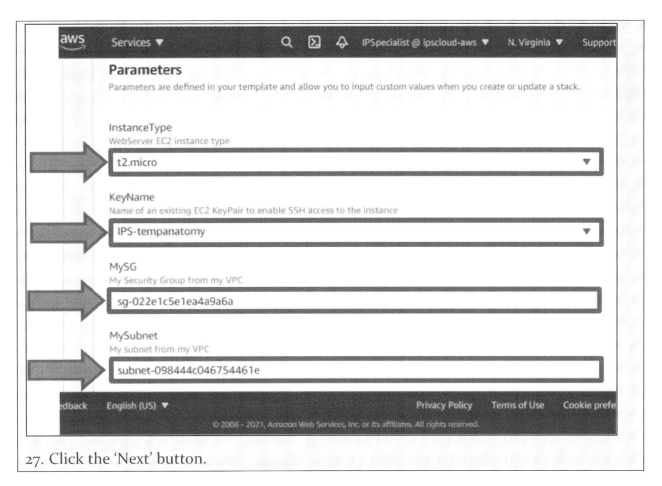

27. Click the 'Next' button.

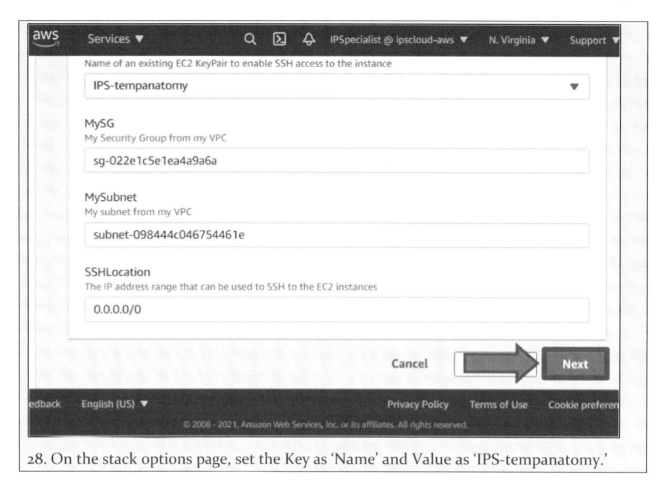

28. On the stack options page, set the Key as 'Name' and Value as 'IPS-tempanatomy.'

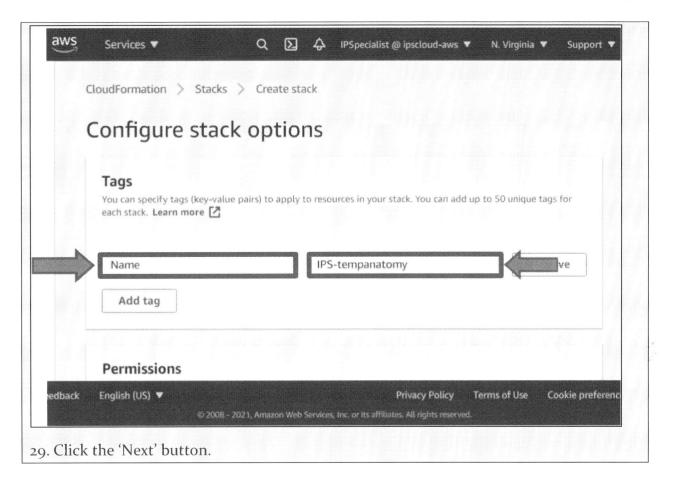

29. Click the 'Next' button.

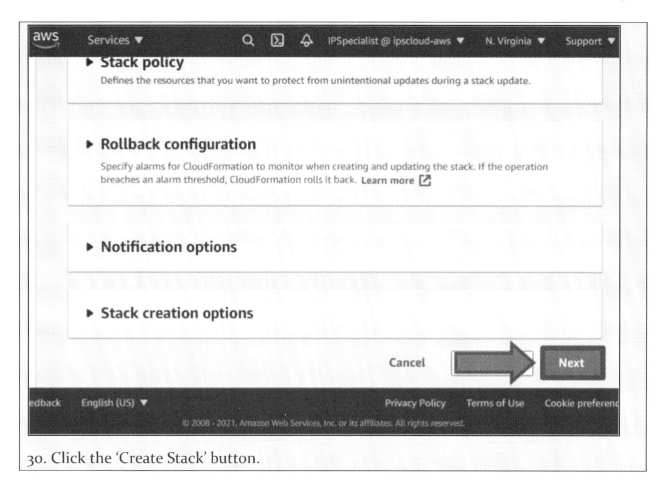

30. Click the 'Create Stack' button.

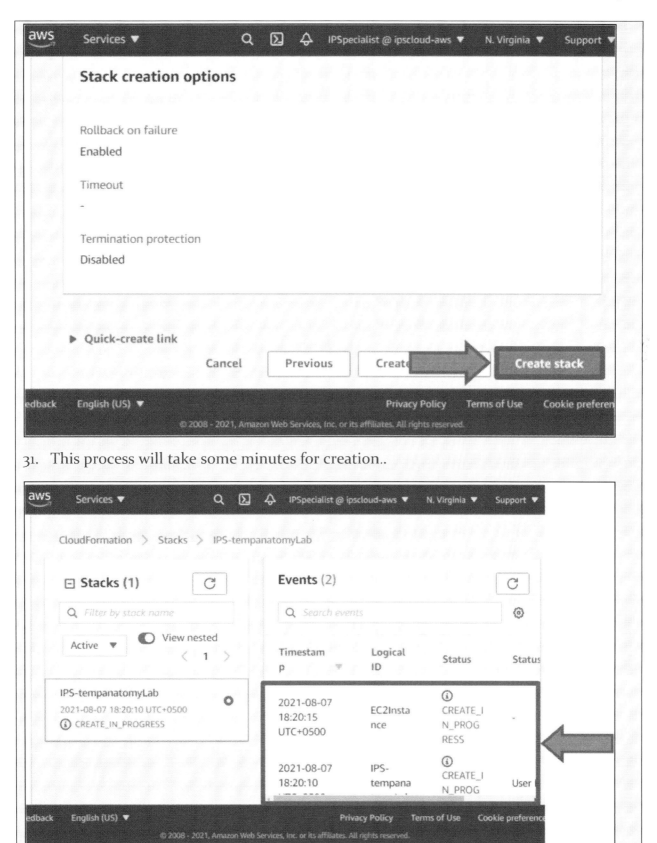

31. This process will take some minutes for creation..

32. Now go to the EC2 tab and click on 'Instances.' You will see an instance initializing with the name 'IPS-tempanatompy.'

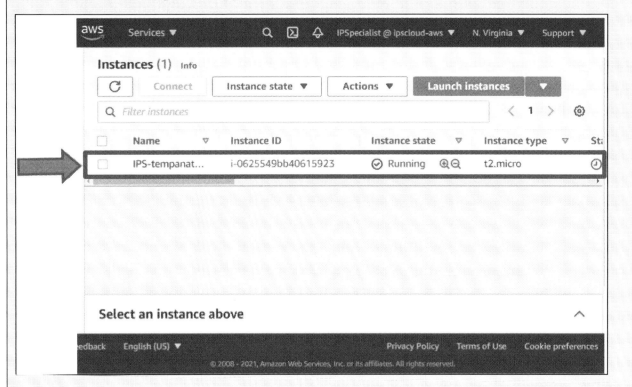

33. Now delete a CloudFormation stack.
34. Once it is created, at the top, click on the 'Delete' button.

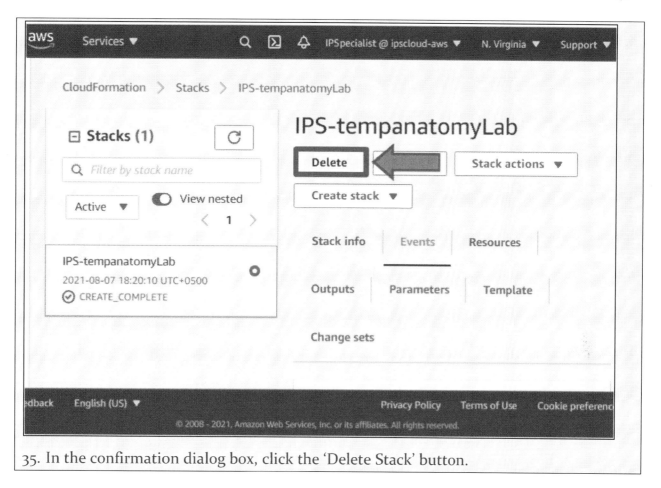

35. In the confirmation dialog box, click the 'Delete Stack' button.

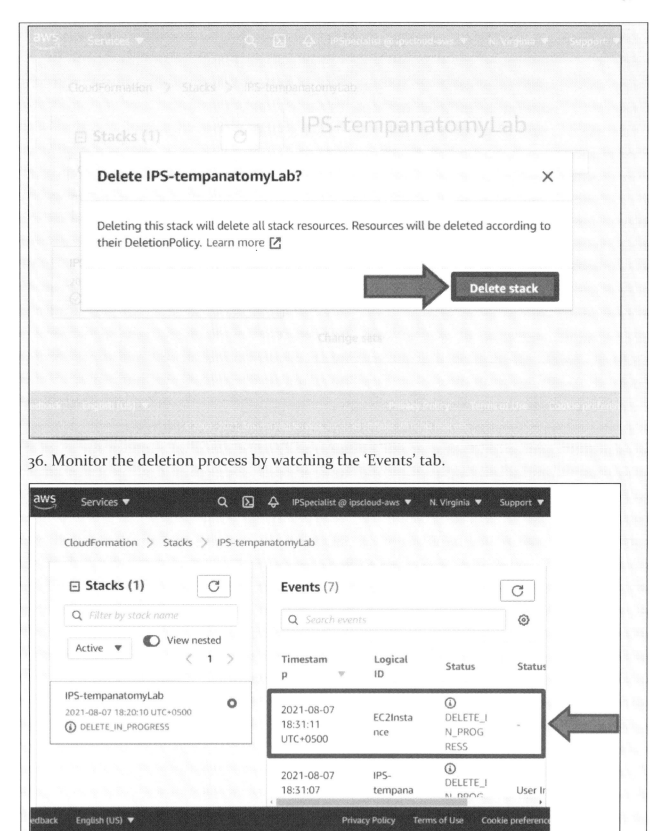

36. Monitor the deletion process by watching the 'Events' tab.

37. Go to the EC2 tab. Click on 'Instances,' and you will see an instance shutting down with the name 'IPS-tempanatompy.'

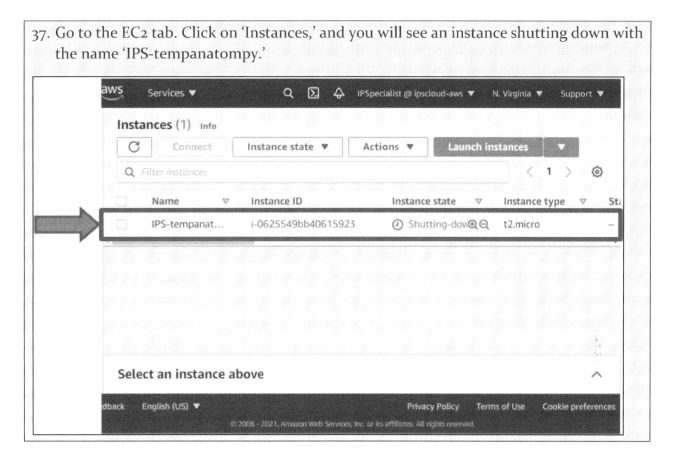

Amazon Elastic Container Service

There are two main container services in AWS, i.e., Amazon ECS (Elastic Container Service) and Amazon EKS (Elastic Kubernetes Service). Both of these are managed highly scalable and available container Platforms. Amazon ECS supports Docker containers and enables a containerized application to be readily operated and scale on AWS. EKS is for Kubernetes. So if you have some existing Kubernetes, then you can easily convert it to EKS.

ECS is easy to learn and use, while EKS is complex and has more rich features with a steep learning curve. ECS leverages a lot of AWS services like ALB, CloudWatch, and Route 53. EKS has a lot of built-in features for the Kubernetes platform, so it handles everything internally.

On ECS, the collection of containers are called "Tasks", these tasks come together to provide service. On EKS collection of containers called "Pods", they can share resources and have better access to one another.

We know that ECS is an AWS creation, so it has limited extensibility. While on EKS, there is a whole library for Kubernetes add-ons that are available to use.

 EXAM TIP: Differences between EKS and ECS can be asked in the exam.

Launch Type

For ECS, there are two launch types, one is EC2 Launch Type, and the other is the Fargate Launch Type. For the EC2 launch type, we have manual control over how we build a fleet of instances to support containers. While in Fargate, everything is controlled by itself for us and automates it.

For the EC2 launch type, you are responsible for upgrading, patching, and care of that EC2 pool. In Fargate, everything is automated, so the provision of compute is as per needs. Optimization of the cluster on EC2 is your responsibility, while Fargate handles that for you.

As you required granular controlling to the resource, then EC2 launch type is the best, whether in Fargate, because of automation, there is limited control over the resources.

> **EXAM TIP:** With EC2 launch type, you have more granular control on the infrastructure as compared to the use of the Fargate launch type.
>
> AWS Fargate is an Amazon ECS Compute engine that can run Docker containers without the need to manage servers or clusters. With AWS Fargate, clusters of virtual machines are not required to scale, deliver or configure the container.

Amazon API Gateway

Amazon API Gateway is a fully managed AWS service that helps developers in creating, publishing, maintaining, monitoring, and securing APIs. Practically, API Gateway lets you create, configure and host a REST API that enables your application to access the AWS cloud. It allows you to create REST APIs that are hosted in a managed and highly scalable fashion. You can also back your APIs in different ways: via Lambda, it can be a proxy for other AWS services or any other HTTP API on AWS or elsewhere. It is region-based, but you can also have API access be edge optimized via CloudFront or use it as privately available.

API Gateway supports API keys, so you can uniquely identify the users. It also supports usage plans, so if you are using API as a service, then you can implement throttling or Quota management, as API gateway uses CloudFront behind the scene, so it has the concept of custom domains and SNI. If you want to make money with your API, then you can publish the API as a product in the market place.

API Gateway Structure

API Gateway is a tool that allows you to develop APIs. With a few clicks on the AWS management dashboard, you may create an API. This API serves as a portal to your backend

systems' functionality. For example, your organization's workload runs on Amazon EC2 instances, and your logic runs on AWS Lambda.

API Gateway manages API calls, including traffic management, authorization, access control, monitoring, and API version management, as well as all the duties involved in accepting and processing thousands of concurrent API requests. There are no fees for setting up APIs; you simply pay for the API calls you get and the quantity of data sent.

Consider an example; client applications have programmatic access to Amazon web services through APIs. These APIs are hosted in the API Gateway, so the client apps are the interface or front-end of the API, while the associated services are working at the API's backend. See the pictorial representation of this example on the next page.

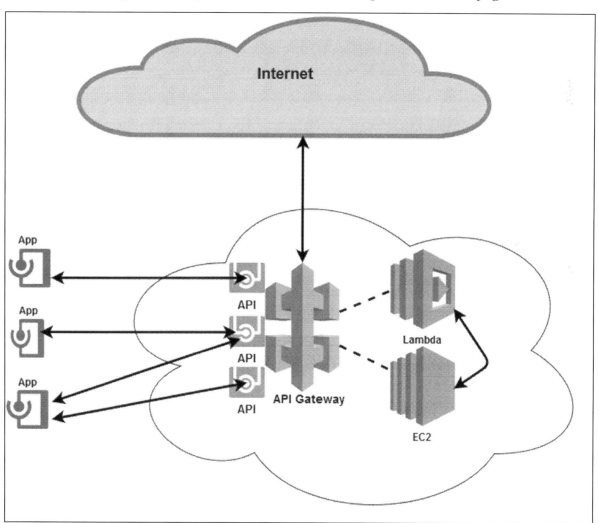

Figure 8-11: Amazon API Gateway Structure

API Gateway has one of the features known as Caching the response. If any request already came before the new request of the same response, then API Gateway instead of sending a

new request to the backend, sends the response which is cached in it. In this way, the performance of the backend becomes better.

> **EXAM TIP:** API gateway is designed to support REST APIs. API Gateway with Lambda can be used for the agility and efficiency of serverless platforms.

Management Tools

There are multiple Management tools that AWS provides; some of them are listed below:

AWS Config

AWS Config is a tool for assessing, auditing and evaluating the configuration of your Amazon Web Services resources. It is useful in the case of the ITIL program's Configuration Management section. It creates a baseline of the system's many configuration settings and files, then compares changes to the baseline over time.

In some ways, AWS Config and CloudTrail are extremely similar. AWS Config is a fully managed service that enables security and governance by providing you with an AWS configuration history, resource inventory, and configuration change notifications. It's the same as capturing everything that happens in the AWS environment all of the time. You can go back in time to see what the security group was doing two weeks ago. It gives you the complete ability to check the AWS environment at any given time. It enables compliance auditing, gives you the ability to do security analysis, and also provides the capability of resource tracking. It also gives you the ability to essentially configure the snapshot of the AWS environment and logs the configuration changes of the AWS environment, and allows you to do automated compliance checking.

Key Components of AWS Config

It is made up of Config Dashboard and Config Rules. The Config Rules are divided into AWS Managed Rules and Custom Rules. It also contains the Resources and Setting options as well. You can also use AWS Config Rules to check the resources for certain desired conditions, and if the condition doesn't match, then that resource is flagged as "non-Complaint".

Some examples of AWS Config Rules are:

- Is backup enabled for an RDS?
- Are EBS volumes encrypted?

> **EXAM TIP:** The purpose of AWS Config rules is to check the resource for whether it is compliant or not by matching the rules.

AWS OpsWorks

Usually, Cloud applications need a group of resources that are related to each other, like an application server or an ELB, so they are built and managed collectively. This collection of instances is called "Stack". AWS OpsWorks allows you to build and manage the stack flexibly and simply along with its linked applications and resources. With the help of OpsWorks, the operational task becomes automated like code deployment, configurations of software, perform upgrades, database setups, and server scaling.

OpsWorks allows you to define application architecture and resource configuration flexibly. It also handles the provisioning of resources for your application. With the help of OpsWorks, you can scale your application depending upon the load and time automatically. You can also do monitoring to identify the issue by troubleshooting and then take action automatically based on resource permission and policy management to make multiuser environment management easier. AWS OpsWorks has three offerings: Chef Automates, Puppet Enterprise, and OpsWorks Stacks.

AWS OpsWorks for Chef Automate and Puppet Enterprise are fully managed hosted versions of these platforms. OpsWorks stack is AWS Creation that uses embedded Chef Clients installed on instances to run Chef Recipes. It also supports on-premises servers as well as agents.

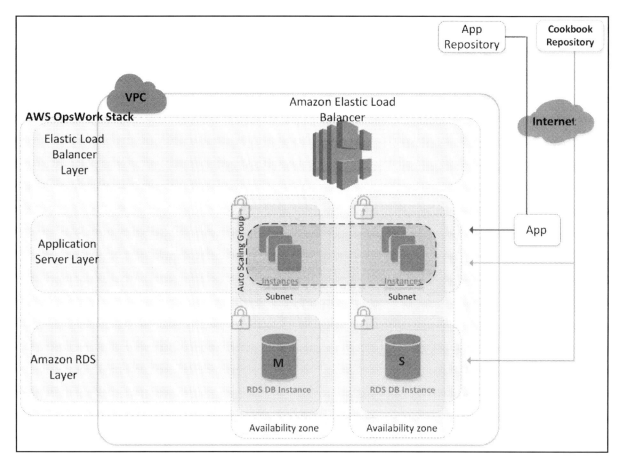

Figure 8-12: Simple Application Server Stack with AWS OpsWorks

Feature

OpsWorks is a graphical user interface for quickly deploying and configuring infrastructure. Because it is a configuration management service, AWS OpsWorks assists in the configuration and operation of the application using Chef and Puppet. It also aids in the provision of high-level tools for managing EC2 instances. Regardless of its architectural plan, OpsWorks can operate with other apps, which is challenging. It provides one configuration management for application deployment in a hybrid architecture. It works with both Linux and Windows servers.

OpsWorks allows you to define application architecture and resource configuration flexibly. It also handles the provisioning of resources for your application. With the help of OpsWorks, you can scale your application depending upon the load and time automatically. You can also do monitoring to identify the issue by troubleshooting and then take action automatically based on resource permission and policy management to make multiuser environment management easier.

Some key concepts are needed to be understood for OpsWorks.

Stack

A stack is a group of resources or a container for the resources, which are managed together like ELB, EC2 instances, EBS Volumes, etc. You can manage these resources fully and specify default configuration settings. In OpsWorks, you can specify individual stacks for different environments or separate applications. Stacks can be cloned only within the region. As we know, OpsWorks is a global service, but when you create a stack, you need to specify the region, and then resources can only be controlled in that region.

Layer

One or more layers in a stack can be used to specify how a group of EC2 instances is configured for a specific task. Layers can be added to define elements in the stack. In OpsWorks, you have built-in layers, which support different standard packages for applications, databases, caching, and load balancing. By modification, in the default configuration, you can modify your layer, or for performing the task, you can add Chef Recipes. Through layer, you have full control over the installed packages, like how they are deployed, configured, and more. OpsWorks can manage the configuration when you create a layer instead of doing these things manually.

> EXAM TIP: You can determine the Chef layer that runs from the layer of the instance it belongs to.
>
> In each layer of the stack, at least one instance must be added, or in each instance of the stack, at least a part of a layer must be added.

App

In OpsWorks, you need to define an app to represent an application type and its related information that is required to deploy that application from the repository. When you deploy an application, it runs deploy recipes on overall instances of the stack, so in this way, instances change their configuration as convenient. You can deploy multiple apps on an individual stack or layer.

Lifecycle Events

There are a group of lifecycle events in each layer that relate to different instance lifecycle stages like the setup, deploy, configure, undeploy and shutdown. Now that Chef Recipes run on each instance to perform a task, they are linked with lifecycle events. You can build a customized recipe or built-in recipe on any lifecycle event to change the configuration script for the application.

Chef

The Chef is a scripted infrastructure that changes the infrastructure into code. With the help of a Chef, you can automate the AWS resources and services in infrastructure. Your infrastructure becomes testable, versionable, and repeatable as an application. Recipes and other configuration data are stored in the Chef server. Servers, virtual machines, networking devices, and containers in the chef are called nodes. On these nodes, a chef-client is installed that polls the server's latest policy and state of the network periodically. If the client finds that any node is out of date, it brings it up to the date.

Difference between OpsWorks Stack and OpsWorks for Chef Automate

OpsWorks for Chef Automate is a configuration management service, allowing you to instantly supply a Chef server, including backups and software upgrades. This service is fully compliant with cookbooks and recipes from Chef's Supermarket. It supports native Chef Tools like Kitchen and Knife.

You can manage applications and servers on AWS and on-site with AWS OpsWorks Stacks. You can design the software as a stack of different layers, such as load balancing, database, and application server, with OpsWorks Stacks. Chef Solo can be run by using chef recipes; it is client software that is installed on an EC2 instance so that you can automate tasks such as packages, language or frameworks, software configuration, and more.

> **EXAM TIP:** AWS OpsWorks is a global service, but you can only manage the resource within the region where you create the stack.

Lab 8-02: Using Chef 11 Stack in OpsWorks

Scenario

An organization hired a solution architect to deploy its applications on the cloud automatically. The files of code are in the repository of GitHub, and the URL of this repository is provided to the solution architect for the deployment of the application. In the application, free compute service, and other services of AWS Cloud are used without any manual management of the application. How can the solution architect deploy the application in the best way possible?

Solution

For this purpose, the solution architect uses AWS OpsWorks with Chef 11 stack because it has built-in cookbooks for application and deployment.

1. Log in to AWS Console and go to "OpsWorks" under "Management Tools".

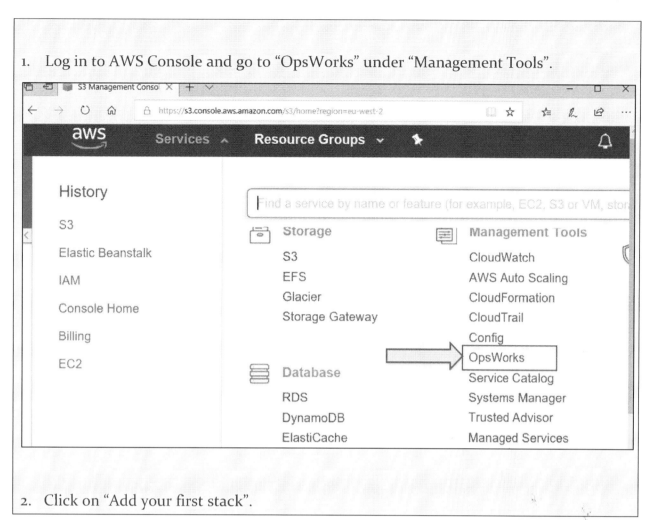

2. Click on "Add your first stack".

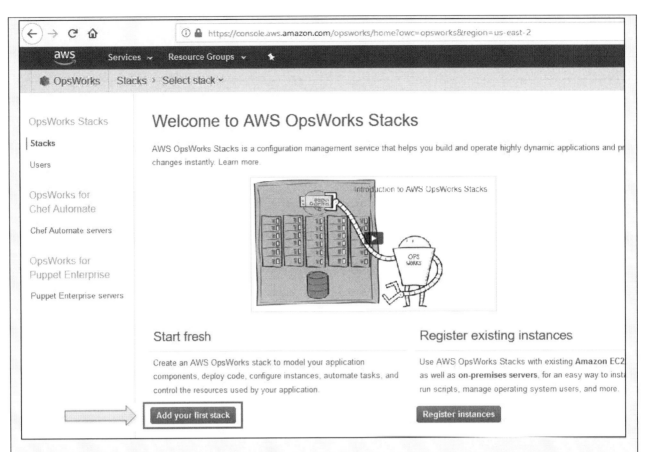

3. Now go to "Chef 11 stack", which uses built-in cookbooks for application and its deployment. If you use Chef 12, then you need to create your cookbook, which is difficult, so chose Chef 11 stack.

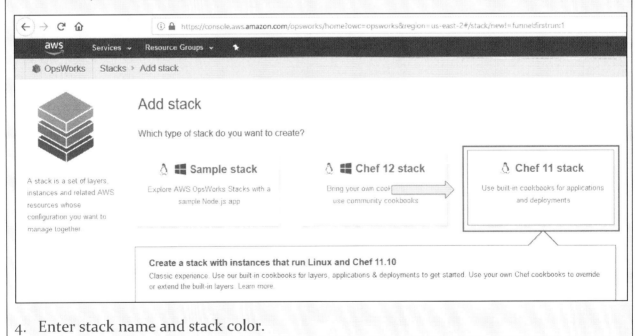

4. Enter stack name and stack color.

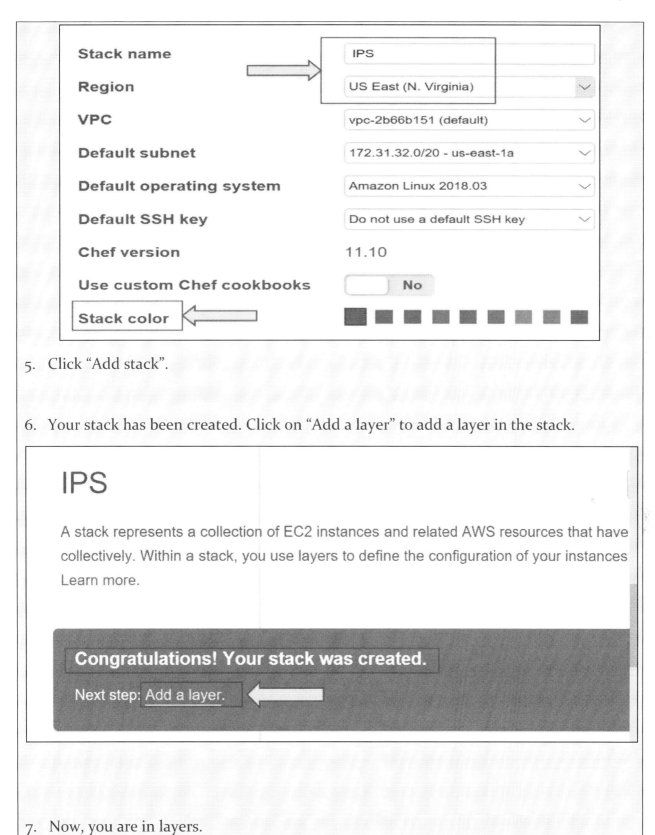

5. Click "Add stack".

6. Your stack has been created. Click on "Add a layer" to add a layer in the stack.

IPS

A stack represents a collection of EC2 instances and related AWS resources that have collectively. Within a stack, you use layers to define the configuration of your instances Learn more.

Congratulations! Your stack was created.

Next step: Add a layer.

7. Now, you are in layers.

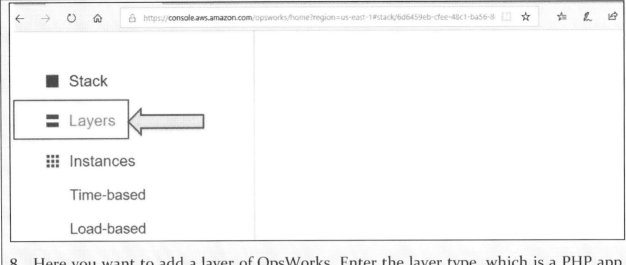

8. Here you want to add a layer of OpsWorks. Enter the layer type, which is a PHP app server here. Click on "Add layer".

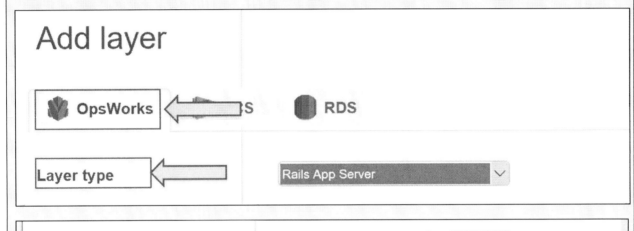

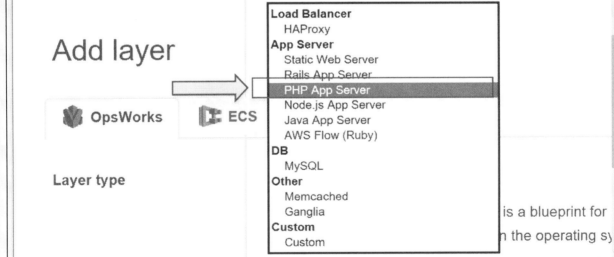

9. Now, your layer has been created. Click on "Add instance" to add an instance to the layer.

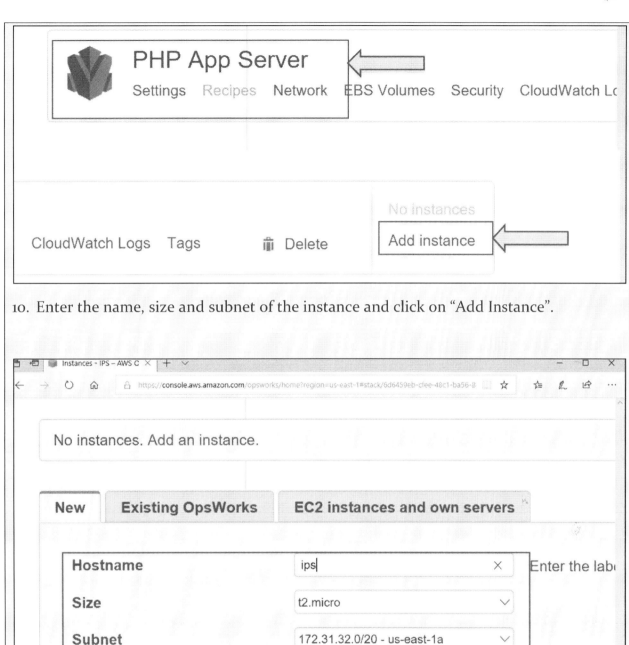

10. Enter the name, size and subnet of the instance and click on "Add Instance".

11. Now your instance has been added and by default, it is stopped. Hence, you will need to start that instance.

12. Now go to apps from the left side to add the code of the application. Click on "Add an app".

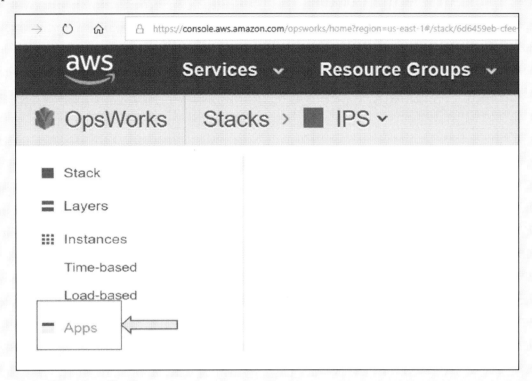

13. Enter the name of the app and select the repository type. Here we will select "Git" because we store codes there. Enter URL of the repository in Repository URL. Leave everything as it is and click on "Add App".

Add App

Settings

Name	PHPserver ✕	Enter the app
Type	PHP ⌄	
Document root	Optional	

Data Sources

Data source type	○ RDS ○ OpsWorks ⦿ None

Application Source

Repository type	Git ⌄
Repository URL	/github.com/IPSpecialist/OpsWorks ✕
Repository SSH key	Optional

Cancel **Add App**

14. Now go to instances from the left side of the window, your instance is online. Click on the instance's IP address and you will see the 403 error because we did not deploy applications yet.

Instances ⓘ 🌑1 | ●1 ⚪0 ⚪0 ⚪0 ⚪0
total online setting shutting stopped errors
up down

PHP App Server

Hostname	Status	Size	Type	AZ
ips	online	⟵ ro	24/7	us-east-1a

S	Size	Type	AZ	Public IP	Acti
	t2.micro	24/7	us-east-1a	34.227.76.93 ⟵	s

← → ↻ ⌂ ⓘ 34.227.76.93/ ☆ ⋆ ℓ

Forbidden

You don't have permission to access / on this server.

15. Go again to apps from the left side of the window and click on "deploy" to deploy the app that you created.

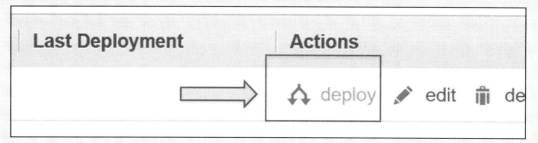

16. Leave everything as it is and click on "Deploy". Once your app is deployed, go back to Instance and click the IP address again and you will be able to see the page whose code is stored in the repository.

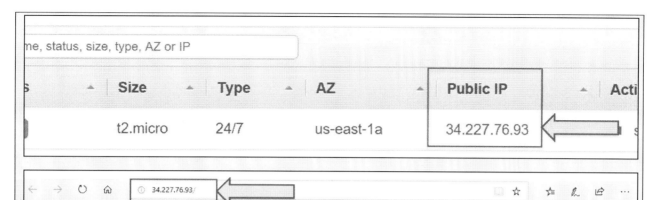

Welcome to your Application

Your AWS OpsWorks *PHP* application is now running on your own dedicated environment in the AWS Cloud

You are running PHP new version

Your Application is now running on the host "ips"; in a new stack and layer in OpsWorks.

This host is running PHP version 5.3.29.

IPSpecialist

17. For your guidance, we have provided the Repository file; the link is here: https://github.com/IPSpecialist/OpsWorks

18. Now we will add a layer for ELB, but for that, you need to go to "EC2" under "Compute".

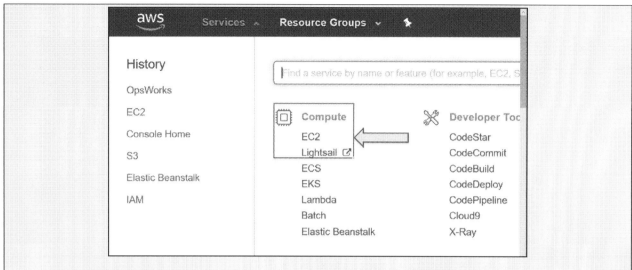

19. Scroll down and go to "Load Balancers" from the left side of the window. Click "Create Load Balancer".

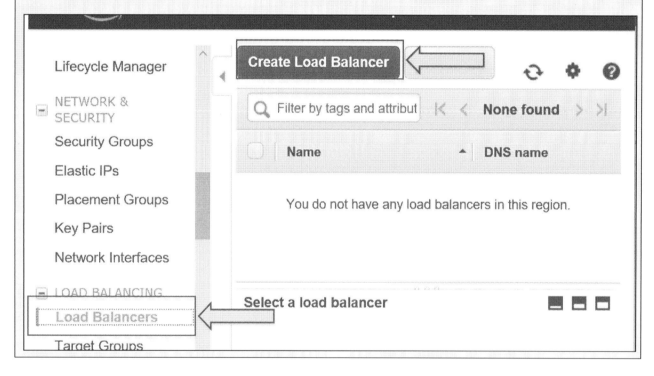

20. Select "Classic Load Balancer" then click "Continue".

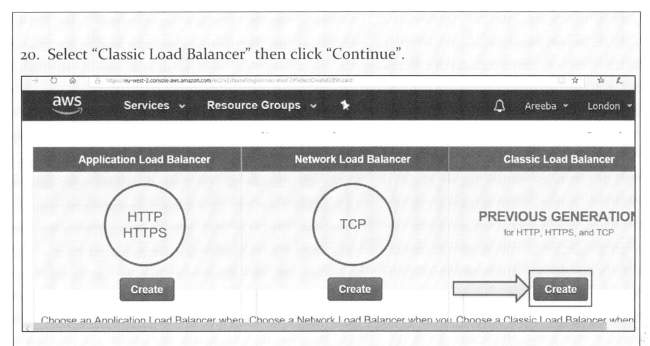

21. Enter the information like name, the threshold of health checks, ping path to PHP and security group. Here, we will add a security group of PHP app server from existing groups.

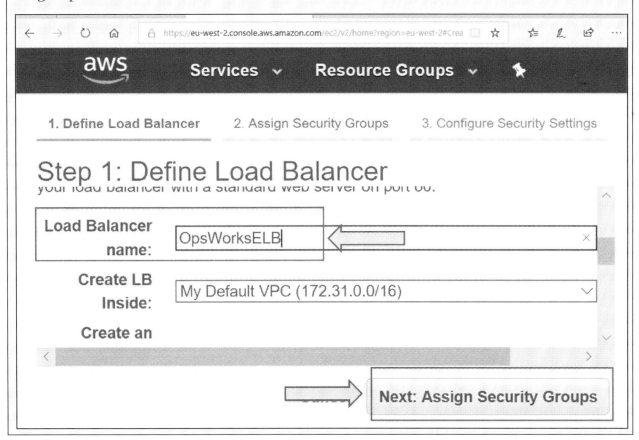

Step 4: Configure Health Check

Your load balancer will automatically perform health checks on your EC2 instances and only route traffic to instances that pass the health check. If an instance fails the health check, it is automatically removed from the load balancer. Customize the health check to meet your specific needs.

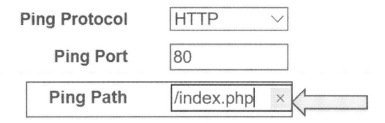

Ping Protocol	HTTP
Ping Port	80
Ping Path	/index.php

Advanced Details

Response Timeout ⓘ	5	seconds
Interval ⓘ	30	seconds
Unhealthy threshold ⓘ	2	
Healthy threshold ⓘ	5	

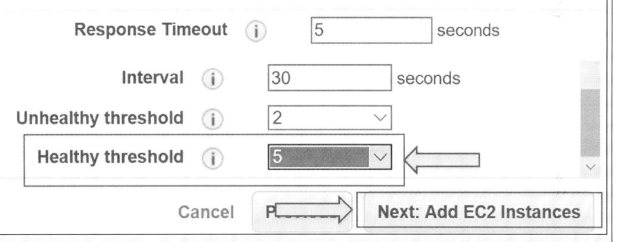

Cancel   P⟹   **Next: Add EC2 Instances**

Step 5: Add EC2 Instances

The table below lists all your running EC2 Instances. Check the boxes in the Select column to add those instances to this load balancer.

VPC vpc-2b66b151 (172.31.0.0/16)

	Instance	State	Zone	Subnet ID
☐	i-00af8aaac390ab9df	● running	us-east-1a	subnet-c79c1b9

Cancel   P⟹   **Next: Add Tags**

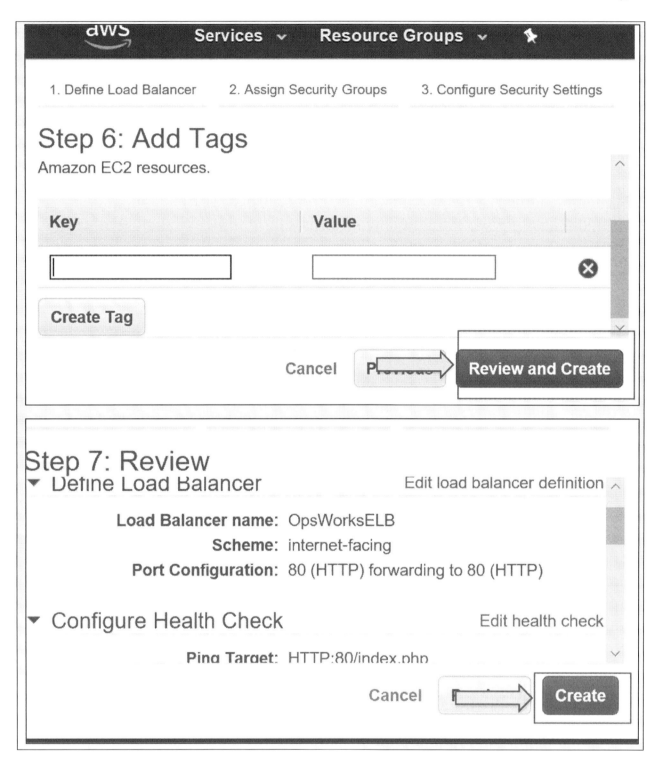

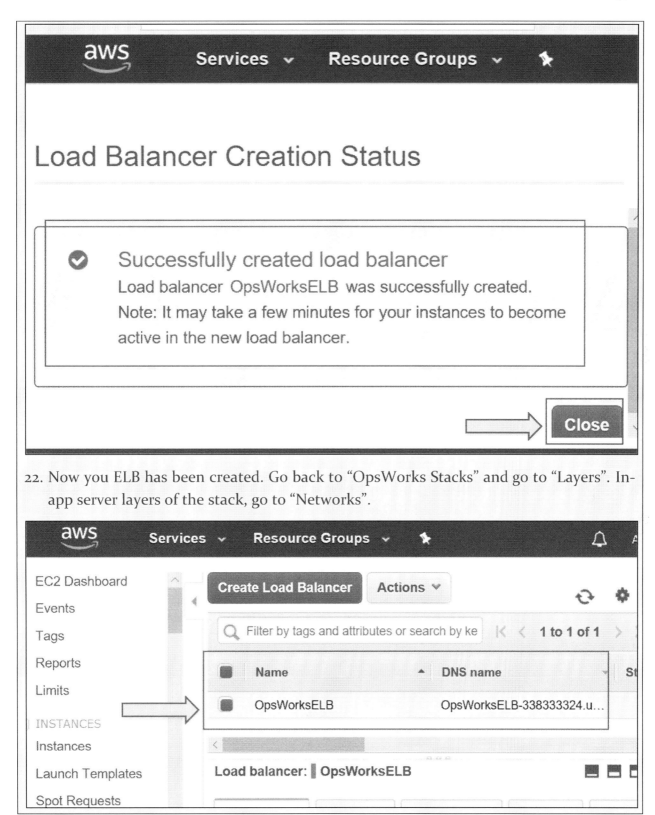

22. Now you ELB has been created. Go back to "OpsWorks Stacks" and go to "Layers". In-app server layers of the stack, go to "Networks".

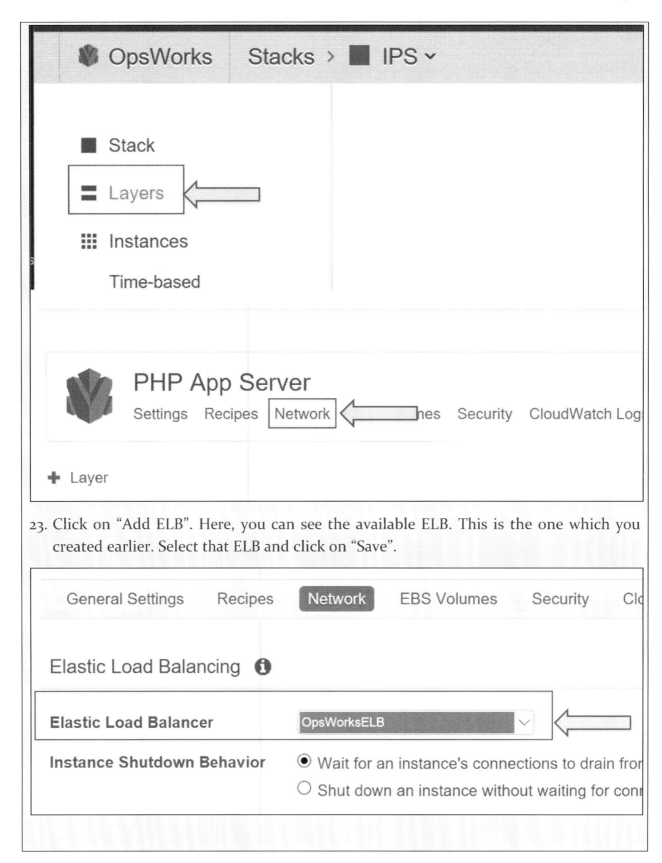

23. Click on "Add ELB". Here, you can see the available ELB. This is the one which you created earlier. Select that ELB and click on "Save".

NOTE: When you create ELB, you do not attach that ELB to EC2 instance because after you attach an ELB to a layer, OpsWorks removes any currently registered instances and then manages the load balancer for you. You can go to that ELB through EC2 console.

24. Now when you go to layers, you can see two layers; one is the ELB layer and other is app server layer.

ELB: OpsWorksELB

OpsWorksELB-338333324.us-east-1.elb.amazonaws.c

PHP App Server

Settings   Recipes   Network   EBS Volumes   Securi

25. For your health check passes for ELB, if you click on DNS name of ELB, it will open the page where the code exists in the repository.

ELB: OpsWorksELB

OpsWorksELB-338333324.us-east-1.elb.amazonaws.com

PHP App Server

Settings   Recipes   Network   EBS Volumes   Security   CloudW

EXAM TIP: Instance type in OpsWorks is by default 24/7, which means it is a baseline instance, but there are two other types, i.e., one is a time-based instance in which instances are started and stopped on bases of a specific schedule, like how much time you want your instance to be online. Another is a load-based instance in which instance start and stop depending on load changes of memory and application on overall instances in the layer.

EXAM TIP: In OpsWorks, Chef and Puppet are automation platforms that allow you to use code to automate the configurations of your servers

AWS Systems Manager

AWS Systems Manager (SSM), formerly known as "Amazon EC2 Systems Manager" or the "Amazon Simple Systems Manager", is a management service provided by AWS to configure and manage Amazon EC2 instances on-premises servers and virtual machines. It can also be used with other AWS resources. It is a simple interface that lets you centralize operational data and automate tasks across your resources. With the systems manager, you can quickly detect and resolve operational problems within your infrastructure. It also gives you a complete view of your architecture's configuration and performance and simplifies the management of resources and applications. By using a systems manager, it is easy to manage your infrastructure on a very large scale. The main component of AWS Systems Manager is SSM Agent, which is installed on instances by default on AWS-provided AMIs and enables System Manager features and supports all OSs. You can also download or install these agents on your on-premises systems and manage them via System Manager.

It is a management service in AWS that assists with collecting software inventory, applying OS patches, creating system images, and configuring OSs. You can manage Hybrid cloud systems (both interfaces and on-premises) from the single interfaces via this service. It also helps in reducing costs. Systems Manager works in such a way that first you group your resources, then view insights and take actions as per requirement. It is a simple interface that lets you centralize operational data and automate tasks across your resources.

On the AWS Systems Manager console, there are also other monitoring services available that you can use separately. You can use the AWS CloudTrail for logging and monitoring all the activities in your account; AWS Config for an audit of your AWS resources; AWS Trusted Advisor for use on many aspects such as cost optimization, performance, and security; and the Health dashboard to notify any issues that might affect your infrastructure.

Features

AWS Systems Manager comes with many features like,

- Run command, which gives secured remote management of instances at scale without login to the service. It will automate the administrative task. To run the command on instances, it uses SSH or remote PowerShell for windows
- State manager, which provides configuration management to maintain the EC2 instances for consistency. It basically creates states that specify when a certain configuration is applied to instances. With this feature, all of the configurations are automatically applied to the instances at a time with a frequency you specified. The configuration is also applied to the groups of instances as well. For example, the instances that have been updated to the current stable version of the Apache server

- Inventory manager feature, which collects the information about the instances and the software installed on these instances. In short, we can say that it will give you an overview of systems and installed applications on them. For example, which instance has what type of Apache server

- The maintenance window helps to schedule a window on time to run maintenance and administrative tasks on all instances. For example, define specific hours for the patch manager

- Patch manager allows you to select and deploy the OS software patches across all instances. Patch manager uses baseline to manage which patches are auto-approved for applying. Pre-defines baseline is provided by AWS for the windows server, or you can create your custom baseline. This pre-defines baseline is also known as "AWS-DefaultPatchBaseline". In this default baseline, there is a timer of 7 days after release

- Automation helps you to automate common and repetitive tasks. For example, stop Dev instances every Saturday and restart on Monday

- Parameter store is a feature that is, in general, a centralized place for storing and managing the configuration data. Parameter data can be tags, config data, passwords, data strings, etc. For example, for storing and retrieving RDS credentials

- The logging feature is also in the Systems Manager, but AWS recently recommended using the CloudWatch Logs agent. Via this, you can stream logs directly to CloudWatch and also use other features of CloudWatch

- Insight Dashboard is also available in Systems Manager, which gives you an account-level view of Config, Trusted Advisor and CloudTrail

- Resource Groups is a feature through which you organize your resources by tagging. Like that the specific resource belongs to the production group

EXAM TIP: AWS Systems Manager can manage both AWS and on-premises systems as long as they are supported OSs.

EXAM TIP: Patch Manager pre-defined baseline acts as a pre-approval gatekeeper.

Systems Manager Documents

Here, we will discuss some Systems Manager Documents, which define the action that the Systems Manager performs. These files are in JSON or YAML format with different steps and parameters you specify. These documents are stored in versions and make it public for other accounts as well.

Type	Used With	Purpose
Command Document	Run Command and State Manager	In run command, it is used to execute the command, while in State Manager, it is used to apply configuration
Policy Document	State Manager	It is used to apply policy on targets. If it is removed, then its actions will no longer be able to perform
Automation Document	Automation	It is a list of tasks or commands that you are applying when using an automation service

Table 8-01: AWS Systems Manager Document Type

Benefits of AWS Systems Manager

- **Quicker Problem Detection**
  You can quickly identify issues in your architecture, as AWS Systems Manager gives you a complete view of your architecture's performance and configuration.

- **Easy Automation**
  Operational tasks can be easily automated by the systems manager, making your teams more efficient. You can automate maintenance and deployment, patching, updates and configuration processes.

- **Visibility and Control**
  You can understand and control the state of your infrastructure more easily. The Systems Manager is integrated with AWS Config, so that you can easily view changes as they occur.

- **Manage Hybrid Environments**

With a unified interface, you can manage all servers running either on AWS or in your on-premises data center. AWS securely communicates with the agent that is installed on your servers to execute management tasks more effectively.

- **Security and Compliance**
  When using AWS systems manager, you can define patch baselines, maintain antivirus definitions and enforce firewall policies. The Systems Manager also maintains security and compliance by scanning your instances regularly, as defined in your configuration and custom policies.

Enterprise Apps

Here, we will discuss some business intelligence and end-user computing tools that AWS provides. There are a variety of services that are aimed for large enterprise customers and as an alternative service to other similar services in the market.

AWS Workspaces and AppStream

Amazon Workspaces and AppStream are quite similar, but there is a little difference between them. AWS Workspace is a fully managed desktop as a service product by Amazon. It is configured to provide fully available and dedicated Windows 7 or Windows 10 desktop in a few minutes. This desktop is accessible via PC on IP software or hardware. The way Workspace is implemented difficult to understand, as it is partially in your account and partially on the on-premises infrastructure.

In AppStream, the application is encapsulated and allows you to access those applications via the browser. So the main difference between both of them is that Workspaces gives you the entire desktop to run an application, while AppStream gives specific applications like engineering applications which are expensive.

Both of them are live on AWS and can be managed and controlled tightly, which is good for a lock-down environment. Consider an example; if your company is concerned about the security of the desktop, you can put WorkSpaces in a VPC and restrict the data from going out to the public internet from within a VPC. This way, you can prevent data theft.

Another use case for WorkSpaces is that you can use it for remote or seasonal workers. Hence, this can be used for such workers by giving them these virtual desktops or applications, which they use on their own PCs.

To sell a product by giving a demo and without giving access to install or download, you can use AppStream for that product.

Amazon Connect

AWS Connect is a fully managed contact center solution with cloud-based configurable call handling, inbound/outbound telephony, interactive voice response, chat bot, and analytics. Many organizations integrate this with their customer management systems.

Amazon Chime

Amazon Chime is an online video and meeting conferencing service. It is a communication service through which you can meet, chat and do business calls within the organization or outside. It has flexible features such as online meetings, business calling and video conferencing with pay-as-you-go pricing. It supports desktop sharing and group chatting as well.

Amazon WorkDocs

Amazon WorkDocs is a fully managed online document storage and collaboration platform. Via this service, you can also create secure content. Amazon WorkDocs allows you to create, edit and share content easily and access them from anywhere on any device since they are central store to AWS. It is like GoogleDrive or Dropbox. With this, you can do versioning and editing with collaboration.

Amazon WorkMail

Amazon WorkMail is a secure and managed business emails and calendar service with desktop and mobile email client support such as Outlook, IMAP, Android, and iOS. Amazon WorkMail can be integrated into an existing directory, email journalization can be used to satisfy the compliance requirements, and you may control both your encrypted keys and your data location key.

Amazon WorkLink

It is a secured reversed proxy, so if you want to access the web application internally, then you can use WorkLink to secure the path, which you can use to access the internal part. When a user accesses a website internally, it is first made available in a browser in a secure AWS container. Then Amazon WorkLink sends the contents of this page as vector graphics to your employees and maintains the functionality and interaction of the page.

Alexa for Business

It is Alexa that can be used in a business setting. Like if you deploy echo devices in the conference room and be able to interact with them through voice. With Alexa for Business, employees will be able to take advantage of Alexa as their intelligent helper for more productive work in meeting rooms and at work desks. It also has some management functionality, which is needed when you try to manage a large number of echoes across the enterprise.

AWS Machine Learning Landscape

There are a number of Machine Learning services that are increasing weekly. The base of the ML landscape is more and minimal services. These are purpose build containers or AMIs that are designed to support popular ML Frameworks like mxnet or TensorFlow.

The next layer is more structured and uses Amazon SageMaker as a core product. SageMaker is an Umbrella for many ML services. First, it is a managed Jupyter Notebook deployment, which is used to deploy many ML models for analyzing data. It is a fully managed Machine Learning service provided by AWS. This service assists data scientists and developers in building and training machine learning models easily and quickly, using special containers called Docker Containers, then deploying these models into a production-hosted environment. Through this model, you can use AWS Built-in Algorithms or use your own. Amazon SageMaker has endpoints that are used to publish the ML models to the apps or other people who consider our ML model.

Then at the top of the stack, we have a variety of services that are encapsulated with ML capabilities into easy-to-use form. The services in AI are for developers without any need for knowledge about ML. Some of these services are given below:

- **Amazon Comprehend**- It takes natural language and translates into that which Machine can read and understand. It is a Natural Language Processing service. The use case for this is sentiment analysis, like identifying whether the person is happy with the post or not on social media

- **Amazon Forecast**- Here, you can add some time-series data, then Amazon Forecast analyses that data and give some predictions about future

- **Amazon Lex**- It is the backbone of Alexa. It takes voice messages and converts them into context or intent

- **Amazon Personalize**- It is the recommended engine which Amazon uses behind the concept of an e-commerce website. Here, you put your customer data in bulk, and this will tell that which customer might like which product

- **Amazon Polly**- It is a text-to-speech service. When you give some text, it produces realistic sounding, speech in many different languages

- **Amazon Rekognition**- It is an image and video processing service. In this, we feed an image, and it will give you information about that image like objects inside the image and emotion

- **Amazon Textract**- It is a high power Optical Character Recognition engine that you feed in a document, and it extracts the details from that physical document and puts it in the database

- **Amazon Transcribe**- It takes an audio file and translates it into text. It is used to produce a transcript in presentation
- **Amazon Translate**- It is a language translation service

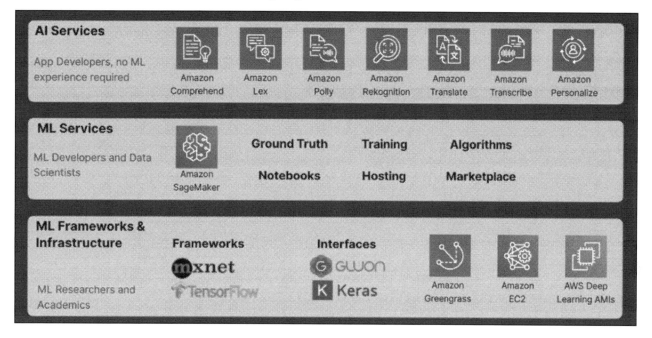

Figure 8-13: Machine Learning Landscape

Lab 8-03: Zero Down Time Deployment

Scenario

A Research and Development company released version 1 of its application. When customers use this application and give their feedback, the company will release version 2. The deployment of version 2 should be without any downtime as the company is not able to tolerate any downtime. How can this be done?

Solution

The first thing that we need to do during this deployment is determined which deployment type is suitable for this deployment by keeping both versions up to and running. So deployment type is Blue/Green Deployment. In the end, also test cutover and rollback.

1. Log in to AWS Console and go to the "Elastic Beanstalk" service.

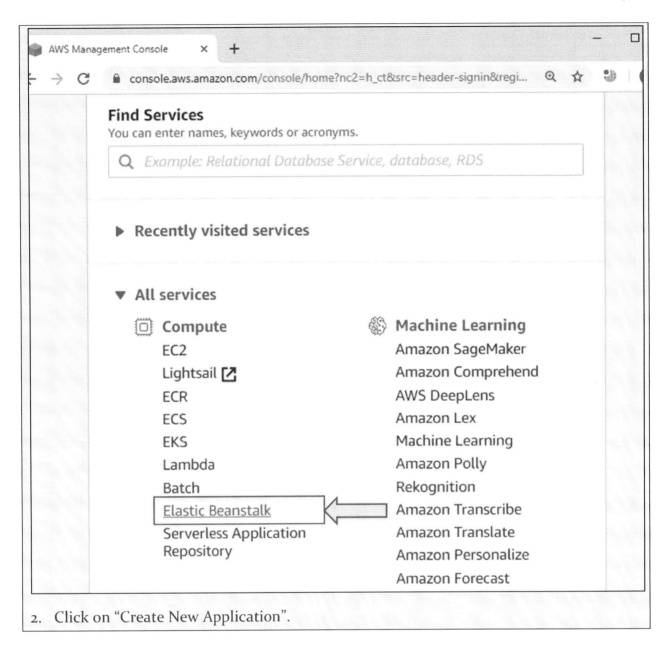

2. Click on "Create New Application".

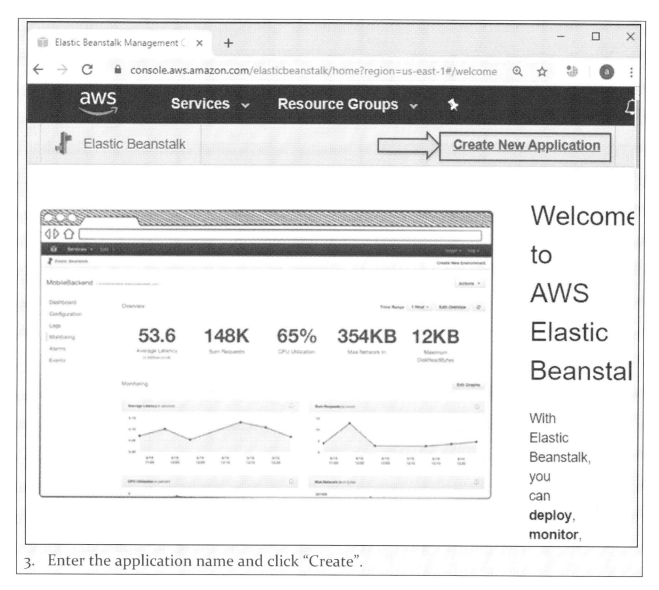

3. Enter the application name and click "Create".

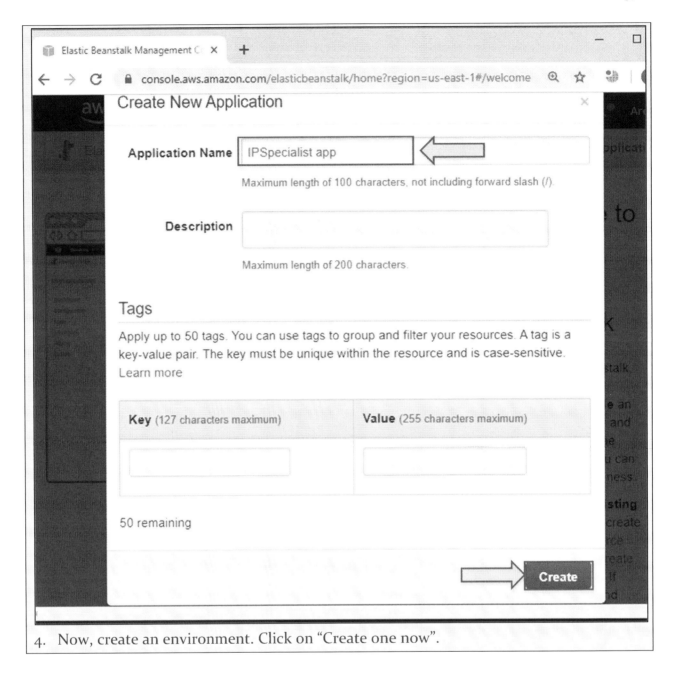

4. Now, create an environment. Click on "Create one now".

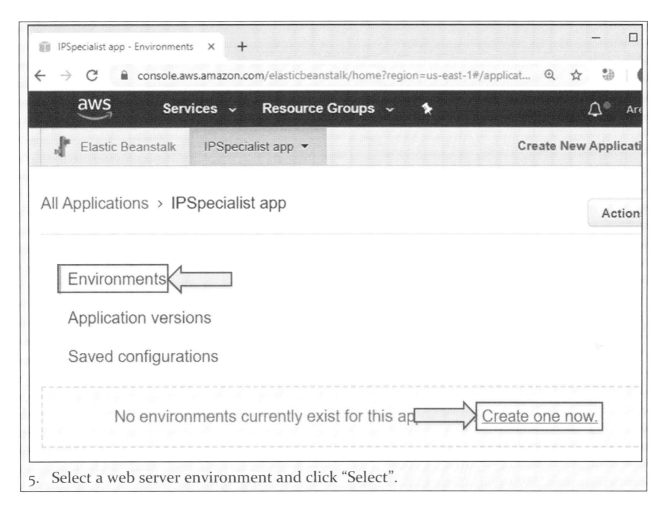

5. Select a web server environment and click "Select".

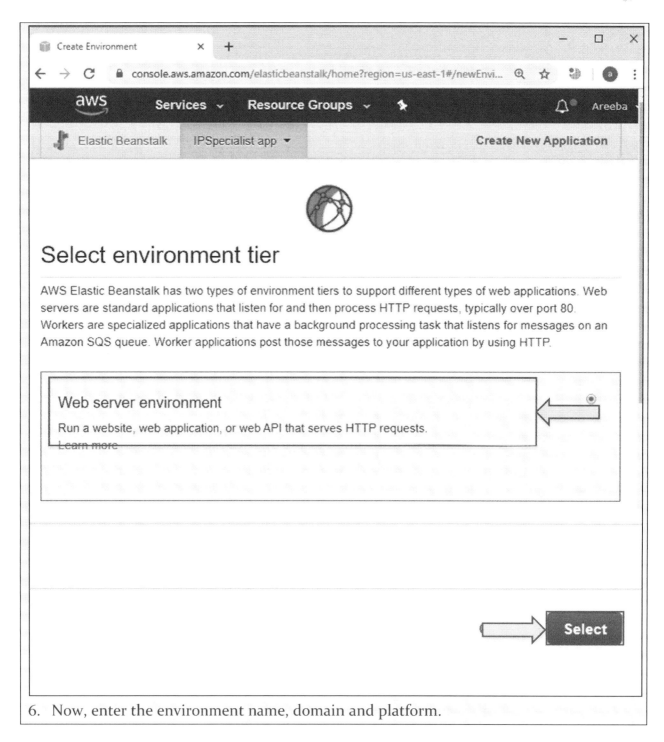

6. Now, enter the environment name, domain and platform.

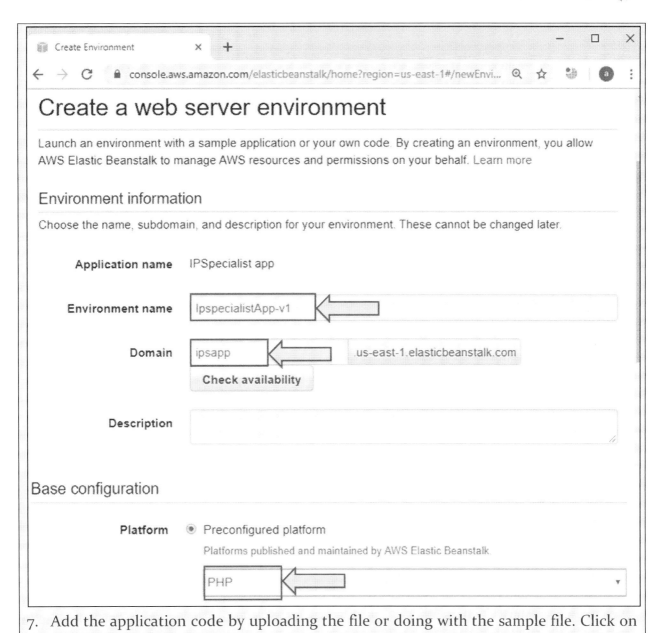

7. Add the application code by uploading the file or doing with the sample file. Click on "Create Environment".

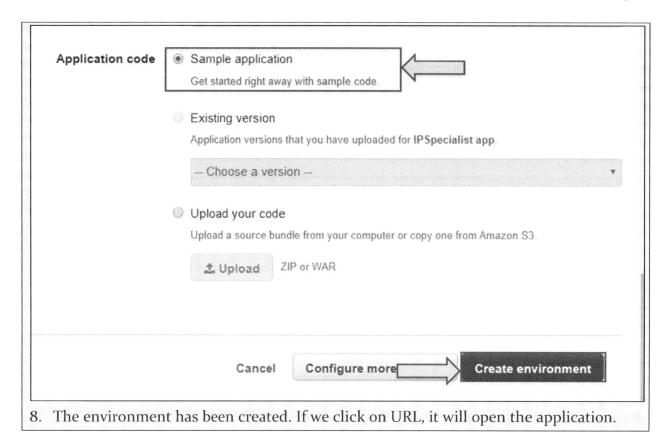

8. The environment has been created. If we click on URL, it will open the application.

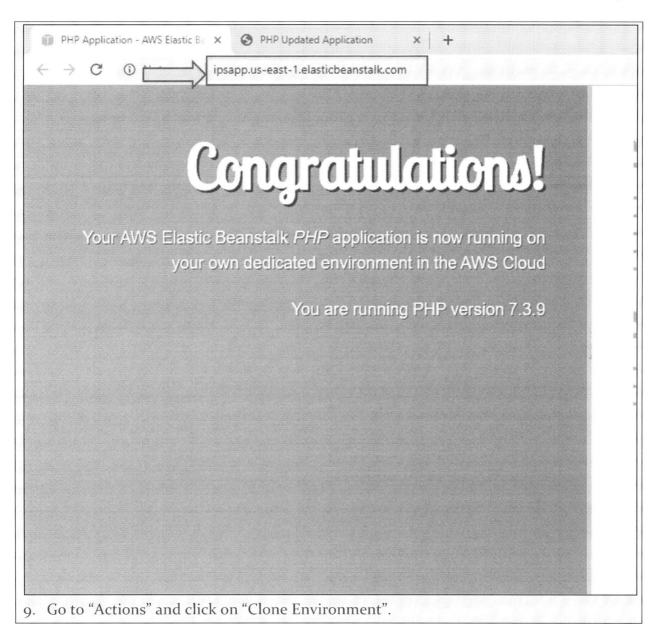

9. Go to "Actions" and click on "Clone Environment".

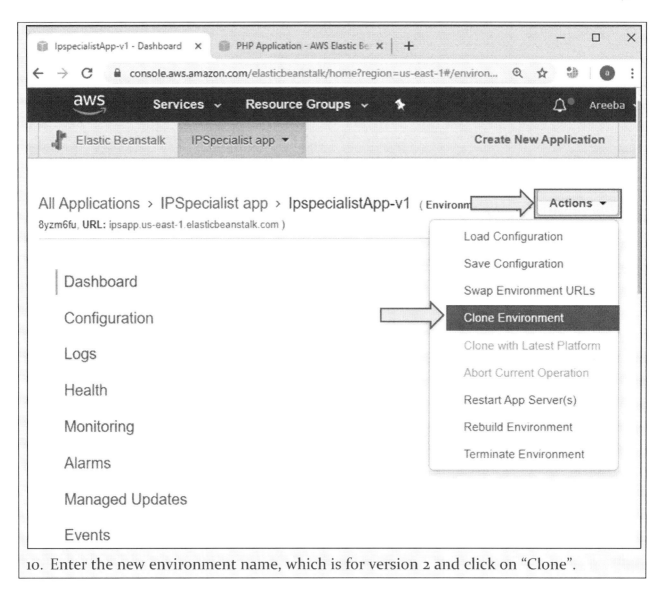

10. Enter the new environment name, which is for version 2 and click on "Clone".

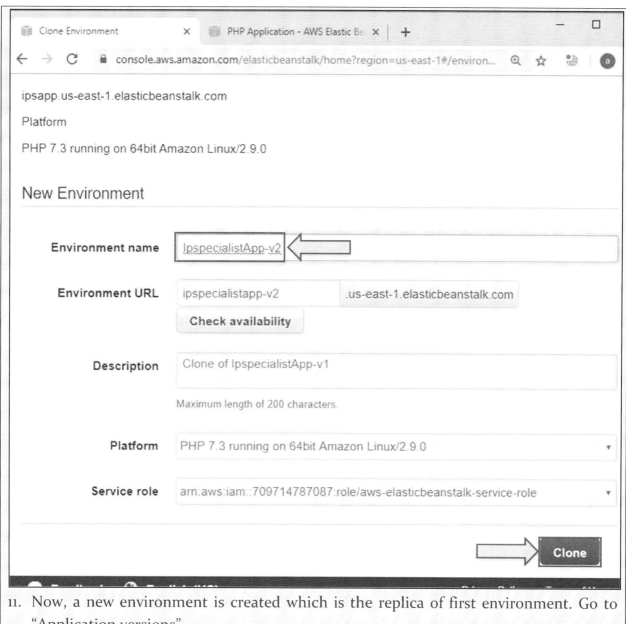

11. Now, a new environment is created which is the replica of first environment. Go to "Application versions".

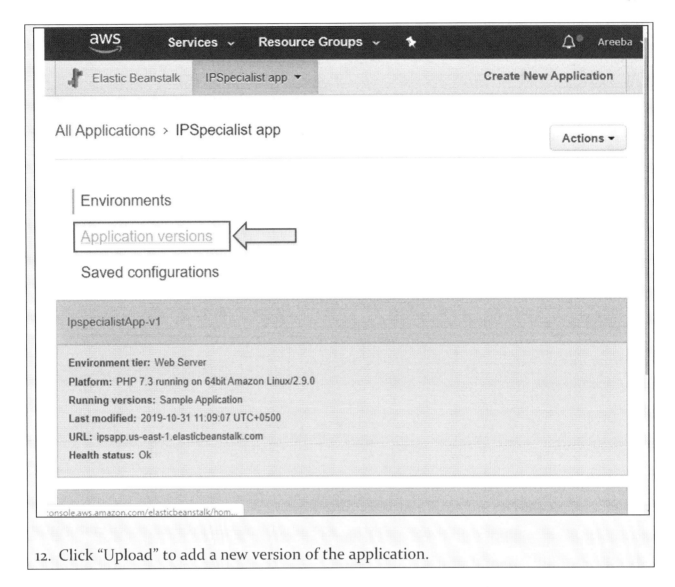

12. Click "Upload" to add a new version of the application.

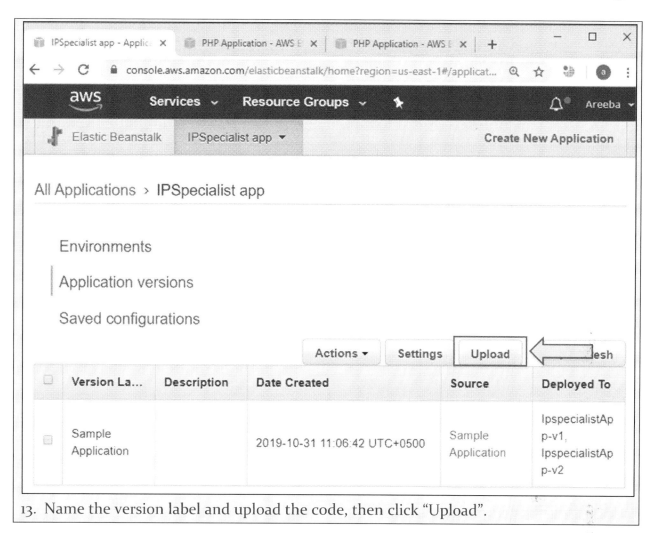

13. Name the version label and upload the code, then click "Upload".

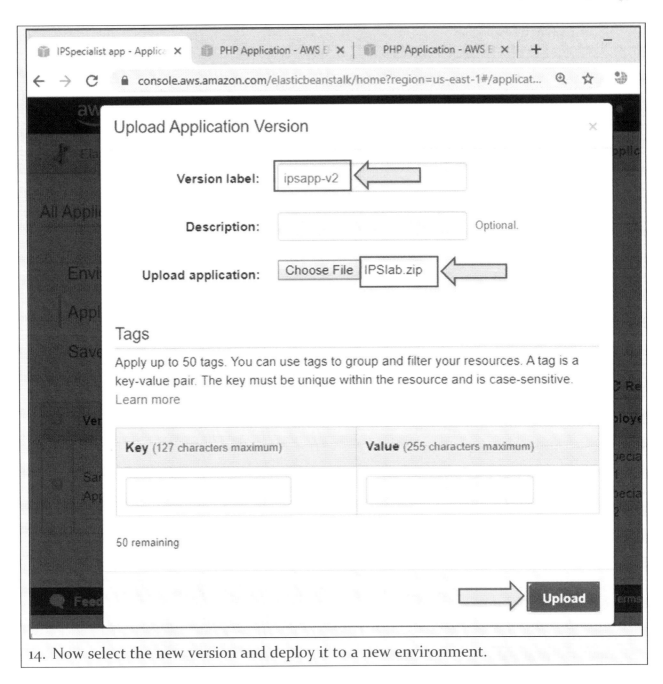

14. Now select the new version and deploy it to a new environment.

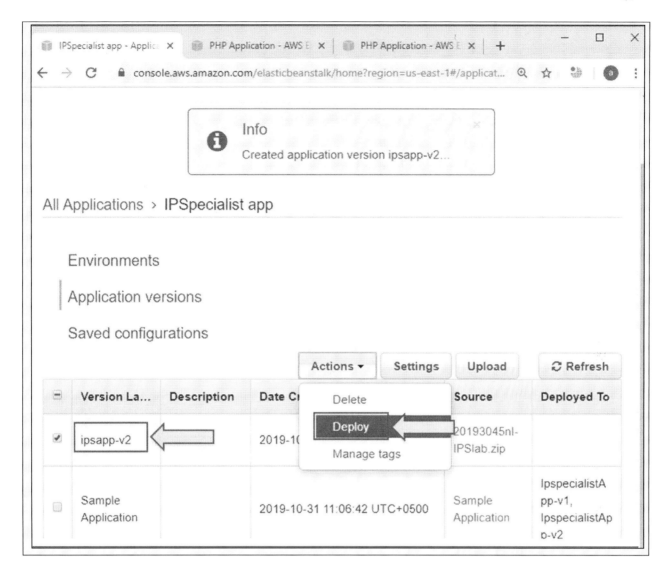

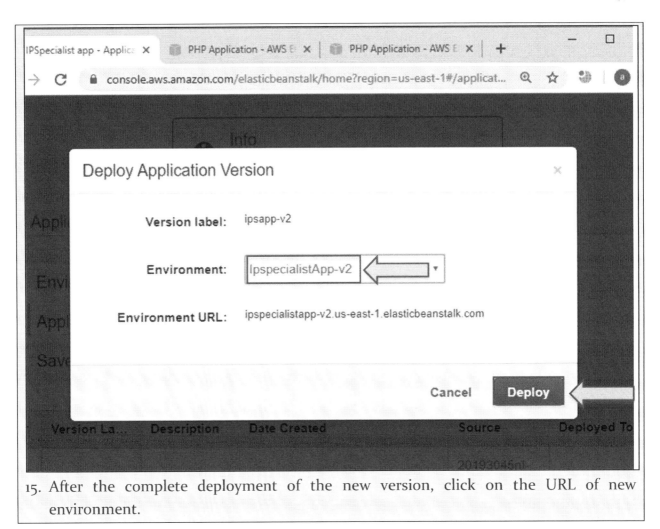

15. After the complete deployment of the new version, click on the URL of new environment.

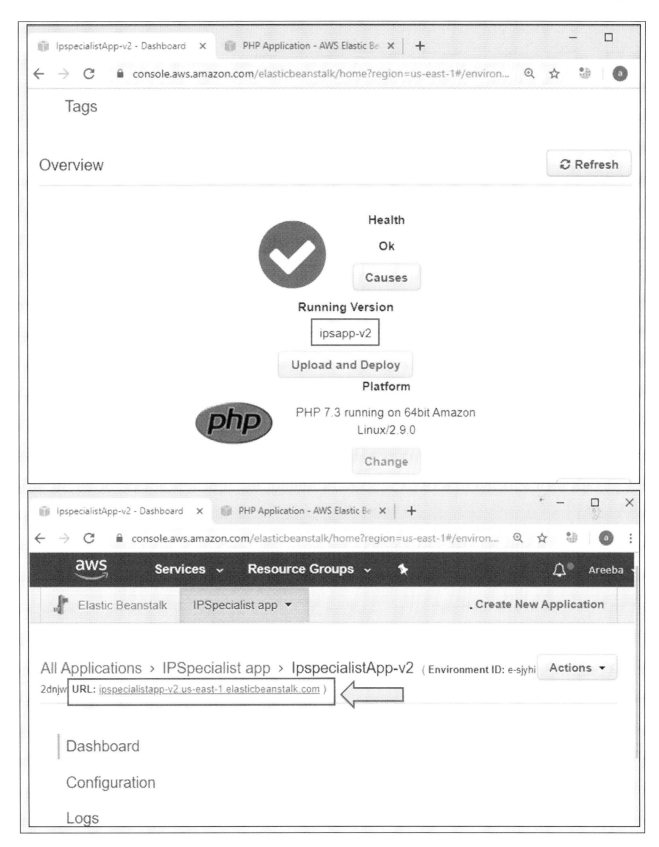

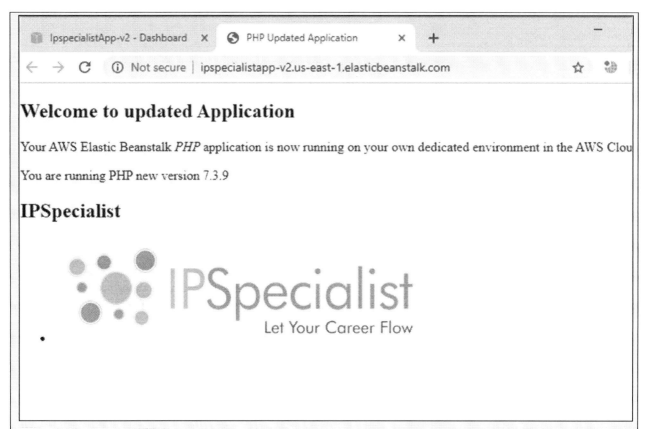

16. Now go to applications, here both environments are showing up and running. Go to action and click on "Swap environment URLs".

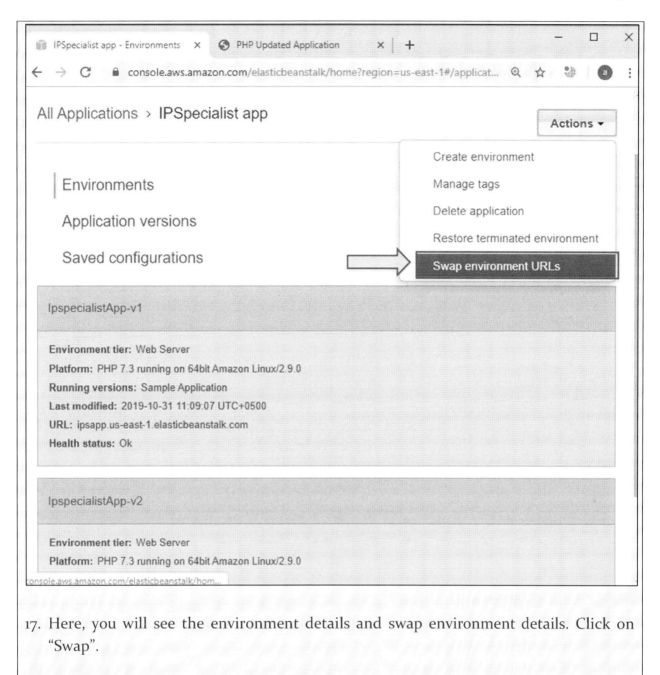

17. Here, you will see the environment details and swap environment details. Click on "Swap".

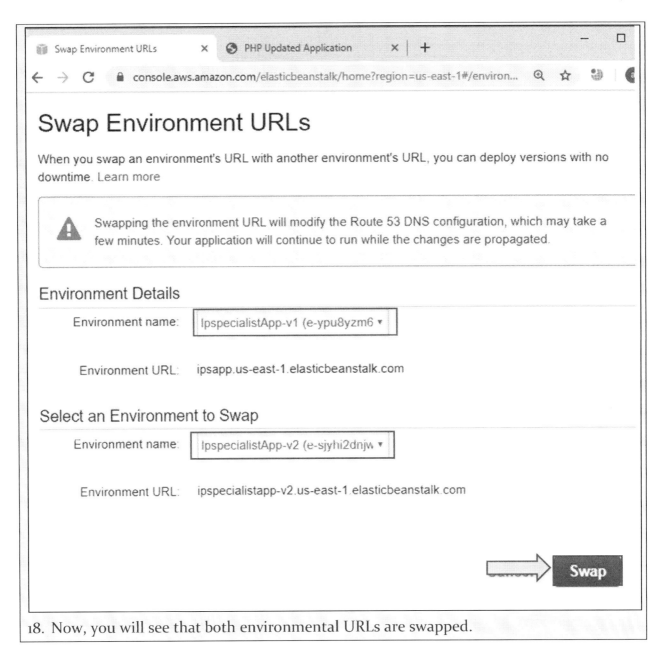

18. Now, you will see that both environmental URLs are swapped.

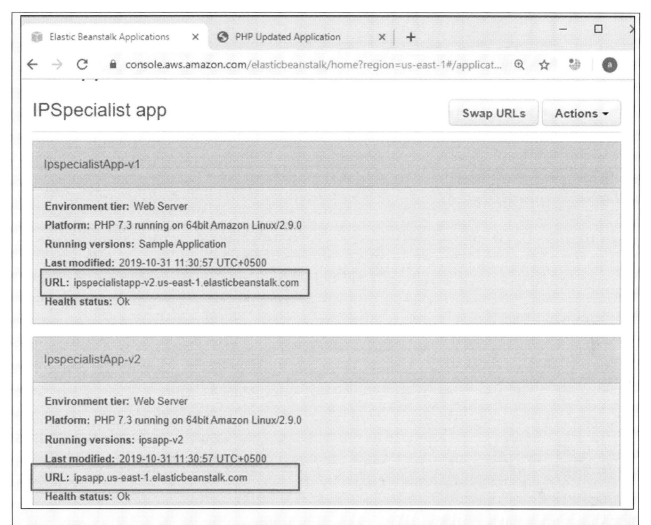

If we open environment URL of version 1 environment, it will open the new version of application and version 2 shows an older version of application.

Note: If you feel any issue occurring in new application version, then Swap URLs again. You can also perform this blue/green deployment via Route 53.

From the given link, you can upload a new version of application "IPSlab.zip" and keep it in zip format.

https://github.com/IPSpecialist/IPElasticBeanstalk

 EXAM TIP:

https://d1.awsstatic.com/whitepapers/overview-of-deployment-options-on-aws.pdf

https://d1.awsstatic.com/whitepapers/DevOps/practicing-continuous-integration-continuous-delivery-on-AWS.pdf

https://d1.awsstatic.com/whitepapers/AWS_Blue_Green_Deployments.pdf

https://d1.awsstatic.com/whitepapers/DevOps/infrastructure-as-code.pdf

Challenge 1

A company IT engineer created a stack in CloudFormation. The stack template is successfully validated. In order to protect the production database, he adds some stack policy to avoid its accidental re-initializes. The policy is given below:

```
{
  "Statement" : [
    {
      "
      "Effect" : "Deny",
      "Action" : "Update:*",
      "Principal": "*",
      "Resource" : "LogicalResourceId/ProductionDatabase"
    }
  ]
}
```

You, as Solution Architect Professional, view this policy. What is your analysis of this policy or recommended action if needed?

   A. The stack policy is lacking a necessary component
   B. Stack policy is fine
   C. Do not do anything in stack policy
   D. Update the faulty policy using console
   E. Stack policy parameter syntax is incorrect
   F. Remove the faulty policy via console
   G. Remove the faulty policy via CLI
   H. Update the faulty policy using CLI

Solution:

By default, stack policy is protecting all the resources. If you want to allow updating on any resource, then you need to explicitly allow it. In the given stack policy, there is a lack of necessary components, which is an explicit allow. We also know that once the stack policy is created, you cannot remove it, so you can only update the policy via using CLI only. So **option A** and **option H** are valid answers.

Challenge 2

An enterprise wants to do new deployment by keeping an application 100% available to the customers. For this deployment, they can use Blue/Green Deployment. The upgrading to the new version needs to be fast, as there are many versions of the application. They also need to quickly roll back to the older version in case of failure in updates.

The documenting of this deployment is in such a way:

Blue stack running the current version, while green is a new version. The new version of the application is used for preparing new AMI, and for using this new AMI, configure an Auto scaling group. Then, you start up the green ELB and attach it to the green Auto scaling Group. What should be the next step used for deployment?

A. Reassign the EIP from the Blue instances to the green instances
B. Change the current launch configuration for the blue auto-scaling group to use the new green AMI, then manually terminate all the instances running the old blue AMI one-by-one, so they restart with the green AMI
C. Once the green ELB and auto scaling pool are healthy, use Route 53's weighted routing feature to route traffic to the green ELB, setting the weight to 1 and set the blue ELB to 0
D. Update the route table in VPC to route all inbound traffic to the new green ELB's IP address. Using CloudWatch, monitor traffic until there are no more requests going to the blue ELB's IP address, then remove it
E. Once the green ELB and Auto scaling pool are healthy, use Route 53's weighted routing feature to route traffic to the green ELB by setting the weight to a number higher than the current weight of 10 for blue ELB
F. Remove the blue ELB from the blue stack, then wait until the TTL expires on the DNS record. Then change the Route 53 entry to point to green ELB.

Solution:

As per the requirement of 100% availability of application during deployment of the new version and also the fastest upgrading, we do not want multiple versions on production at the same time. For the next step, we need to use Route 53, which is the most suitable solution for the requirement.

Option A is not valid because we ELB, so we do not assign any EIP to the instances behind ELB.

Option B could work, as it is known as a rolling upgrade, but it takes long duration than Route 53's option. The question also explains that we create a green Auto scaling group, so there is no need to make any changes in the blue Auto scaling Group. Hence, this option is also not valid.

Options C and **E** both are using Route 53's weighted routing feature. It works in such a way that it takes the total of all weights for a given DNS name and then route traffic on the basis of ratio; each record has some ratio of the total. Option E still keeps some amount of the total traffic, while Option C allocates the weight 0 to blue ELB and stops sending traffic to blue ELB. In this way, all traffic goes to green ELB. So **Option C** is the correct answer.

Option D is also invalid because we never refer to ELB by IP address, as it is referred by Domain name, and also VPC route table is not used to control inbound traffic to public ELB.

Option F is not valid since it requires down time as the blue stack is removed from ELB, and the user whose DNS still holds Blue ELB will not be able to take that to the application.

Mind Map

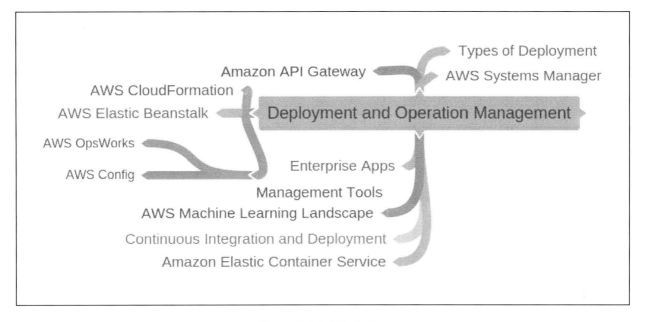

Figure 8-14: Mind Map

Practice Questions:

1. Your organization uses Chef heavily for its deployment automation. What AWS cloud service provides integration with Chef Recipes to start new application server instances, configure application server software, and deploy applications?
   a) AWS Beanstalk
   b) AWS OpsWorks
   c) AWS CloudWatch
   d) AWS CloudFront

2. To convert hardware structure into a code, which AWS service is used?
   a) AWS Trusted Advisor
   b) AWS Elastic Beanstalk
   c) AWS CloudFormation
   d) AWS Kinesis

3. In Elastic Beanstalk Environment type is divided in to _____.

a) 3
b) 2
c) 4
d) 5

4. With the help of CloudFormation, you can create_____ and assign them.
   a) IAM Users
   b) IAM Groups
   c) IAM Policy
   d) IAM Roles

5. CloudFormation service in AWS is _____.
   a) $5 per month
   b) $10 per month
   c) Free
   d) $0.5 per day

6. What are the formats of the template in CloudFormation? (Choose 2)
   a) XML
   b) JSON
   c) Html
   d) YAML

7. How many elements of the template are there?
   a) 2
   b) 3
   c) 5
   d) 8

8. Using CloudFormation, you must ensure that the order of provisioning is set in your script, or the stack will fail to be provisioned. True or false?
   a) False
   b) True

9. Which deployment tool is good for developers who do not know much about AWS?
    a) CloudFormation
    b) OpsWorks
    c) Elastic Beanstalk
    d) None of the above

10. In CloudFormation, you can create multiple _____ in a single template.
    a) Users
    b) VPC
    c) Layer
    d) Stack

11. To get notified about health and event, Elastic Beanstalk uses which AWS service?
    a) CloudTrail
    b) CloudWatch
    c) CloudFront
    d) Redshift

12. In Elastic Beanstalk, fault tolerance is enabled for_____.
    a) Single region for multiple AZ
    b) Multiple regions for single AZ
    c) Multiple regions for multiple AZ
    d) All of the above

13. Which service of AWS allows you to build and manage the stack flexibly and simply along with its linked applications and resources?
    a) EC2
    b) OpsWorks
    c) S3
    d) CloudFront

14. Which of the following in AWS OpsWorks can be used to specify how a group of EC2 instances is configured for a specific task?
    a) Stack
    b) App
    c) Lifecycle event
    d) Layer

15. How many types of lifecycle events in each layer relate to different stages of instance lifecycle?
    a) 2
    b) 4
    c) 5
    d) 7

16. Which service of AWS is generally a GUI used to deploy and configure the infrastructure faster?
    a) OpsWorks
    b) EC2
    c) IAM
    d) Redshift

17. To make sure that certain items are not deleted upon a CloudFormation stack being deleted, you can _____.
    a) Create deletion policy on CloudFormation that stack will not delete at any cost.
    b) Create deletion policy on those resources.
    c) Manage the resources independently of CloudFormation.
    d) All of the above

18. Which term in OpsWorks is a group of resources or like a container for the resources?
    a) Stack
    b) App
    c) Lifecycle event
    d) Layer

19. With the help of Elastic Beanstalk, you can deploy_____.
    a) RDS Instance
    b) CloudFormation Template
    c) OpsWorks Stack
    d) All of the above

20. In a CloudFormation template, which of the following is mandatory?
    a) Version and format of the template
    b) Resources along with its configuration
    c) Resources and output values
    d) Input values

21. From the following given options, which is not an advantage of Continuous Delivery?
    a) Improved code quality
    b) Automated software releases to production
    c) Deliver updates faster
    d) Automated and consistent release preparation

22. Which deployment technique takes the shortest time in deployment?
    a) Rolling with Batch
    b) Immutable
    c) Blue/Green
    d) All at once

23. In which upgrade type a new release is deployed to the new instance and terminates the old instance?
    a) Disposable
    b) Parallel
    c) In place
    d) Multi-stage

24. Which feature of CloudFormation is used to review any potential impact of changes on the process?
    a) IAM Roles
    b) Template Linting

c) Stack Policies

d) Change Sets

25. OpsWorks allows you to clone stacks to other regions as well as within the same region. True or false?

a) True

b) False

Chapter 09: Costing Management

Introduction

In this chapter, we will discuss some business costing related terms and that how we can optimize the costs by using different strategies. We will also discuss tagging resource groups, which helps you to identify your resources easily. As we have different pricing options for EC2 and RDS, so these will be discussed as well to know that where and what pricing options are used for certain requirements. To manage your organization accounts, AWS gives you a service, AWS Organization which will also be discussed briefly. In AWS, to access the roles and permissions of one account from another AWS account, "Cross Account access" is used; this will be discussed at the end of the chapter.

Concepts

To understand business related terms in costing, there are some terms that you need to know, which are defined below:

Capital Expenses (CapEx)

Money spent on long-term assets is known as Capital Expenses, such as expenditure for property, buildings, and equipment.

Operational Expenses (OpEx)

Operational expense means spending money to keep the business running, and this can also be termed as a variable expense.

CapEx Budgeting

All businesses require a budget for their future expenses and to purchase the resources with the maximum capacity to use. The future is unpredictable, so either they can avail that budget, they can save from that budget, or there might be the possibility that emergency reasons increase the expenses from the set budget. If you buy a resource of high capacity and do not use it at its full capacity, this under-utilization of resources is also an overhead.

OpEx Cost Model

OpEx cost model uses variable cost, which means you will pay for what you will use. If a service is down or you have stopped or started a server because of load management, you will only be paying for the time the services were running; this is not possible when you buy resources. Pay as you go cloud computing also provides the same benefit.

Pay as you go model does not require long term contracts.

Total Cost of Ownership (TCO) and Return on Investment (ROI)

Total Cost of Ownership (TCO) includes all the costs for a selected option. It includes both direct and indirect costs involved in the package. ROI is the total cost that is expected to be returned. It is not always positive. It can be more, less, or equal to the invested money.

For TCOs and ROI, you need to be very careful because most of the companies are not good in handling the full on-premises datacenter costs like power, cooling, fire suppression, etc. The real state is involved in supporting the datacenter.

Also, soft costs are rarely tracked as most companies do not pay any attention to the soft cost. Soft cost means the overhead or extra time that is needed to maintain something, which is rolling the subscription. It is known as a tangible expense.

When you migrate to the cloud, the learning curve will vary from person to person, and most of the companies do not pay enough respect or enough runway for the people to get enough speed. So when you are initially in the process of migrating to the cloud, your expenses and time need to be more than on-premises.

Most business plans include a lot of assumptions, which in turn require other assumptions, which again require other assumptions. This way, the IT team of the organization is several layers down an assumption chain.

Cost Optimization Strategies

Following are the cost optimization strategies:

- Appropriate Provisioning
- Right-Sizing
- Purchase Options
- Geographic Selection
- Managed Services
- Optimized Data Transfer

Appropriate Provisioning

- Only provision those resources that you need. For example, stop or terminate those instances that are not in use
- Consolidate for greater density and lower complexity where it is possible. For example, consolidate the bunch of small read and write databases in one big database (multi-database RDS, containers)
- Use CloudWatch, which enables you to monitor the utilization of resources

Right-Sizing

- Choose the resources that have lower cost and provide the technical requirements
- Design in such a way that you will make use of resources consistently and avoid spikes and valleys
- Create loosely coupled architecture by using SNS, Lambda, SQS, and DynamoDB. These can smoothen demand and help to achieve more predictability and consistency

Purchase Options

- AWS offers different types of purchase options having different costs for permanent and variable use of resources
- Reserved instances are best to use when you are working for a permanent application or needs
- For temporary horizontal scaling, the use of spot instances is a cost-effective solution
- AWS offers EC2 Fleet, which gives you the option of defining target comprising of spot, reserved, and on-demand instances

Geographic Selection

- AWS pricing is different for every region
- Select the region having low price if you do not require the service same as your current region
- Use Route53 or CloudFront to compete with the latency due to resources in other regions

Region	S3 Standard Storage for First 50TB
us-west-2	$0.023 per GB
us-west-1	$0.026 per GB
ap-northeast-1	$0.025 per GB
sa-east-1	$0.0405 per GB

Table 9-01: S3 Storage Cost

Managed Services

- Use managed services instead of self-managed services. For example, you can use MySQL RDS instead of MySQL on EC2
- Reduce the complexity and manual interventions, would result in cost saving
- Examples of fully managed services are RDS, Redshift, Fargate, and especially EMR

Optimization Strategies

- Data IN is free of cost while data OUT is charged
- DirectConnect is cost-effective long run solution providing good volume and speed

 EXAM TIP: Go through the following whitepapers:

https://d1.awsstatic.com/whitepapers/architecture/AWS-Cost-Optimization-Pillar.pdf

https://d1.awsstatic.com/whitepapers/total-cost-of-operation-benefits-using-aws.pdf

https://d1.awsstatic.com/whitepapers/introduction-to-aws-cloud-economics-final.pdf

Tagging and Resource Groups

Tagging

Tags are key-value pairs that are attached to AWS resources. They are labels that you assign to an AWS resource, and they contain "metadata", which is the information about data.

Features

The tag limit varies with the resource, but most can have up to 50 tags. With most AWS resources, you have the option of adding tags when you create the resource, whether it is an Amazon EC2 instance, an Amazon S3 bucket, or any other resource. You can also add, change, or remove those tags from one resource at a time within each resource's console. Whereas adding tags to multiple resources at once can be done by using Tag Editor. Tags are sometimes inherited, which means that when provisioning AWS services like CloudFormation, Auto-scaling, and Elastic Beanstalk create other resources, they tag the resources that they created. If you delete a resource, tags for the resource are also deleted. You can also perform editing of tag keys and values and remove tags from a resource at any time. With Tag Editor, you search for the resources that you want to tag and then add, remove, or edit tags for the resources in your search results. Tag Editor provides a central, unified way to easily create and manage your user-defined tags across services and regions.

The tags function like properties of a resource, so they are shared across the entire account. This enables your AWS resources to be categorized in different ways like, by environment purpose or owner. When you have a lot of resources of the same type, you can quickly identify a specific resource based on the tags you have assigned to it. With the help of tagging, you can organize your resources, enabling yourself to simplify resource management, access management, and cost allocation.

Assigning tags to resources allows higher levels of automation and ease of management. You can execute management tasks at scale by listing resources with specific tags, then

executing the appropriate actions. For example, you can list all resources with a particular tag and value, then for each of the resources, either delete or terminate them. This is useful to automate the shutdown or removal of a set of resources at the end of the working day. Creating and implementing an AWS tagging standard across your organization's accounts will enable you to manage and govern your AWS environments consistently and uniformly.

Resource Groups

With the help of Resource Groups, you can easily create, maintain and view a collection of resources that share one or more common tags or portions of tags. You can use resource groups to organize your AWS resources by marking resources from multiple services and regions with a common tag, and then view those resources together in a customizable pane of the AWS Management Console.

To create a resource group, you identify the tags that contain the items that members of the group should have in common. The resource group contains information like Regions, Names, and Health checks, or it can display metrics, alarms, and configuration details and make it easier to manage and automate tasks on large numbers of resources at one time. It can also contain specific information depending upon the resources, which you can dump in the CSV file.

Lab 9-01: Resource Group and Tagging

Scenario

An organization needs to keep track of resources to know which department uses what resources. Using AWS, how can they achieve this?

Solution:

With the help of resource groups and tagging, they can keep track of resources.

1. Log in to AWS Console and go to "EC2" under "Compute Service".

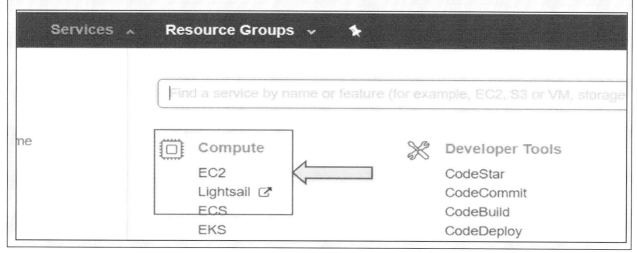

2. On "EC2" dashboard, click the "Launch Instance" button.

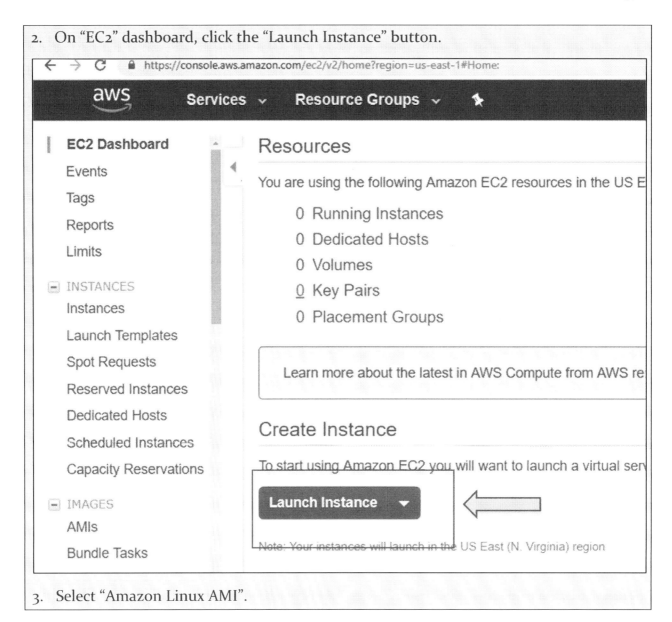

3. Select "Amazon Linux AMI".

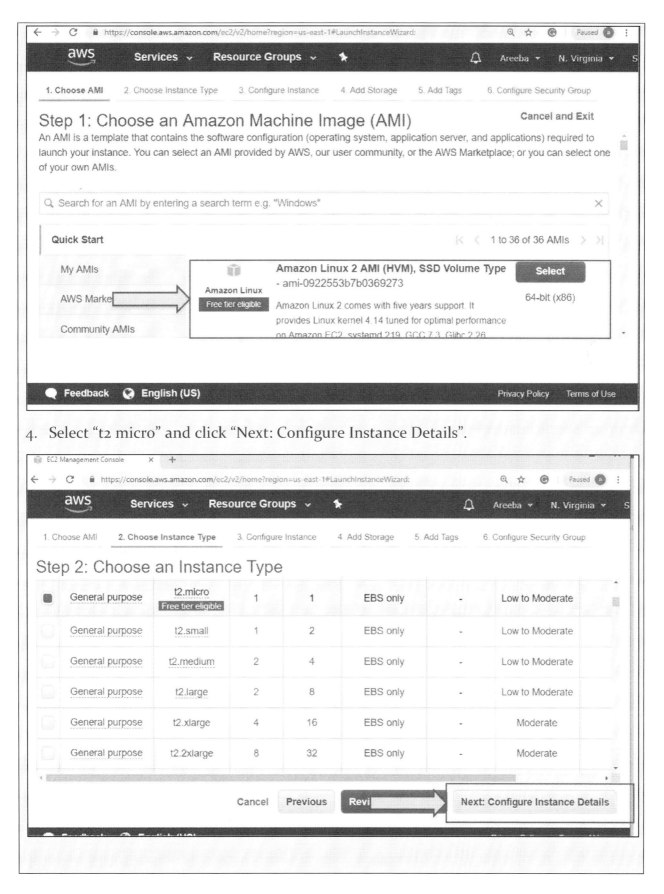

4. Select "t2 micro" and click "Next: Configure Instance Details".

5. Click "Next: Add Storage".

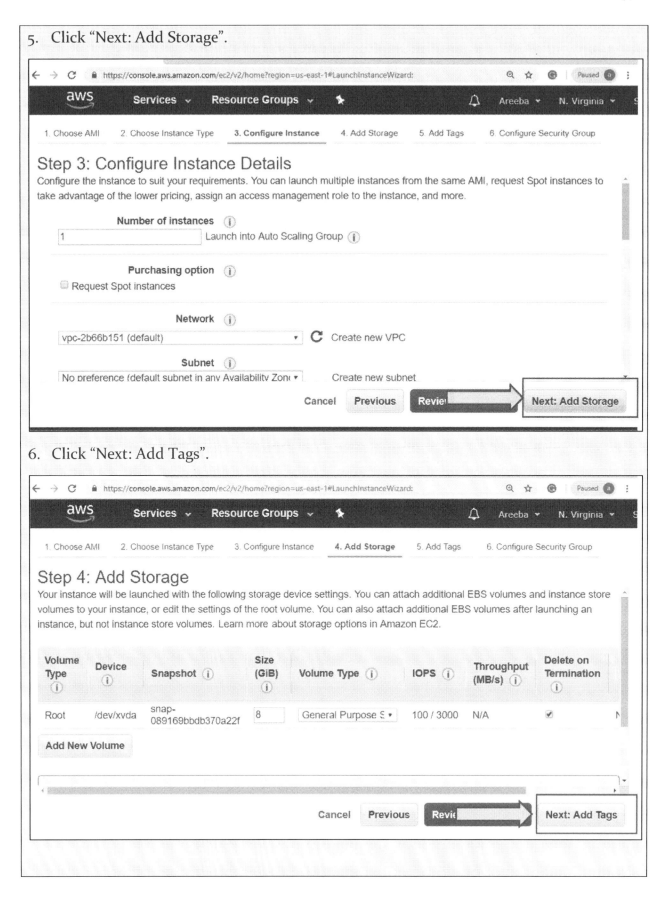

6. Click "Next: Add Tags".

7. Click "Add Tags". Now add tags and click "Next: Configuration Security Group".

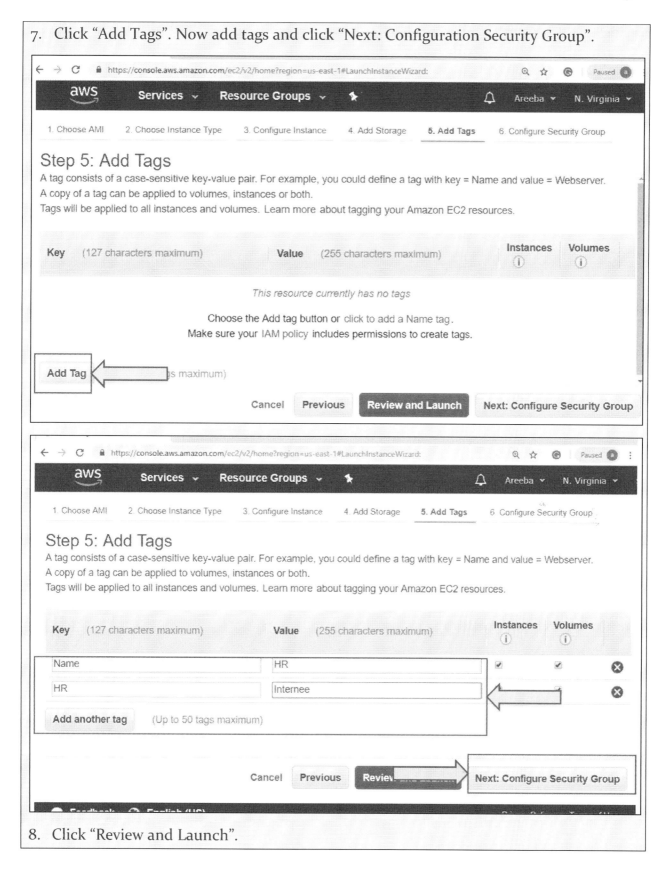

8. Click "Review and Launch".

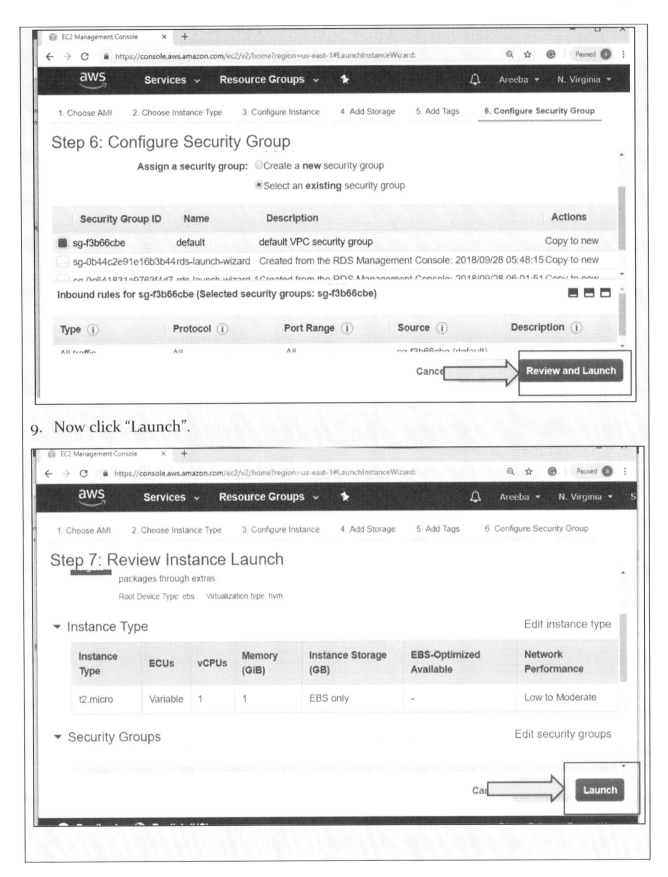

9. Now click "Launch".

10. Now select "An existing key pair", or you can select "New key pair". Click "Launch Instances".

Select an existing key pair or create a new key pair   ✕

A key pair consists of a **public key** that AWS stores, and a **private key file** that you store. Together, they allow you to connect to your instance securely. For Windows AMIs, the private key file is required to obtain the password used to log into your instance. For Linux AMIs, the private key file allows you to securely SSH into your instance.

Note: The selected key pair will be added to the set of keys authorized for this instance. Learn more about removing existing key pairs from a public AMI.

Choose an existing key pair ▾

Select a key pair

HR ▾

☑ I acknowledge that I have access to the selected private key file (HR.pem), and that without this file, I won't be able to log into my instance.

Launch Instances

11. Your instance is now launching. Click on "View Instances".

Launch Status

✔ Your instances are now launching
The following instance launches have been initiated: i-05da46f5aaf16c8ff   View launch log

ℹ Get notified of estimated charges
Create billing alerts to get an email notification when estimated charges on your AWS bill exceed an amount you define (for example, if you exceed the free usage tier).

How to connect to your instances

Your instances are launching, and it may take a few minutes until they are in the **running** state, when they will be ready for you to use. Usage hours on your new instances will start immediately and continue to accrue until you stop or terminate your instances.

Click **View Instances** to monitor your instances' status. Once your instances are in the **running** state, you can **connect** to them from

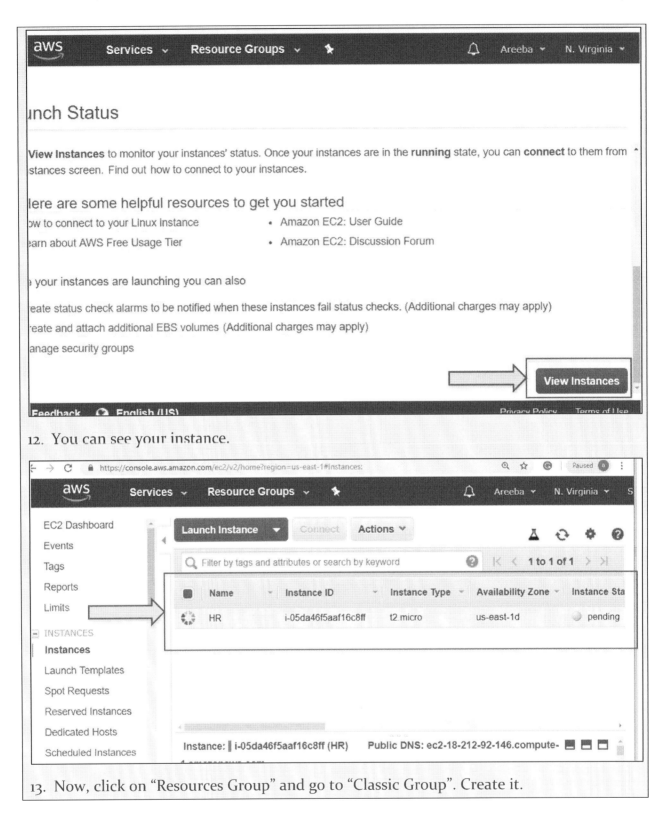

12. You can see your instance.

13. Now, click on "Resources Group" and go to "Classic Group". Create it.

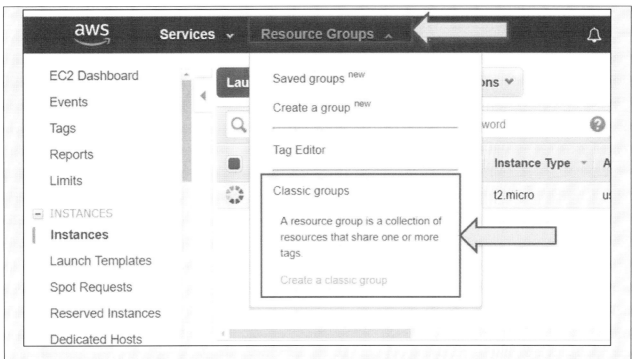

14. Enter the details of the resource group like name, tags, region and resource types. Then click "Save".

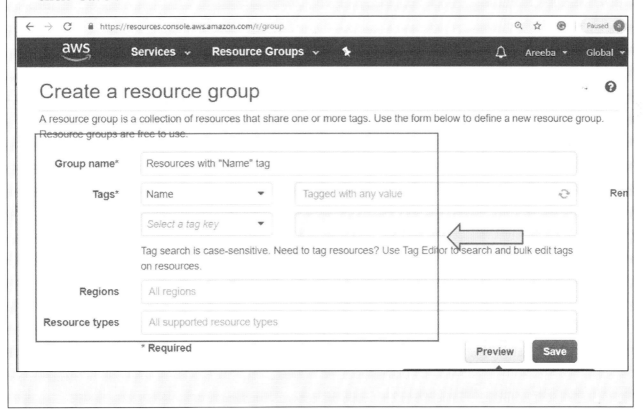

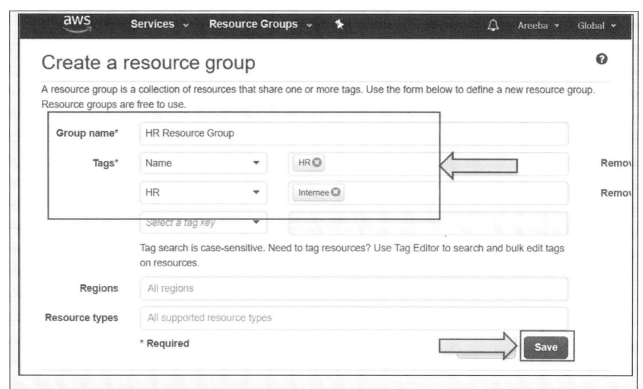

15. Now your resource group has been created. On the left side, you can see all the resources of AWS.

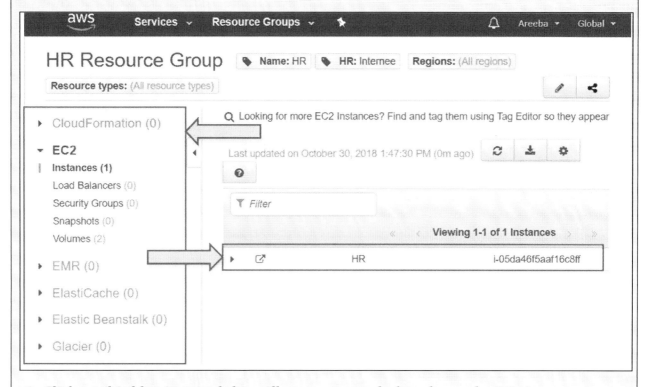

16. Click on this blue icon and this will open a new tab that shows the EC2 instance.

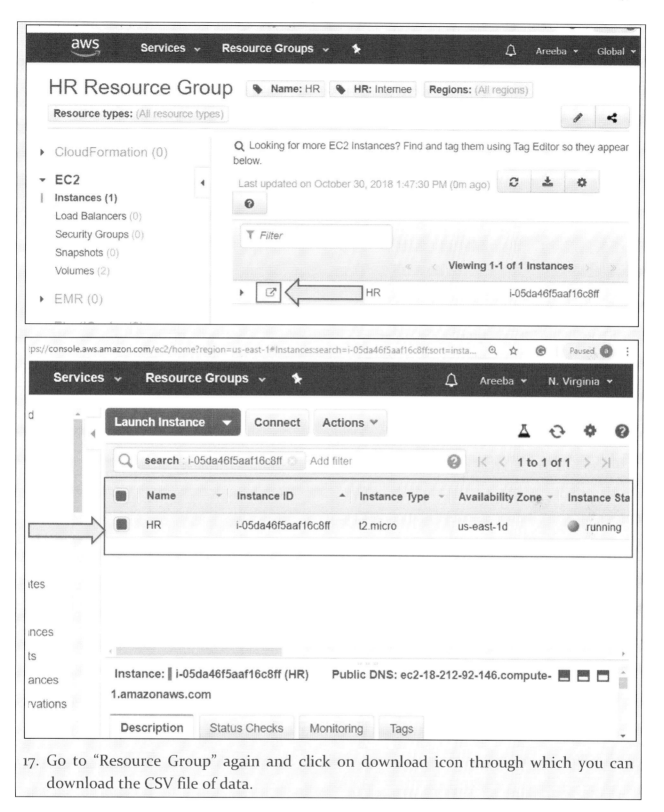

17. Go to "Resource Group" again and click on download icon through which you can download the CSV file of data.

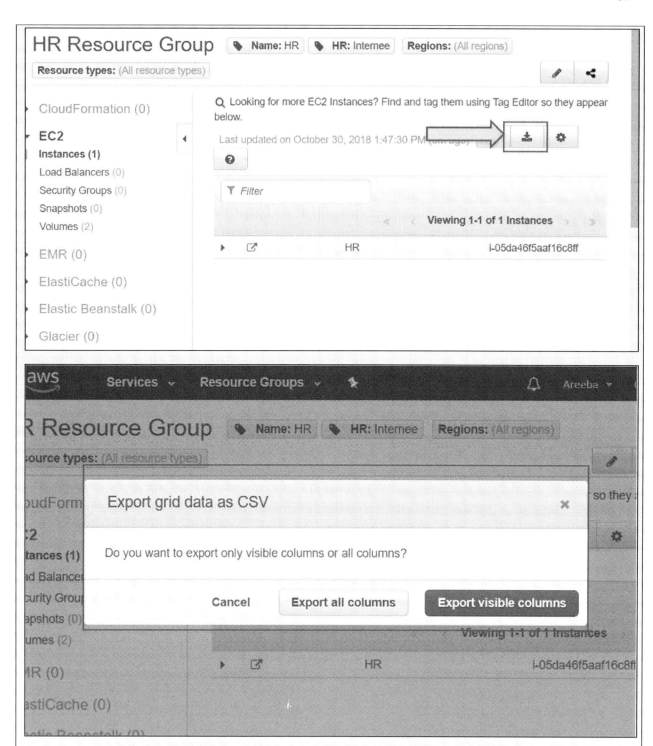

18. Now click on the setting icon if you want to see other metrics. Select the metric and you will see that metric in the window.

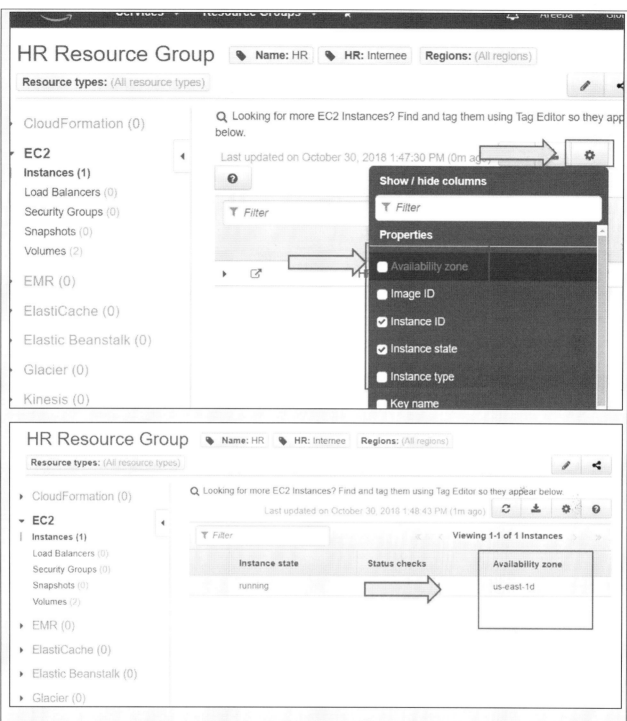

19. You can also use tag editor instead of resource group for tracking of resources and for that, you need to select "Tag Editor" in "Resource Groups" or you can also choose this highlighted line.

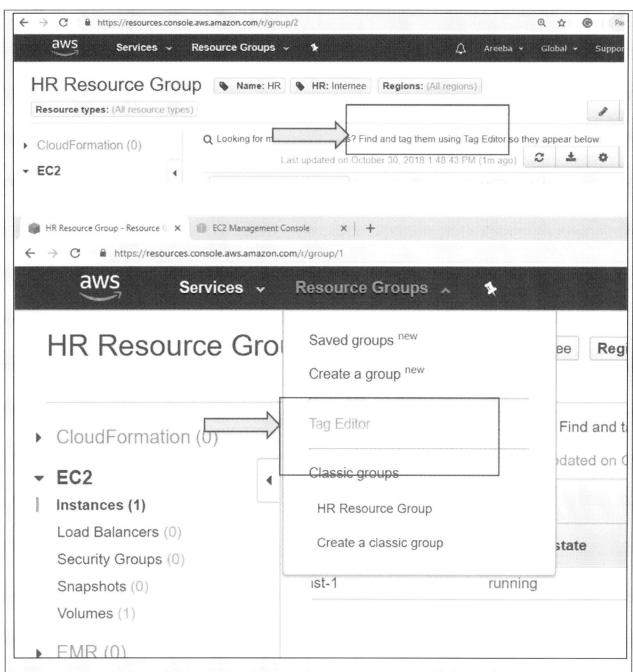

20. Here, you can see the list of regions where your resources can be used. In the bottom of the window, you can see the resources with tags.

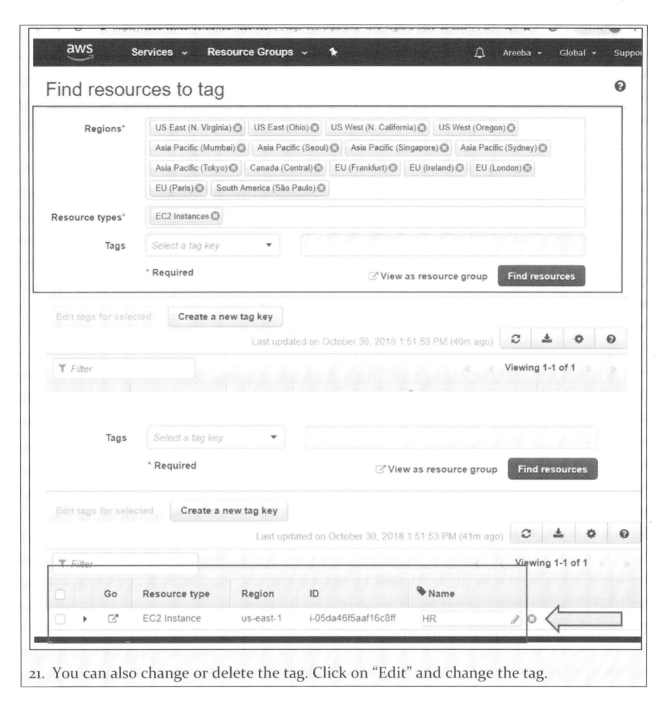

21. You can also change or delete the tag. Click on "Edit" and change the tag.

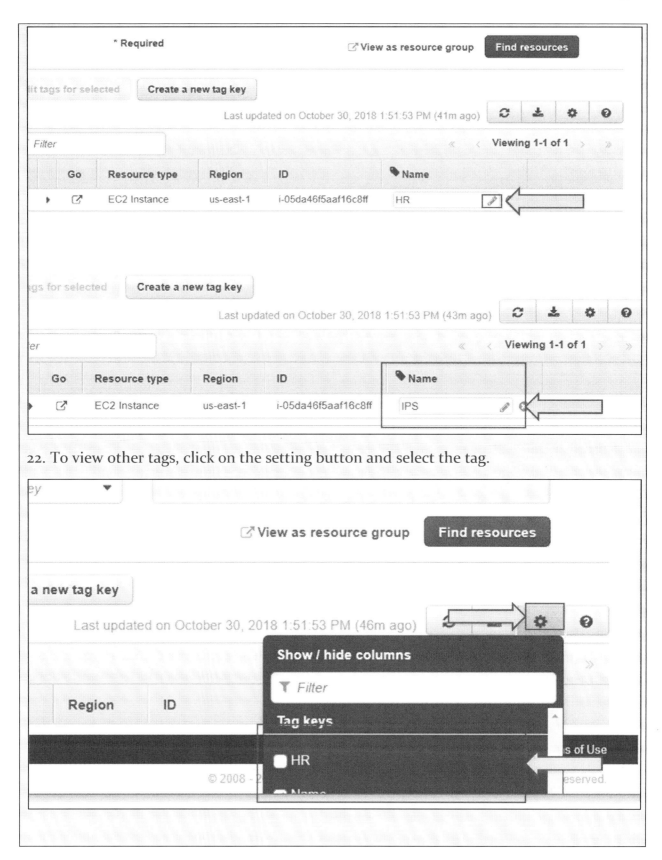

22. To view other tags, click on the setting button and select the tag.

23. Now you can see that both tags are shown. You can do this similarly for more tags if you define it during instance launching.

Create a new tag key	Last updated on October 30, 2018 1:51:53 PM (47m ago)

24. You can also view resource types by going to option in "Resource Types".

Pricing Options for EC2 and RDS

EC2 Pricing Options

For Amazon EC2 instances, there are four different price choices, each with a different cost per hour. The four alternatives are as follows:

On-Demand Instances

The pricing for On-Demand instances is represented by the per-hour price for each instance type listed on AWS. It does not require any upfront commitments, and the user has complete discretion over when the instance is started and stopped. As a result, it is the

most cost-effective alternative. Although it is the least cost-effective of the three price choices, users can save money by supplying a variable computing level for unpredictable workloads. These types of instances are used during the testing of the applications.

Reserved Instances

Reserved Instances (RIs) allow users to set aside computer resources for a certain workload. When a user purchases a reservation, they specify the instance type and AZ, for instance, and they receive a cheaper, effective hourly pricing for that instance for the duration of the reservation. Within the confines of consolidated billing, reserved instances can be shared with other accounts. You can sell your reserved instances in the Reserved Instance Marketplace when you no longer need them.

Term Commitment is the duration of the reservation. It can either be 1 or 3 years. The longer the commitment is, the bigger the discount.

You can modify your reserved instances when your computing needs change; modifications do not change the remaining term of the reservation. There is no fee for modification of RIs. The adjustment can be made in several ways, such as:

> Switch Availability Zones within the same region
> The change between EC2-VPC and EC2-Classic
> Change the instance type within the same instance family (Linux instances only)

 EXAM TIP: You can move RIs from one AZ to another AZ but not between regions.

Normalization Factor

The normalization factor is a factor of instance type and amount of instance in reservation for finding the size of the footprint of the instance. If the footprint size of the target configuration is not the same as the original configuration, then the modification request does not process. The footprint is measured regarding the unit in the EC2 console.

Example:

Instance Type	Normalization Factor
Micro	0.5
Small	1
Medium	2
Large	4

Xlarge	8
2xlarge	16
4xlarge	32
8xlarge	64

Table 9-02: Normalization Factor

In table 9-02, you can see different types of EC2 instances with their normalization factor. Consider you are using three large instances; the footprint here is the number of instances multiplied by the normalization factor.

- $3^*4=12$

Then, you can change that in either one xlarge instance and one large (1*8) + (1*4) or 10 small and one medium instance meaning (10*1) + (1*2) or similarly other ways. However, if you have a small value of footprint, then it will be difficult to change it to a different type. Therefore, it is better to reserve large instances for enough capacity to purchase more instances.

EXAM TIP: Always purchase more RIs with a larger capacity than your requirement because it helps you to grow easily.

Types of RIs

1. **Standard RIs** provide a significant discount (up to 60%) compared to the On-demand hourly rate. You can change attributes of your Standard RIs by sending modification requests and then processing the request if provided. The footprint remains the same as the targeted footprint. The size of the footprint is calculated by the Normalization factor. You can modify the standard reserved instance within the same family.

EXAM TIP: You can modify standard RIs only if they are from the same family and its normalization factors are equal.

2. **Convertible RIs** provide a discount (up to 54%) compared to the On-demand hourly rate by changing the attributes of RIs as long as exchange results in the creation of Reserved instances of equal or higher value. Standard and convertible RIs are for steady-state usage. In Convertible RIs, you can change instance families like from t2 to m3, OS like from Linux to windows, tenancy, and pricing option. Therefore, it is the most flexible option.

3. **Amazon EC2 Scheduled RIs** allow you to launch an instance in a time window, which you reserved to meet the reserved capacity with the predictable recurring schedule, which requires a portion of a day, week, or month.

> **EXAM TIP:** During the exam, always read first if they have asked for a commercially feasible way, then choose spot instance, and if they have asked for high availability, then go for the on-demand instance.

RI Attributes

- Instance Type: Define memory, CPU, and networking capabilities
- Platform: Linux, SUSE Linux, Microsoft Windows, Microsoft SQL server
- Tenancy: Shared tenancy(default) or dedicated tenancy
- Availability Zone (optional): If AZ is selected, then the RI is reserved, and discounts only apply to that AZ (Zonal RI). RI is not reserved to any region if you do not select any region; the discount is applied to any instance in the family, in any AZ, in the region (Regional AZ).

To change Zonal RI to Regional RI, use console or ModifyReservedInstance API. RI size flexibility is only available for Linux or Unix Regional RIs with default tenancy; they are not available Windows, RHEL, and SLES.

Payment Option

1. <u>All Upfront:</u> Pay the entire reservation charges in advance. There will be no monthly fee during the term. It provides the largest discount.

2. <u>Partial Upfront:</u> Pay a part of the reservation charges beforehand, and the rest will be paid in monthly installments. It provides a medium-level discount like the hourly rate of the reserved instance.

3. <u>No Upfront:</u> Pay complete reservation charges in monthly payments. This provides the least discount but is cheaper than on-demand instances.

The more customer pays upfront, the more the amount of discount.

> **EXAM TIP:** The largest account is applied for all upfront payment options up to 75%.

Spot Instances

Spot instances are the excess EC2 capacity, which AWS sells on a market exchange basis. Spot instances offer the greatest discounts for workloads that are not tied critical and interruption tolerant. Customers can specify the price they are willing to pay for a specific instance type. These instances will operate just like other instances, and the customer will pay the spot price for the hours that instance(s) run. The instances will run until:

- The user terminates them
- The spot price reaches above the customer's bid price
- The required computing capacity is not available

If Amazon needs to terminate a spot instance, a notice of termination will be received, providing a two-minute window before Amazon terminates the spot instance. For the possibility of interruption, it is recommended that spot instances should be used for interruption-tolerant workloads like analytics, big data, media encoding, financial modeling, scientific computing, and testing. It can be used on applications with flexible start and end times or when the user requires a huge amount of additional capacity for computing.

Spot requests can be of three types: Fill and Kill, Maintain, and duration-based. Fill and Kill is when your bid price is higher than the other prices you get the instance, and when the price gets low, your instance is terminated. In "Maintain", when the prices are higher than your bid price, the instance is terminated, and when the price is lower than your bid price, a new spot instance is created. "duration-based" allows you to purchase the instance for the time that you define and after that time is over, the instance is terminated.

"Fill and Kill" spot requests "One-Time Request", which results in loss of ephemeral data once the instance is terminated. When "Request and Maintain", then the instance can be terminated, stopped, or hibernated until the price meets your bid price. This will prevent you from data loss.

💡 EXAM TIP: If Amazon EC2 terminates a spot instance, you will not be charged for a partial hour of usage, while if you terminate it by yourself, you will be charged for a complete hour in which instance is running.

Dedicated

An EC2 dedicated host is a server with Amazon EC2 instance capacity entirely dedicated to a single user's use, which means it is not for multitenant virtualization. Dedicated hosts help users reduce costs by allowing them to use their existing server-bound software licenses. It can be purchased on-demand or as a reservation for up to 70% off the on-

demand price. Dedicated hosts are different from dedicated instances in that dedicated instances can be launched on any hardware dedicated to an account. Dedicated instances are those instances, which run in VPC on hardware, dedicated to a single user. Dedicated instances are isolated physically at the hardware level, from those instances that are not dedicated and also from those that belong to other AWS accounts.

Dedicated Instance vs. Dedicated Host

Dedicated Instance	Dedicated Host
Virtual Instance on hardware dedicated to you	Physical servers dedicated for your use
Hardware can be shared with other non-dedicated instances in the same account	Have full control over which instances are deployed on that
Available as On-Demand, Reserved, and Spot instances	Available as On-Demand or with Dedicated Host Reservation
An additional $2 per hour per region is charged	Each dedicated host can run one EC2 instances size and type only
	It is useful in the scenario when you have server-bound software licenses that use metrics like per-core, per-socket, or per-VM

Table 9-03: Dedicated Instance vs. Dedicated Host

EC2 Instance Types

In Amazon EC2, you have a wide variety of instance types that are optimized for different scenarios. Instance types consist of varying combinations of CPU, memory, storage, and networking capacity with one or more instance sizes, giving you the flexibility to select computational resources according to the requirements of your targetted workload.

The instance type is the virtual hardware, which is supporting an Amazon EC2 instance. The classification of these instance types is as below:

- Virtual CPUs (vCPUs)
- Memory
- Storage (size and type)
- Network performance

Family	Specialty	Use Cases
D2	Dense Storage	Fileservers/Data Warehousing/Hadoop

R4	Memory Optimized	Memory Intensive Apps/DBs
M4	General Purpose	Application Servers
C4	Compute Optimized	CPU Intensive Apps/DBs
G2	Graphics Intensive	Video Encoding/3D Application Encoding
I3	High-Speed Storage	NoSQL DBs, Data Warehousing, etc.
F1	Field Programmable Gate Array	Hardware Acceleration for your code
T2	Lowest cost, General purpose	Web Servers/Small DBs
P2	Graphics/General Purpose GPU	Machine Learning/ Bitcoins mining etc.
X1	Memory Optimized	SAP HANA/Apache Spark etc.
A1	General Purpose	Scale out workloads such as web servers, caching fleets
T3	Burstable General Purpose	Micro-services, virtual desktop
M5	General Purpose	Microsoft Sharepoint, Cluster computing, etc.
M5a	General Purpose	Running backend servers for SAP, Microsoft Sharepoint
T3a	General Purpose (Coming soon)	Development environment, code repositories, etc.
C5	Compute Optimized	Compute intensive workloads such as High Performance Computing
C5n	Compute Optimized	HPC, video editing, etc.
R5	Memory Optimized	Memory intensive applications like high performance databases
R5a	Memory Optimized	Memory intensive applications such as real time big data analysis
X1e	Memory Optimized	High performance databases, in-memory databases, and memory intensive applications
High Memory	Memory Optimized	Large enterprise databases, production installation of SAP HANA

zıd	Memory Optimized	Electronic design automation
P3	Accelerated Computing	Machine deep learning, HPC

Table 9-04: Instance Types

Instance families are a collection of EC2 instances that are grouped according to the ratio of memory, network performance, CPU size, and storage values to each other. For example, the m4 family of EC2 provides a balanced combination of computing, memory, and network resources. Different instance type families are designed to accommodate different types of workloads, but they all have the same linear scale-up behavior within the family.

On customer demand and need, AWS occasionally introduces new instance families. You can check the list of the latest instance families in AWS documentation.

RDS Reserved Instances

Like Amazon EC2 reserved instances, in RDS reserved instances, there are three pricing options. With the help of a Reserved RDS instance, you can reserve a DB instance for the duration of 1 to 3 years and get a significant discount on pricing as compared to the on-demand instance. All reserved instances are available for MySQL, Oracle, MariaDB, PostgreSQL, Aurora, and SQL Server DB engines. The reservation of instance has the following attributes:

1. DB engine
2. Instance class for DB
3. Deployment type
4. License model
5. Region

When you reserve the instance, this reservation is only applied to the DB engine with the same attributes for reservation terms. If you change any attributes on the running instance before the reservation term, then it charges an hourly rate for the DB instance to on-demand rates.

When you decide to modify the running DB instance attributes after some duration to meet it with the original reservation or create a new DB instance with similar attributes of the original reservation, then pricing of the reservation will be applied to it up until the end of the reservation term. RI is also for RDS multi-AZs and read replicas, but for read replicas, it must be in the same instance class and region. Each RI is in a specific region that is fixed and cannot be changed for a lifetime, but you can move it in AZs that are associated with those regions.

EXAM TIP: You can have reserved RDS instances and move them to AZs but not regions. Read replicas are also reserved, but they are in the same region.

AWS Organizations

It is an account management service that allows you to consolidate multiple AWS accounts into an organization, enabling you to create a hierarchical structure that can be managed centrally.

With AWS Organizations, you can create multiple groups of AWS accounts known as the Organizational Units and then apply policies to those Organizational Units, commonly referred to as Service Control Policies (SCPs). These policies centrally control the use of AWS services across multiple AWS accounts without the need for custom scripts and manual processes. Entities in the AWS accounts can only use the AWS services allowed by both the SCP and the AWS IAM policy for the account.

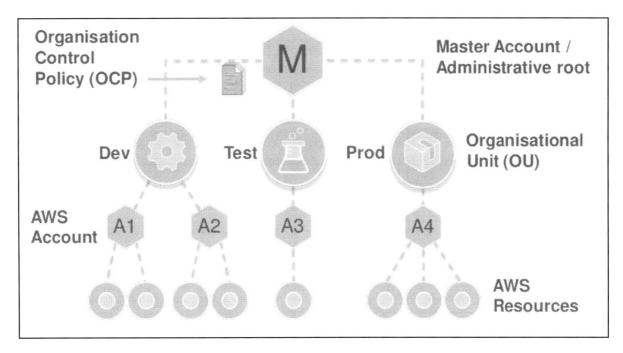

Figure 9-01: AWS Organization

AWS Organizations is available to all AWS customers at no additional charge in two feature sets:

- <u>Only Consolidated billing features:</u> This mode only provides the consolidated billing features and does not include the other advanced features of AWS Organizations, such as the use of policies to restrict what users and roles in different accounts can access

- <u>All features:</u> This mode is the complete feature set that includes all the functionality of consolidated billing in addition to the advanced features that provides more control over the accounts in your organization

Lab 9-02: AWS Organizations

Scenario

A software house has a huge number of employees, and they all are using cloud services. Now, they need to keep track of usage by individual employees and also want to restrict the departments about the usage. If a new employee is hired for a particular department, how will he be added to a specific department?

Solution

With the help of AWS organization service, the organization can keep track of each individual employee and also attach a policy to a specific organization unit, that is its department. With the help of this service, they can also add new accounts on specific organization units.

1. Go to AWS console and click on "Create an Organization".

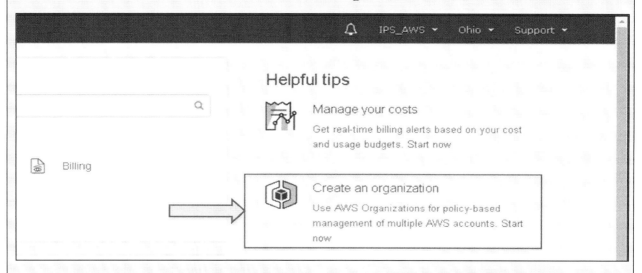

2. If you want to work on an existing account, select it from the list of existing accounts. If you are a new member, then add an account by clicking on "Add account".

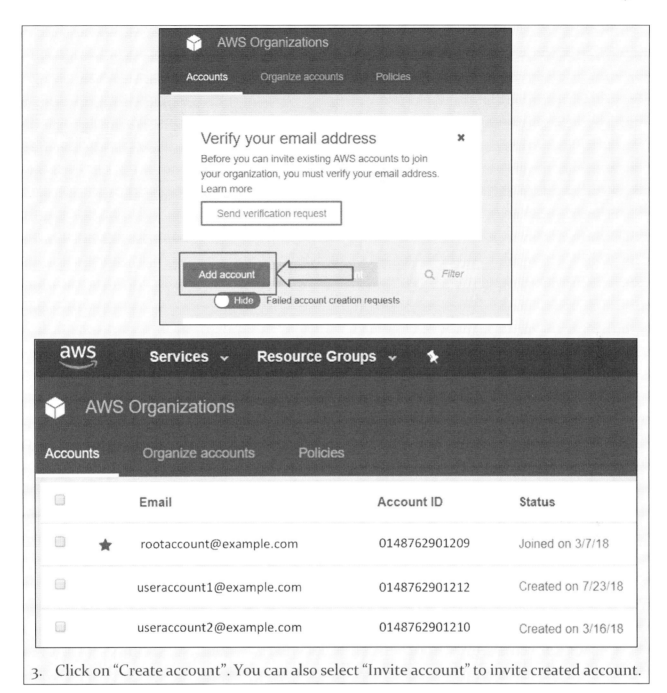

3. Click on "Create account". You can also select "Invite account" to invite created account.

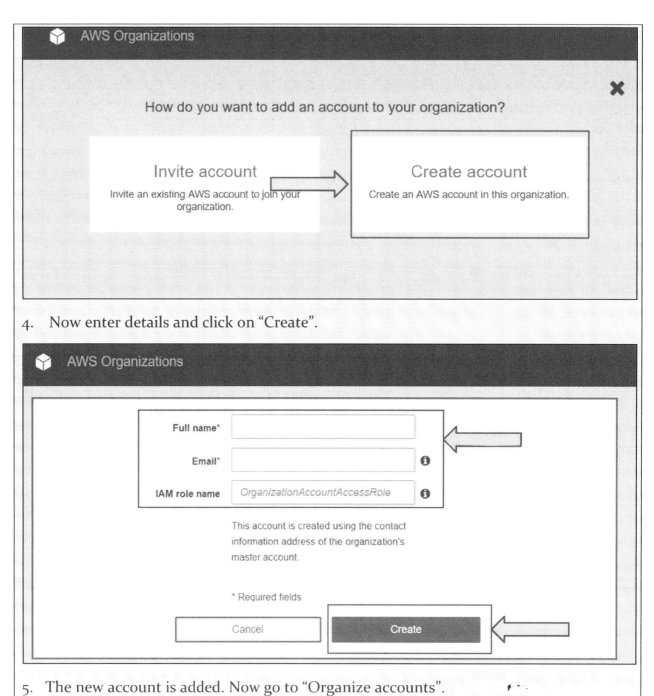

4. Now enter details and click on "Create".

5. The new account is added. Now go to "Organize accounts".

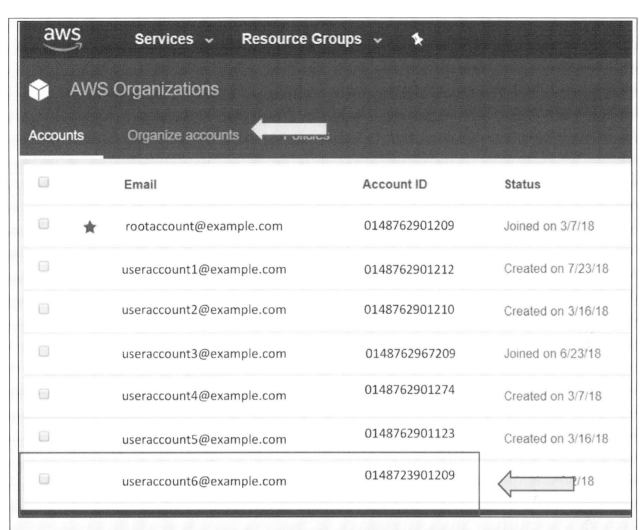

6. Here, you can see the organizational units are created. You can also create new OU to manage the new account. Click on "New Organizational Unit".

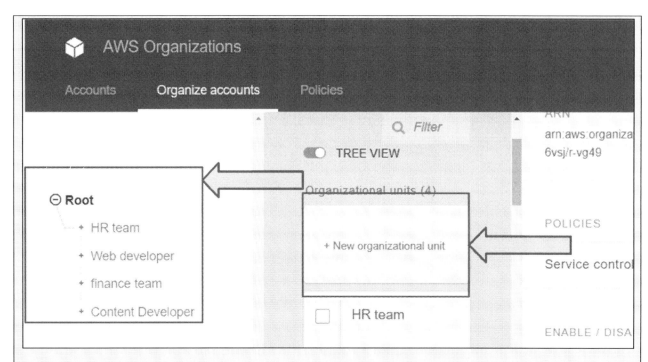

7. Enter the name of OU that you want to create. Click "Create Organization unit".

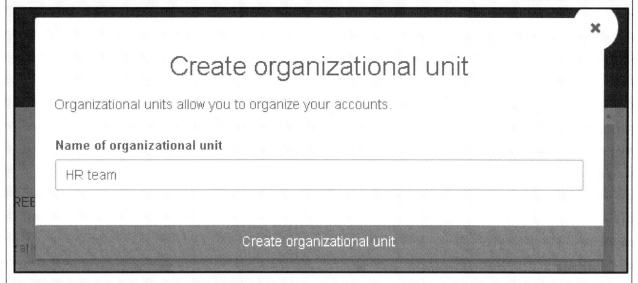

8. Go to "Accounts" in the root account. Select the account and click "Move" to move the account to the OU.

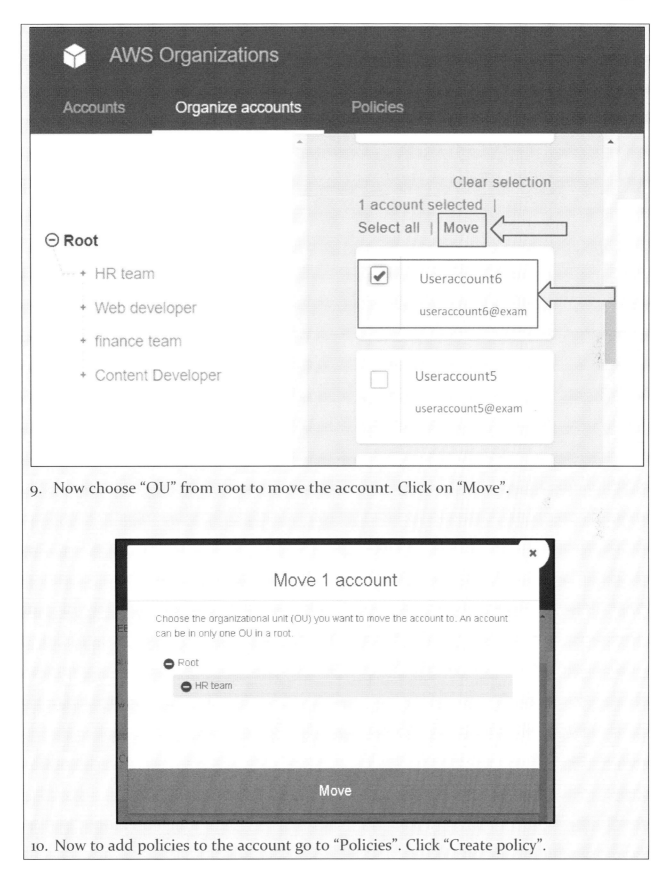

9. Now choose "OU" from root to move the account. Click on "Move".

10. Now to add policies to the account go to "Policies". Click "Create policy".

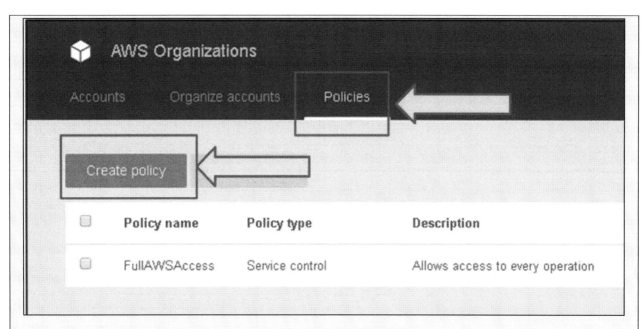

11. Enter the policy name and choose whether you want to allow or deny effects.

12. Click on "Statement Builder" and select the option of your own choice.

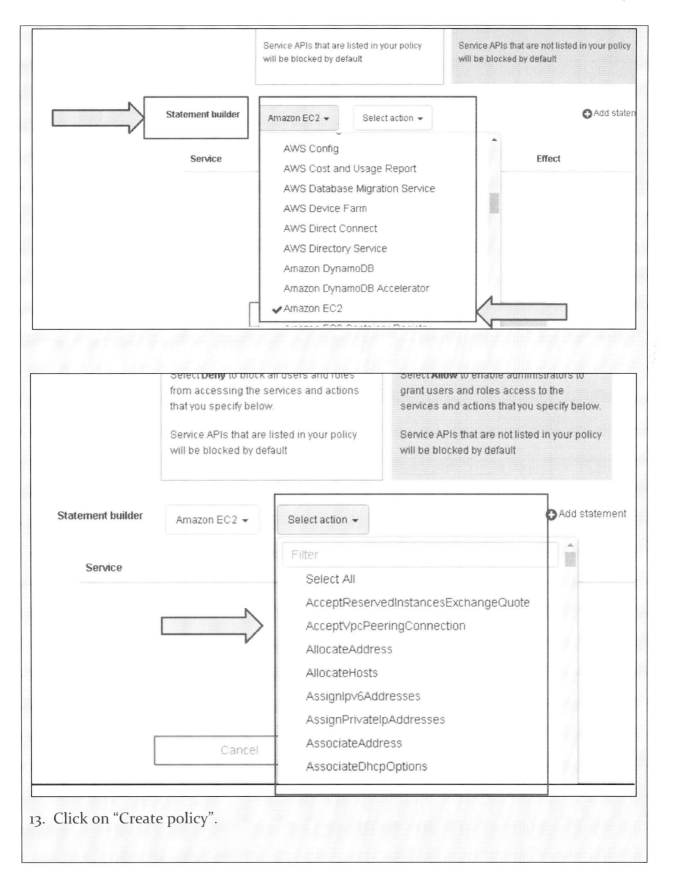

13. Click on "Create policy".

14. The policy has been created.

15. Select the policy you want to add on the account and go to "Accounts" from the right side of the screen.

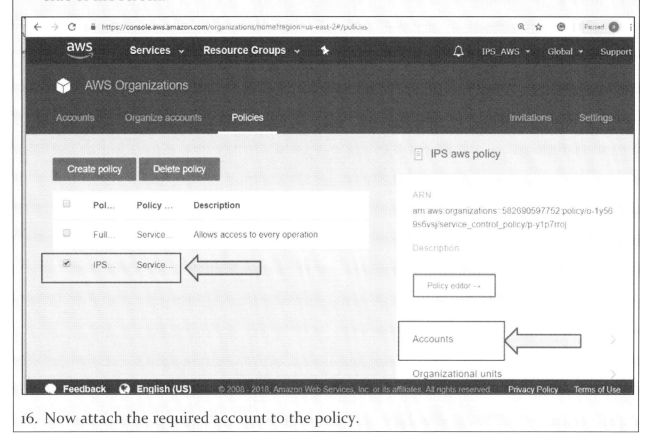

16. Now attach the required account to the policy.

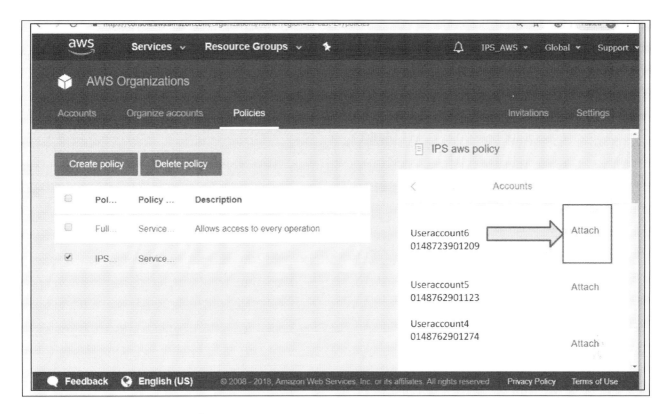

Cost Management Tools

AWS Budgets

You can set your budget limit, and AWS Budgets will notify you whenever spending is near the defined budget or exceeds the budget. The budget can be based on total cost usage, Reserved Instance utilization, or Reserved Instance coverage. Defining a budget is useful in delivering cost and usage awareness and responsibility to platform users.

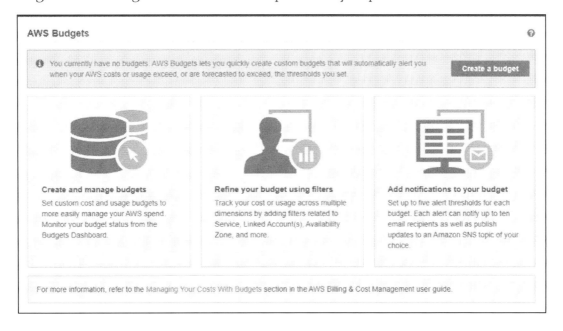

Figure 9-02: AWS Budget Console

Consolidated Billing

One of the most important features of AWS Organizations is the billing consolidation of all your AWS accounts, where you have a single AWS account as the paying master account linked to a group of all other AWS accounts to build a simple one-level hierarchy. You get a consolidated view of all of your AWS accounts' charges at the end of the month. It also generates a cost report for each of the member accounts linked to the master paying account. Consolidated billing is provided at no extra charge.

You can manage and track billing for several AWS accounts under a master account using the Consolidated billing capability. This allows you to simplify accounting and take advantage of low-cost services. In consolidated billing, you can attach up to 20 accounts to the master account, and you cannot have two master (paying) accounts in the same organization. As we know that the master account is the main account, we need to secure the account for which you will need to use MFA and a strong, complex password. Always try to use the master account for paying purposes, not for using resources, which is the best practice. You can also enable root account monitoring in consolidated billing, which allows you to watch billing data for all accounts, or you can establish billing alerts for particular accounts to monitor. You can do auditing with consolidated billing by using CloudTrail per AWS account and enabling per region by pushing combined logs to the centralized S3 bucket, but you will need to enable CloudTrail in the master account, define a policy for cross-account access, and enable CloudTrail in all other accounts first.

EXAM TIP: Paying Account should be used for billing purposes only. Do not deploy resources to the Paying Account. On the Paying Account, monitoring is enabled through that billing data for all linked accounts are included. You can also create billing alerts for individual accounts separately.

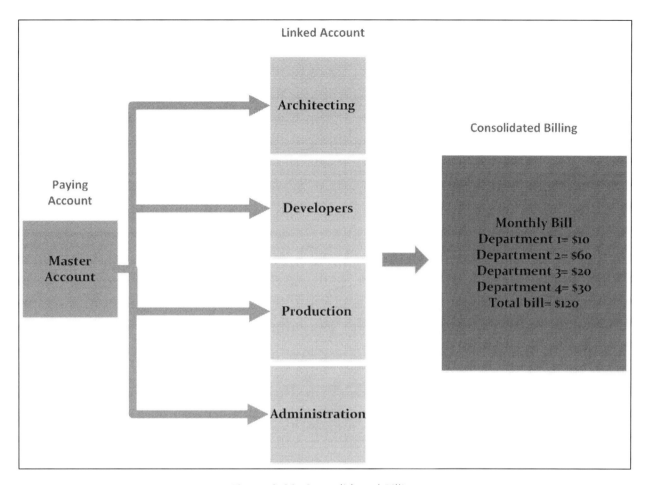

Figure 9-03: Consolidated Billing

Each member account is independent of the other member accounts when only the aggregated billing option is enabled. Unless the master account uses policies to explicitly restrict linked accounts, the owner of each member account can access resources, sign up for AWS services, and use AWS Premium Support independently. Account owners use their own IAM username and password with independently assigned account permissions in the organization.

EXAM TIP: AWS CloudTrail is a service used to monitor account activity and deliver generated event logs to the associated account S3 Bucket. You can aggregate Log Files from multiple regions to a single S3 bucket of the Paying Account.

Example of Consolidated Billing:

Standard Storage S3	Pricing
First 1TB/month	$0.0300 per GB
Next 49TB/month	$0.0295 per GB
Next 450TB/month	$0.0290 per GB
Next 500TB/month	$0.0285 per GB

Table 9-05: Pricing of S3

The table above shows standard storage pricing. If the organization has four departments and each department's usage is the following:

Account Name	Usage
Architecting	300GB
Developers	400GB
Production	600GB
Administration	700 GB

Table 9-06: Example

Then without consolidated billing, the bill is:

- 300*$0.03= $9
- 400*$0.03= $12
- 600*$0.03=$18
- 700*$0.03=$21
- Total bill = $60 for 2TB of storage

With consolidated billing, the bill is:

- 1TB*$0.03=$30
- Next 1TB*$0.0295=$29.5
- The total bill of 2TB is $59.50

As a result, you can save money by using consolidated billing. AWS Organizations treat all linked accounts as a single account; therefore every member account can benefit from the hourly cost-benefit of Reserved Instances purchased by any other member account within the organization.

Only nine instances will be charged on the organization's consolidated account, with five of them being Reserved Instances and the remaining four being ordinary On-Demand Instances. Six On-Demand Instances and five Reserved Instances would have been charged if the accounts were not tied to a single aggregated bill.

The linked accounts receive the cost-benefit from each other's Reserved Instances only if the launched instances are in the same Availability Zone, having the same instance size, and belonging to the same family of instance types.

> **EXAM TIP:** Consolidated Billing allows you to get volume discounts on all your accounts. When consolidated billing is enabled, unused reserved instances for EC2 are applied across the group.

AWS Trusted Advisor

AWS trusted advisor is a service of AWS, which provides you real-time guidance that ensures the AWS resources are provisioned and managed correctly. It is an online resource that helps in reducing cost, increasing performance, and improve security by optimizing your AWS environment. The advisor will advise you on cost optimization, performance, security, and fault tolerance. It has a whole bunch of core checks and recommendations and splits into two different service levels, named as Business Trusted Advisor and Business Companies.

It has categories and provides reports for these categories, which gives an overview of your account. With the help of this report, you can identify what thing you need to fix or change in case of the existence of any issue. From these below reports, some of them are free, while for some, you need to pay.

- **Cost optimization**- it is a category that shows if you are paying too much and how you can save your money
- **Performance**- it will tell you about the utilization of resources, whether they are underutilized or over-utilized
- **Security**- it tells you about the security of your account, and if you are missing any security aspects, it will tell you about that
- **Fault tolerant**- it will tell that how well you are prepared for any incident
- **Service limits**- it will tell you that how close you are to breaching the service limit

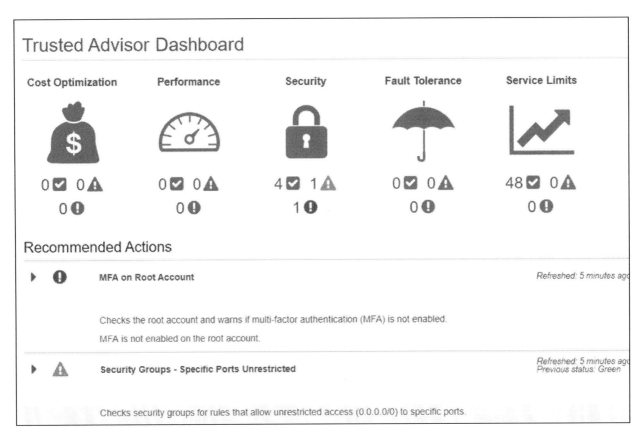

Figure 9-04: AWS Trusted Advisor Console

The Basic and Developer get access to 7 core Trusted Advisor checks, while Business and Enterprise get access to all Trusted Advisor checks.

Cross-Account Access – Roles and Permissions

Cross-Account Access is allowing access of resources from one account to trusted federated users or IAM users of a different account, which means multiple customers can use individual accounts for its production and development resources. Therefore, through this, you can separate different resources with security benefits.

With the help of Cross-Account Access, you can work easily and effectively in a multi-account AWS environment by switching roles in the AWS Console. Through cross-account access, you can share resources among different accounts. This means that you can log in with an IAM username and move towards another account via console, without any need for another username and password to access the resources that are in a different account via roles, or you can use policy directly attached to the resources. For granting cross-account access, there are some general steps you need to follow:

- ✓ Identify the account number of both accounts
- ✓ Create a group and user in Account A

- ✓ Log in to Account B
- ✓ Create policy and add this policy to the role
- ✓ Log in to Account B
- ✓ Create a new Inline policy and apply it to a group in Account A
- ✓ Log in as user and switch accounts

IAM User

The "Identity" aspect of Amazon web services Identity and Access Management helps you with the question, "Who is that user?" often referred to as authentication. Instead of sharing your root user credentials with others, you can create individual Identity and Access Management users within your account that correspond to users in your organization. Identity and Access management users are not separate accounts, i.e., they are users within your account. Each user has

their own password for access to the Amazon Web Service's Management Console.

IAM Policy

Identity and Access Management users are identities in the service. When you create an Identity and Access Management user, they cannot access anything in your account until you permit them. You can grant permissions to a user by creating an identity-based policy, which is a policy that is connected to the user and allows the user to access the resources defined in the policy. Identity-based and resource-based policies are the two sorts of policies. Permission policies attached to a principal or identity, such as an Identity and Access Management user, role, or group, are known as identity-based policies. Permission policies that are connected to a resource, such as an Amazon S3 bucket, are known as resource-based policies.

Identity-based policies control what actions the identity can perform on which resources and under what conditions. Identity-based policies can be further classified:

- Managed Policies
- Inline Policies

Managed policies

They are self-contained identity-based rules that you may apply to numerous roles, users, and groups in your Amazon Web Services account. Managed policies are divided into two categories:

- **AWS Managed Policies**: Policies that are created and administrated by AWS
- **Customer-Managed Policies**: Identity-based policies that you create

Inline policies

Policies that you create and control, which are embedded directly into an individual role, user, or group.

IAM Group

You can organize Identity Access Management users into Identity and Access Management groups and attach a policy to that group. In this case, single users still have their own credentials, but all the users in a group have the permissions that are connected to the group. Use groups for easier permission management.

IAM Roles

An IAM role is similar to a user. It is an AWS identity with permission policies that control what an identity can and cannot do in AWS. A role cannot be assigned to just one person. Anyone who requires a role can assume it. There are no common passwords, access keys, or long-term credentials for a role.

Lab 9-03: Cross-Account Access

Scenario

An organization has different departments for which they have different accounts. A deployment department employee needs to use some resources like the S3 bucket that are in use of the HR department. Now this company does not have enough budget to purchase the same resources for each department. How will one department gain access to the resource of the other department? How can they achieve this using AWS?

Solution

Through IAM, they can achieve their requirements.

1. Log in to account A and go to "IAM" service under "Security, Identity and Compliance" in AWS Console.

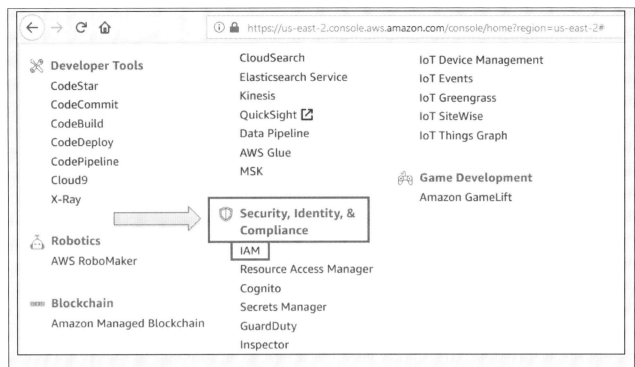

2. Create a group in account with required built-in policy by following the steps given below.

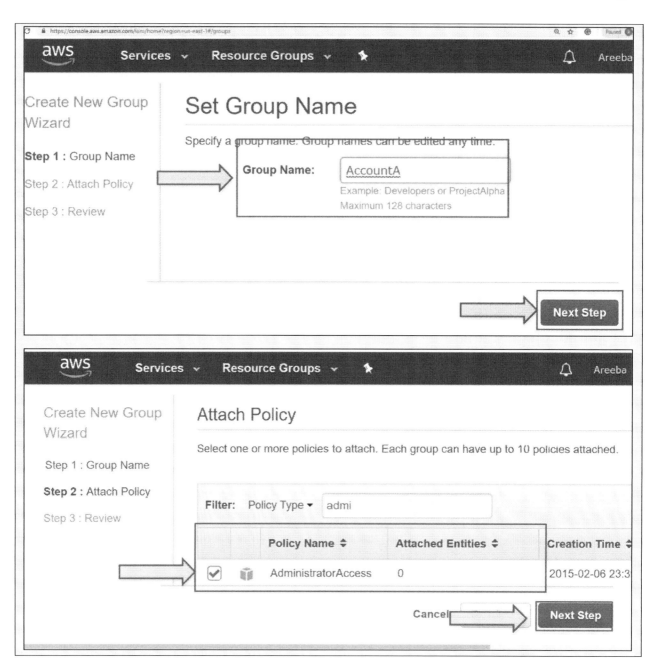

3. Go to "Users" and create a user. The user password access type must be "AWS Management Console access" with a custom password and enable the reset password option.

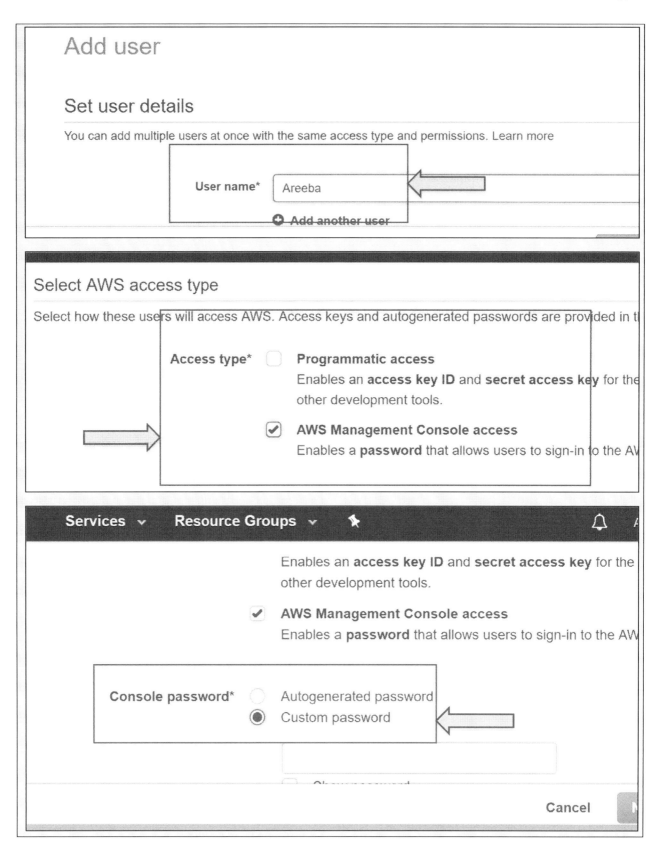

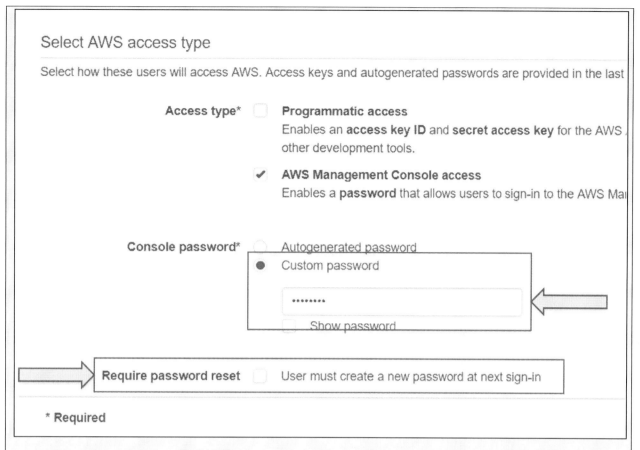

4. Click on "Next: Permissions" and add this user to the group. Then click "Next: Review".

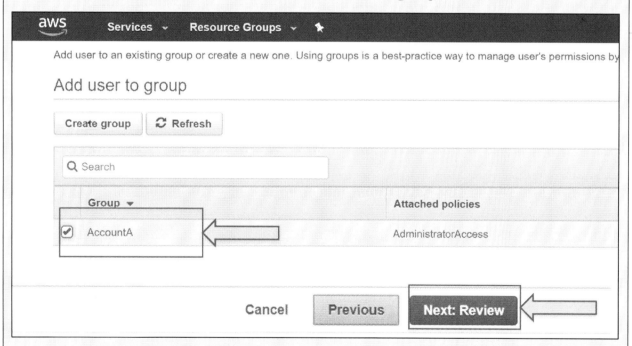

5. Click on "Create user" after reviewing. Now, the user has been created. Save URL of the user in a separate place.

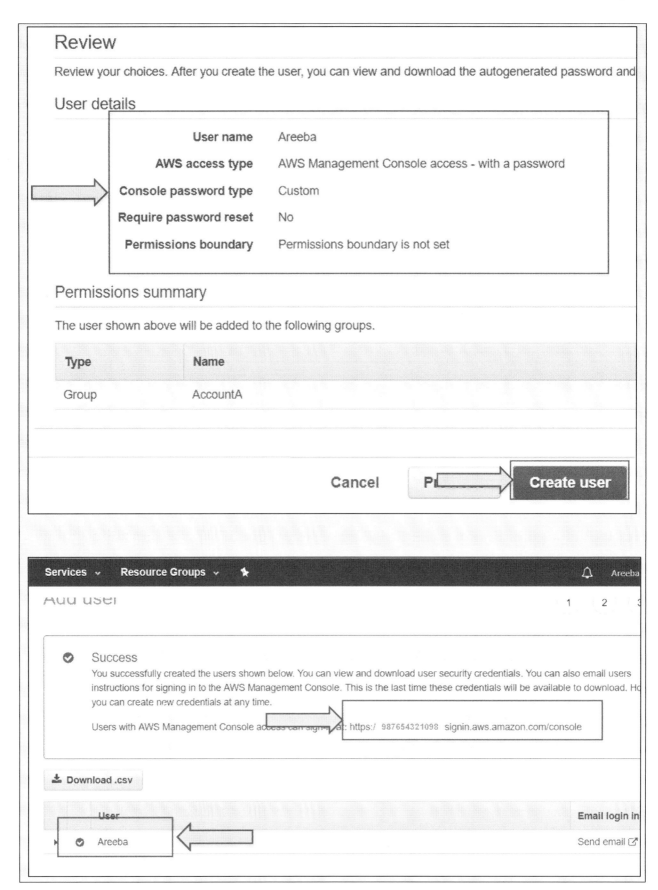

6. Save the account ID from your account information for further use and you will get this by going into "My Account".

aws   Services ˅   Resource Groups ˅   ★   🔔   Areeba ˄

AWS Management Console

My Account
My Organization
My Billing Dashboard
My Security Credentials

Sign Out

AWS services

Find services
You can enter names, keyword or acronyms.

🔍   *Example: Relational Database Service, database, RDS*

---

aws   Services ˅   Resource Groups ˅   ★

Dashboard

Bills

Cost Explorer

Budgets

Reports

Cost Allocation Tags

Payment Methods

▼ Account Settings

Account Id: 987654321098
Seller: AWS Inc.
Account Name: Areeba
Password: *****

▼ Contact Information

7. Now, log in to Account B.

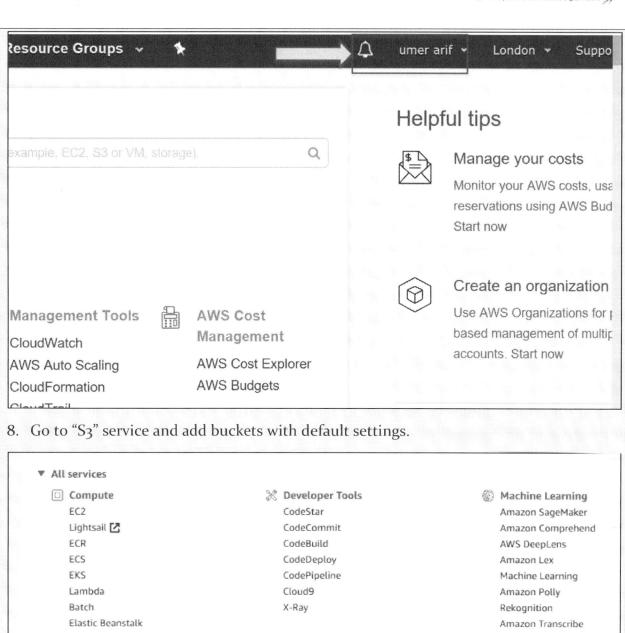

8. Go to "S3" service and add buckets with default settings.

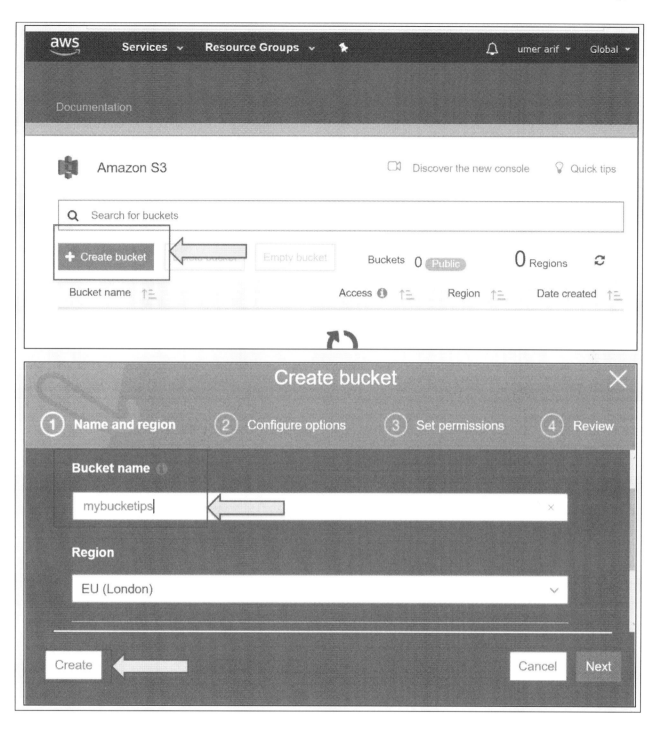

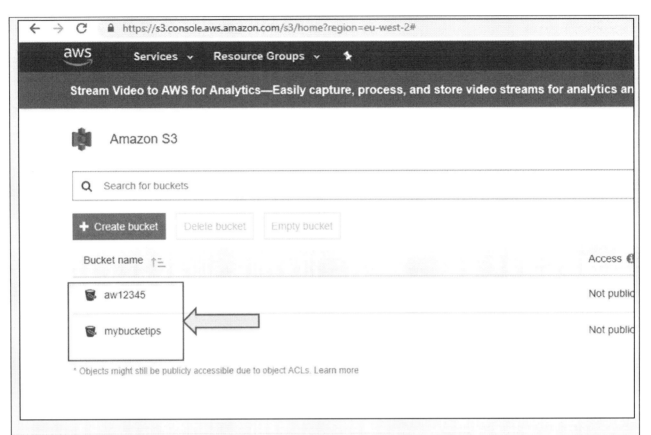

9. Go to "IAM" then to "Policies".

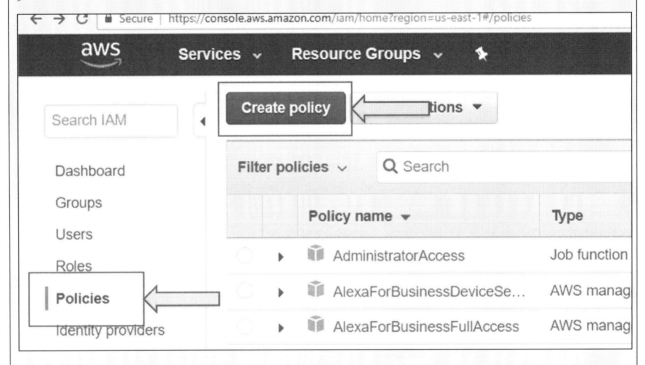

10. Now create a policy by your own in JSON format. In this policy, you need to write ARN of Bucket whose access you need to allow in "Resource".

```
{
    "Version": "2012-10-17",
    "Statement": [
        {
            "Effect": "Allow",
            "Action": "s3:ListAllMyBuckets",
            "Resource": "arn:aws:s3:::*"
        },
        {
            "Effect": "Allow",
            "Action": [
                "s3:ListBucket",
                "s3:GetBucketLocation"
            ],
            "Resource": "<ARN of bucket>"
        },
        {
            "Effect": "Allow",
            "Action": [
                "s3:GetObject",
                "s3:PutObject",
                "s3:DeleteObject"
            ],
            "Resource": "<ARN of bucket>/*"
        }
    ]
}
```

ARN of the bucket is copied from here.

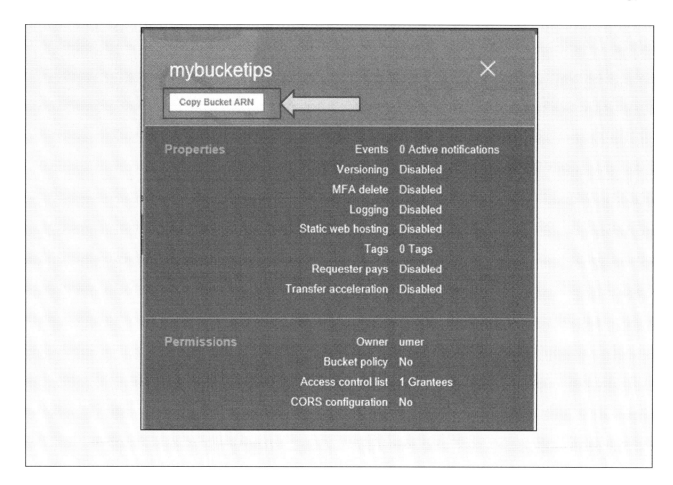

Go to "Review policy" at the bottom of the page.

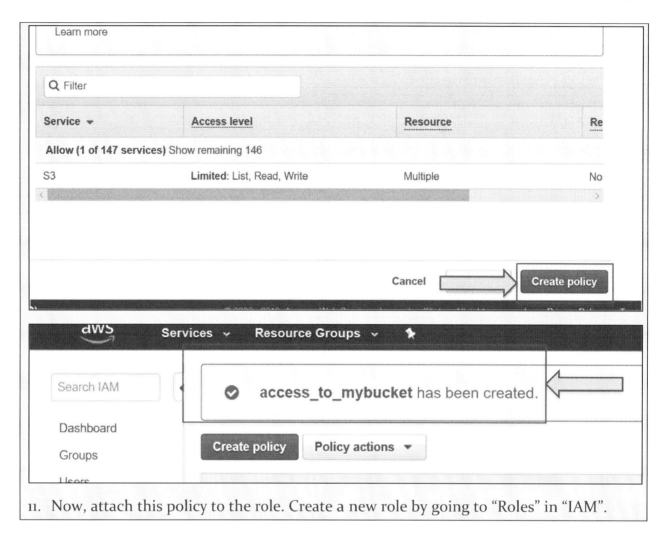

11. Now, attach this policy to the role. Create a new role by going to "Roles" in "IAM".

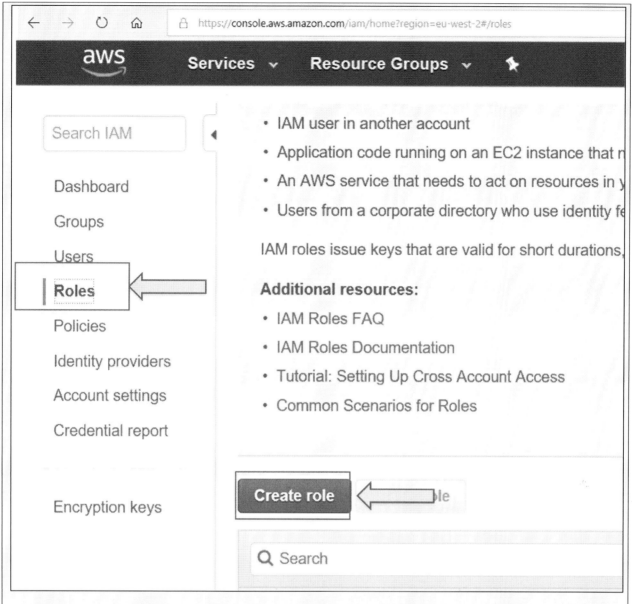

12. Select role type to "Another AWS account". Now, enter account ID of Account A that you stored in a separate place. Click "Next: Permissions".

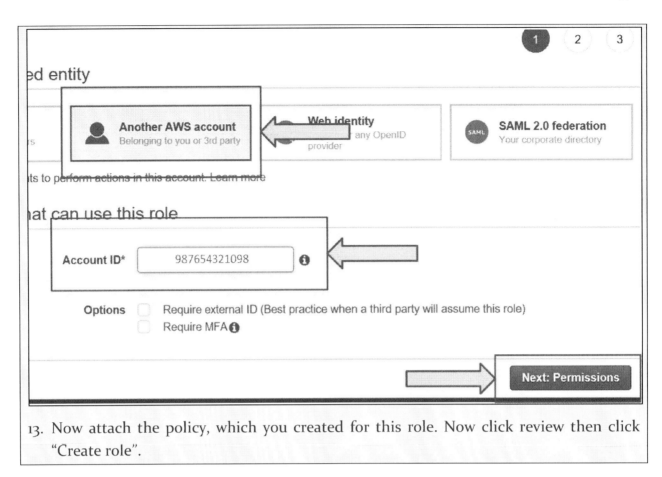

13. Now attach the policy, which you created for this role. Now click review then click "Create role".

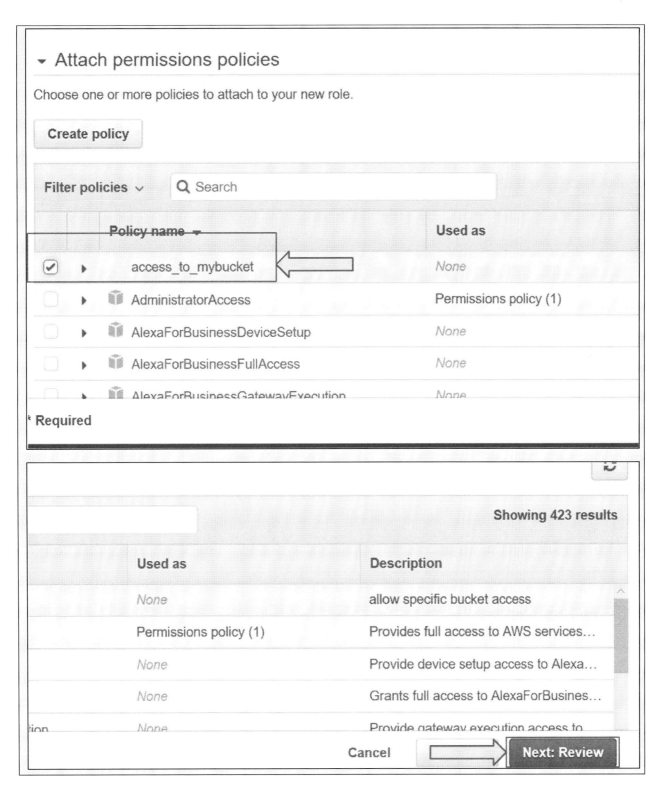

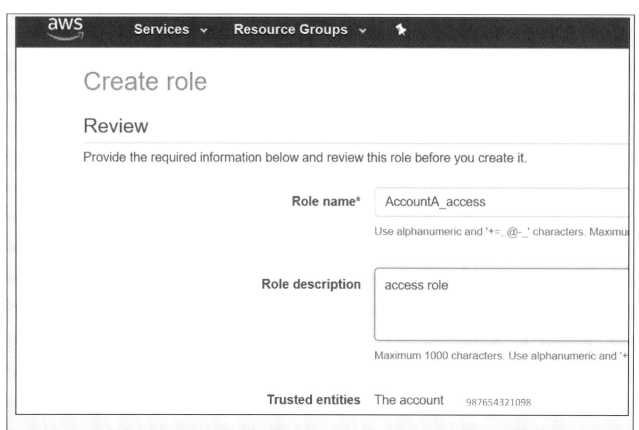

Now, click on the "Create Role" button at the bottom of page.

14. The role has been created.

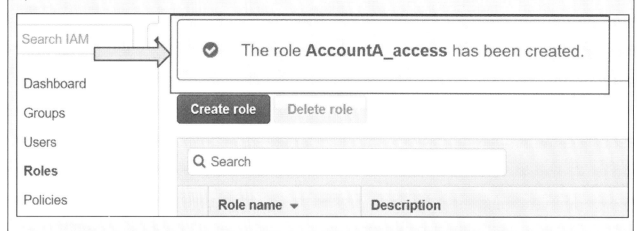

15. Log in again to Account A. Go to "IAM" service and then to "Groups". Select the group that you created.

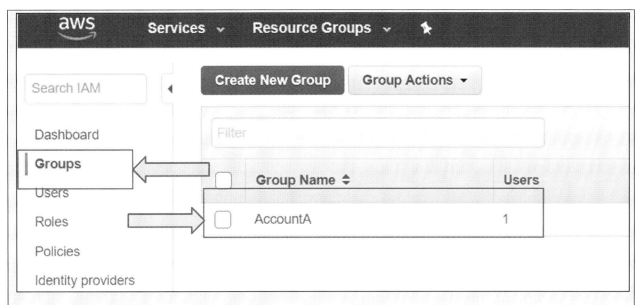

16. Go to "Permissions" of your created group and here you can see the "Inline Policies" option. Drop down to "Inline policies" and click on "click here".

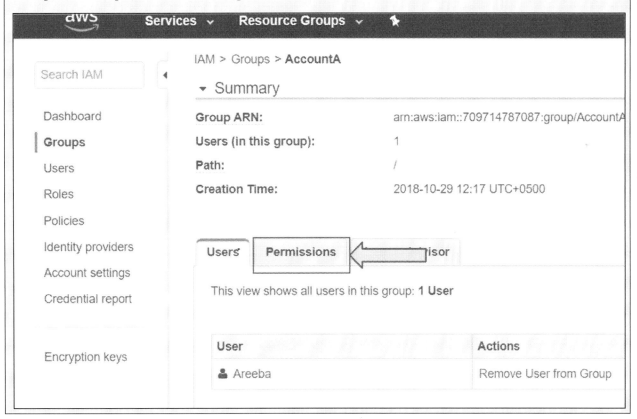

17. Go to "Custom Policies" and click "Select" then write the policy. Now in the policy, you need to enter account ID of account B, which can be obtained in the same way you get into account A and the role that is created in account B.

{

"Version": "2012-10-17",

  "Statement": {

    "Effect": "Allow",

"Action": "sts:AssumeRole",

"Resource": "arn:aws:iam::<ACCOUNT-ID of_AccountB>:role/<enter role that you created in account B>"

  }

}

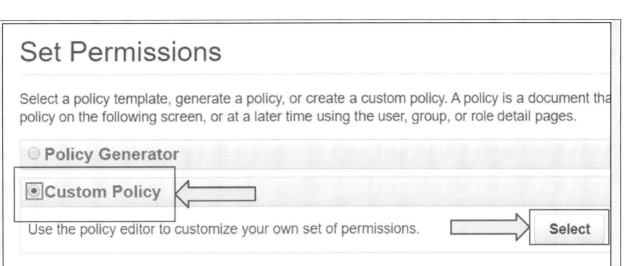

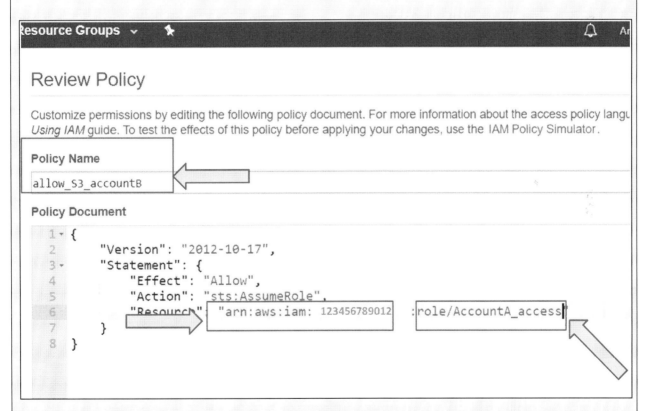

18. Click on "Apply Policy", this policy will be applied as an inline policy to the group.

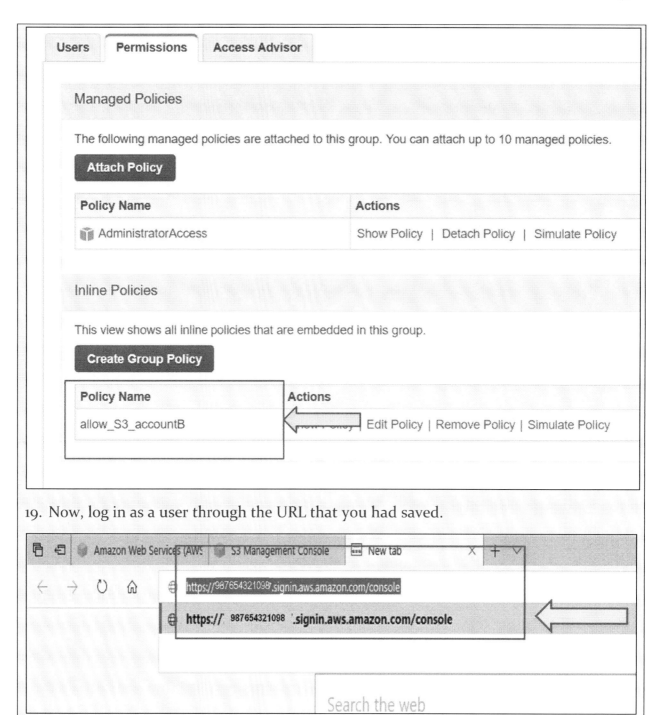

19. Now, log in as a user through the URL that you had saved.

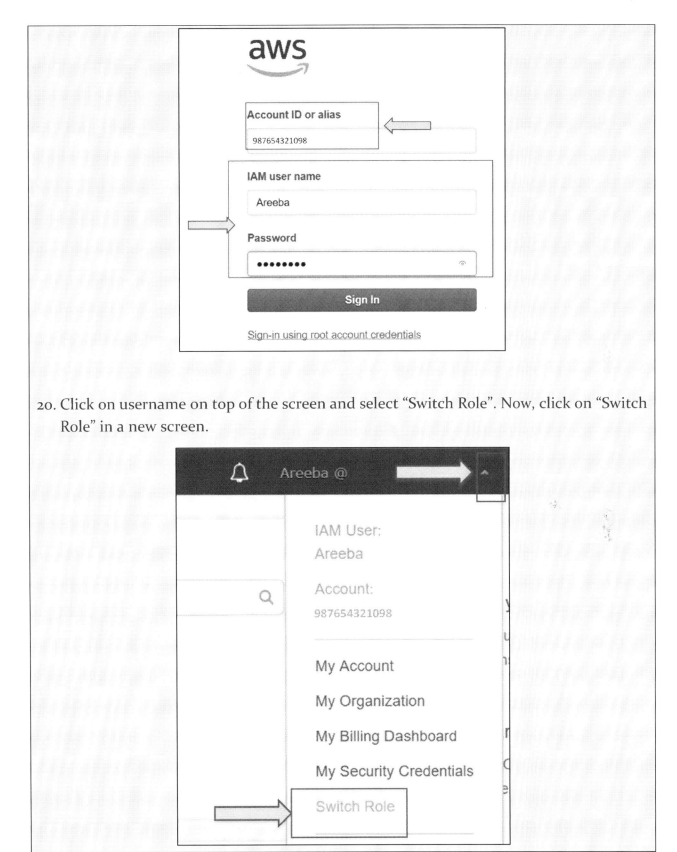

20. Click on username on top of the screen and select "Switch Role". Now, click on "Switch Role" in a new screen.

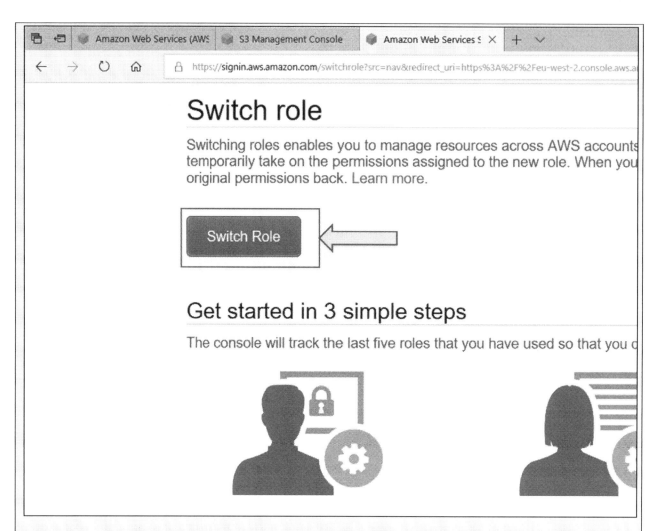

21. Enter the account number of Account B and the role created in Account B. Select the color of your choice. Now click "Switch Role".

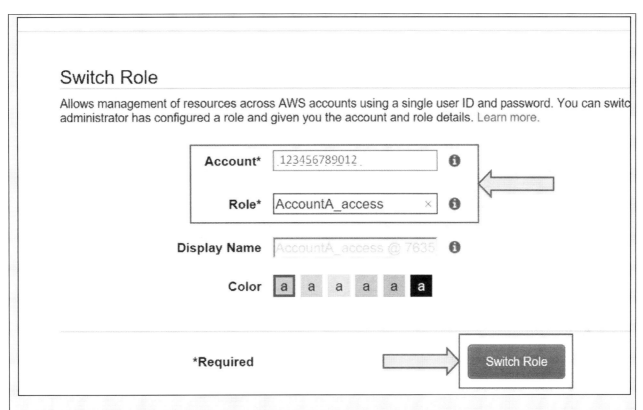

22. Here you can see that you have switched to the role.

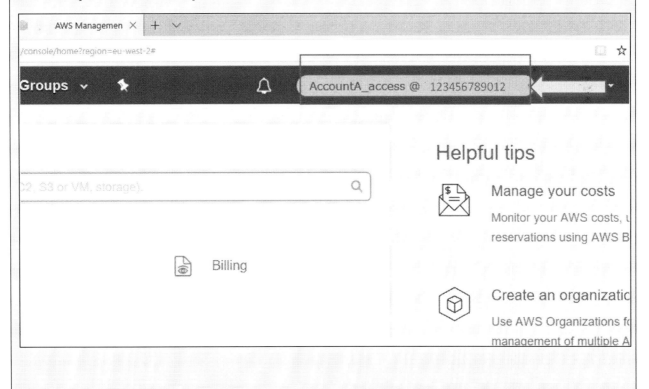

23. Now go to "S3" and you can see the bucket that you created. Select the bucket whose ARN is attached in the role.

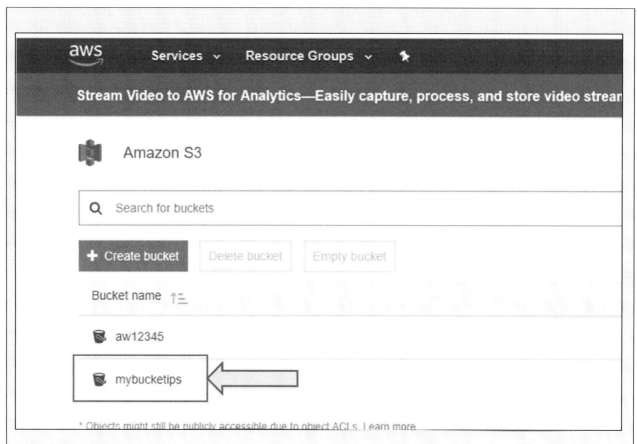

24. Upload object in the bucket. You have only the permission to add an object in this bucket.

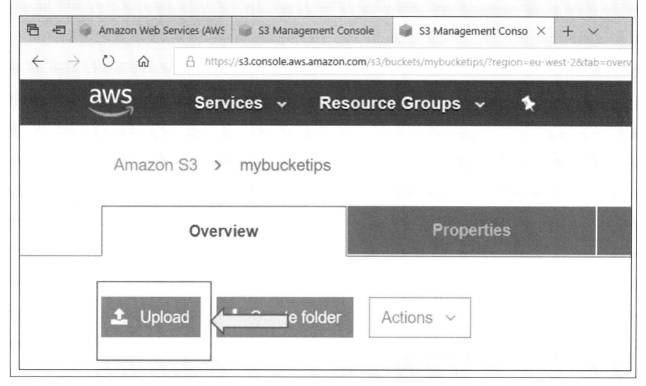

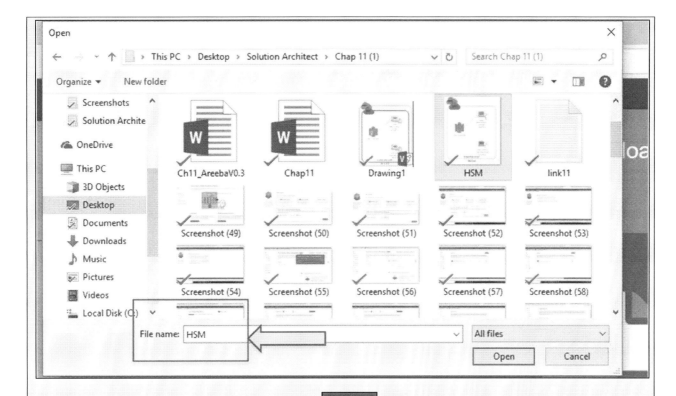

A dialogue box will appear having button Upload

25. If you try to upload an object in another bucket, you will not get the access to upload because its ARN is not defined in the Role.

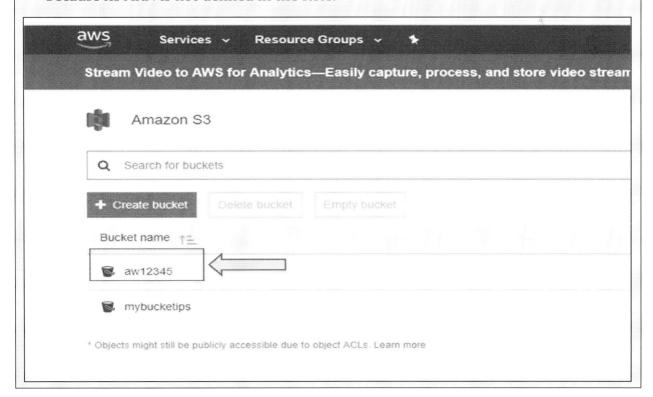

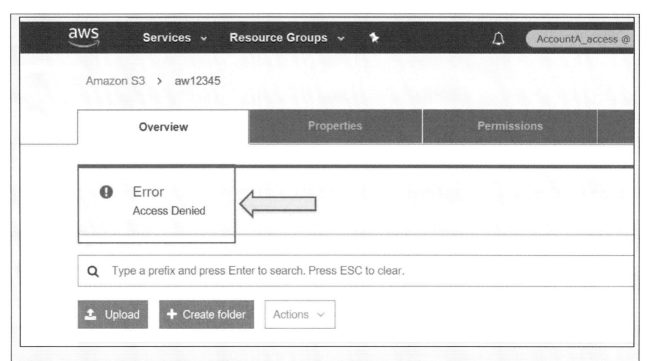

26. You can also switch back to account A, just go to name on top and click on "Back to <user>".

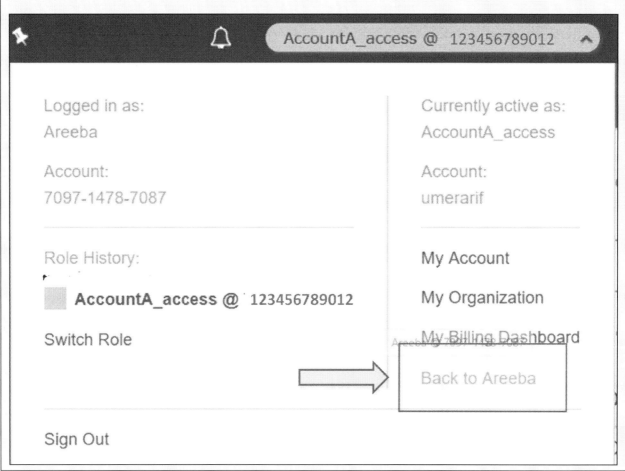

Challenge 1

A decree is issued by your CFO that due to a declining economy, all budgets should be reduced by 40% for next year.

You have to find out the ways to minimize the cost of your existing AWS landscape without compromising the durability of data, the integrity of applications and services running on AWS.

Which of the following ideas are reasonable for the required purpose?

- A. Setup CloudTrail to collect usage logs to determine which instances can be scaled back
- B. Configure your website's Auto-Scaling group to use spot instances rather than on-demand instances
- C. Purchase dedicated instances for those applications that will continue as part of the roadmap for the next year
- D. Consolidate many smaller RDS instances into a single large RDS instance
- E. Use the S3 Lifecycle feature to transition infrequently accessed data to different storage classes
- F. Create an EBS snapshot lifecycle process to delete outdated snapshots
- G. Migrate an EC2-based DB2 Database to RDS

Solution

In this challenge, the main task is to reduce cost without affecting the durability of data, the integrity of applications, and running services.

Option A is not valid because the problem with this option is that CloudTrail is the service to monitor API access, whereas CloudWatch is used to collect machine statistics. Therefore, CloudTrail cannot be used.

Option B will create a problem when the price of spot instances rises and does not allow auto scaling. This will also affect durability and integrity. You can use some reserved instances then scale spot instances.

Option C cannot be considered because the company did not demand dedicated instances, and it will also include extra premium charges.

Option D is not suitable, as this will not save money.

Option E is a valid option, as the transition of storage class would not affect durability and surely reduce some costs.

Option F is also a suitable way to save cost, as outdated snapshots are not of any use

Option G is not valid because DB2 Database does not support RDS.

Challenge 2

You are working in a company that has an e-commerce production landscape hosted in us-west-2 and using all 3 AZs. You noticed that occasionally performance falls below the acceptable levels by using a performance monitoring method that uses synthetic transactions.

The first issue that comes in the mind is the scaling problem. Which of the following things will you consider to address this problem in a cost-effective way?

A. Purchase Reserved Instances without selecting a specific availability zone so the reserved capacity can cover all AZs
B. Make sure your VPC subnets have a sufficient IP address range available for scale-out
C. Submit a Reserved Instance Modification Request to move RIs from us-east-2 to us-west-2
D. Purchase some Scheduled Instances for the most common poor performance times
E. Purchase a Dedicated Host in us-west-2 and ensure that instances spun up in the auto-scaling groups get assigned Dedicated Hosts
F. Enable cross-zone load balancing on your ELB

Solution

In this challenge, it is mentioned that the problem occurs occasionally.

Option A will cause a problem because if no availability zone is specified, then availability is not guaranteed.

Option B will depend on the subnet mask that if it is very small, then we cannot scale out. (You have to check for the number of IPs you have).

Option C is wrong because moving Reserved Instances between regions is not possible.

Option D cannot be considered because we have no idea of any schedule of load.

Option E is invalid because Dedicated Host cannot be used in Auto-Scaling groups.

Option F can be a solution, as cross-zone load balancing ensures that the requests are equally distributed across all targets, regardless of AZs.

Mind Map

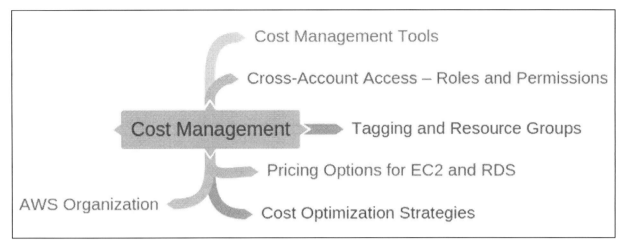

Figure 9-05: Mind Map

Practice Questions

1. How are resources of one account accessible from another account?
   a) By making it public
   b) By using cross-account access
   c) By using direct memory access
   d) By using open access

2. Which IAM feature is used to avoid sharing root credentials to other users?
   a) Role
   b) Group
   c) User
   d) Policies

3. Identity based policy is divided into _____ different categories.
   a) 4
   b) 3
   c) 1
   d) 2

4. Which of the following policy types is connected to the resource, not to the identity?
   a) Resource-based

b) Managed policy

c) Inline policy

d) Customer-based policy

5. Which IAM feature is used to manage the IAM users that have the same policy?
   a) User
   b) Role
   c) Policy
   d) Group

6. Which AWS service allows you to consolidate multiple AWS accounts into an organization?
   a) AWS CloudTrail
   b) AWS S3
   c) AWS Organization
   d) AWS EC2

7. Which feature of AWS organization is used to make a single AWS account as the paying master account linked with a set of other AWS accounts to form a simple one-level hierarchy?
   a) Consolidated Billing
   b) Load Balancing
   c) CloudFormation
   d) CloudFront

8. You can use the Consolidated-billing feature for _____.
   a) $0.5/month
   b) $0.025/day
   c) Free
   d) $0.075/hour

9. What type of EC2 pricing option can you use for the application, which is used on a continuous basis?

a) Reserved Instance

b) On-Demand Instance

c) Spot Instance

d) Spot + Reserved instance

10. Through which service of AWS can you monitor accounts and forward logs to S3?

a) AWS CloudFormation

b) AWS CloudFront

c) AWS CloudTrail

d) AWS ElasticBeanstalk

11. With the help of consolidated billing, you can get_____.

a) Volume discount

b) Extra resources

c) Extra policies

d) None of above

12. With the help of a payee account in consolidated billing, you can also provide resources to linked accounts. True or false?

a) False

b) True

13. How many accounts can you link to the paying account in consolidated billing?

a) 10

b) 20

c) 30

d) 5

14. To organize your AWS resources by marking resources from multiple services and regions with a common tag, which AWS service is used?

a) S3

b) EC2

c) Resource group

d) CloudTrail

15. _____ are the key-value pair that are attached to AWS Resources.
    a) Name
    b) Time of creating a resource
    c) Date
    d) Tags

16. For unpredictable workloads, which EC2 pricing option is used?
    a) Reserved
    b) On-Demand
    c) Spot
    d) Dedicated

17. For predictable workload, which EC2pricing option is used?
    a) Reserved
    b) On-Demand
    c) Spot
    d) Dedicated

18. The size of footprint of an instance can be calculated by _____.
    a) Personal footprint calculator
    b) Normalization factor
    c) Ecological footprint explorer
    d) Carbon footprint calculator

19. The size of footprint for target configuration should be _____ as original configuration.
    a) Equal
    b) Less than
    c) Greater than
    d) None of the above

20. Standard RI provides _____ discount as compared to on-demand instance.
    a) 20%
    b) 30%
    c) 75%
    d) 50%

21. Which type of RI is able to convert instance from one family to another?
    a) Standard RI
    b) Convertible RI
    c) Scheduled RI
    d) All of the above

22. In which type of payment option of RI do you need to pay all reservation charges in advance?
    a) No Upfront
    b) Partial Upfront
    c) All Upfront
    d) None of the above

23. What type of pricing option is for workloads that are not tied critical and interruption tolerant?
    a) Spot
    b) Dedicated
    c) Reserved
    d) On-demand

24. What type of instance pricing option can you use for a 2-week task in a cost-effective way and with high availability?

    a) Spot instance+ On-demand
    b) On-Demand+ Reserved
    c) Reserved
    d) On-demand

25. For intensive workload, what type of instance family can you use?

a) Storage Optimized
b) General Purpose
c) Memory Optimized
d) Compute Optimized

26. Select the services that can most directly help with right-sizing your landscape. (Choose 2)
    a) AWS CloudTrail
    b) AWS Budgets
    c) AWS Trusted Advisor
    d) AWS Shield
    e) AWS CloudWatch

27. The organization is assessing a cloud migration's financial implications. What should be their first step?
    a) Recruit an experienced project manager
    b) Update the architecture roadmap to better align with cloud technologies
    c) Ensure governmental or regulatory constraints are cloud-compatible
    d) Get a clear understanding of current costs

28. Choose the option that is not a feature of AWS Organizations?
    a) Granular configuration of Security Groups within a VPC
    b) Hierarchical based control over groups of IAM users and roles within multiple Accounts
    c) Grouping all of your AWS accounts into Organizational Units (OUs) as part of a hierarchy
    d) AWS accounts that are members of the Organization can have the benefit of Consolidated Billing

29. Select the features of Consolidated Billing. (Choose 3)
    a) Charging is based per VPC
    b) Account charges can be tracked individually
    c) Multiple standalone accounts are combined and may reduce your overall bill
    d) A single bill is issued containing the charges for all AWS Accounts

30. Your company's initial analysis showed that on-premises costs are substantially lower than cloud deployments. Which items are you supposed to check for parity? (Choose 3)
    a) Ensure the model assumes making use of managed services on the cloud
    b) Make sure the cloud cost model includes OpEx tax credits
    c) If amortization is being used for on-premises assets, using a Reserved Instance cost is more realistic than On-Demand
    d) Ensure that soft costs are somehow accounted for in both models
    e) Dedicated instances should be used to most closely resemble on-premises IT assets

31. Which of the following options is the primary AWS value proposition around cost?
    a) AWS offers agility without large upfront investments
    b) AWS lets you spend less time on IT management
    c) AWS allows organizations to migrate to the cloud
    d) AWS puts cost data in the hands of everyone

32. In one AZ, you have some extra unused RIs, but you need them in another AZ. What can you do if you want to use them in the other AZ? (Choose 2)
    a) If these are Zonal RIs, you cannot use them in another AZ
    b) If these are Zonal RIs, you first need to modify the zone
    c) If these are Standard RIs, you cannot use them in another AZ
    d) If these are Regional RIs, you do not need to do anything
    e) If these are Convertible RIs, you cannot use them in another AZ

33. The application of your company has to process a very volatile inconsistent flow of data inbound in order. Choose the option that would be most reliable and cost-effective?
    a) Use SQS to receive the inbound messages and a spot fleet to process them
    b) Use SQS to receive the inbound messages and use a single reserved instance to process them
    c) Use SNS to receive the inbound messages and use a single reserved instance to process them
    d) Use SQS to receive the inbound messages and a dedicated host to process them

34. Which of the following expectations is something that you should NOT set with your stakeholders for cloud migration?

a) Existing business processes will need to be modified

b) We will require downtime for some applications to move them to the cloud

c) Overall costs will decrease as soon as we start using cloud assets

d) New business processes will need to be defined

35. Choose one from the following options that is NOT a direct use of tagging.

a) Security

b) Grouping

c) Cost Allocation

d) Automation

e) Purchasing

36. Which potential economy-of-scale benefit is offered by consolidated billing?

a) Clear visibility on what business units are spending

b) Leveraging tiered pricing

c) Automated notifications when an account exceeds its budget

d) All charges appear on the same invoice

37. Select true statements about Dedicated Instances and Dedicated Hosts. (Choose 2)

a) Dedicated Hosts are more cost-effective than Dedicated Instances

b) Dedicated Instances are required to run on Dedicated Hosts

c) Dedicated Hosts reserve capacity

d) Dedicated Instances reserve capacity

e) Dedicated Instances can run as spot instances

Answers

Chapter 06: Architecting to Scale

1. **C** (CloudFront)

Explanation: Amazon Cloud front gives developers and your business an easy and cost-effective way to distribute data with a high data transfer rate and low latency without any limitation of users.

2. **A** (True)

Explanation: Amazon CloudFront supports the delivery of Dynamic content via the use of HTTP cookies. CloudFront is a service of AWS through which you can distribute your website completely along with its static, dynamic, streaming, and interactive content with the help of an edge location that is global.

3. **B** (Web) and **C** (RTMP)

Explanation: Amazon CloudFront has two types of distribution Web and RTMP. The limit of Web distribution per account is 200 and of RTMP per account is 100.

4. **B** (Geo restriction)

Explanation: Geo-restriction means you can restrict your content access in countries where you do not want to show your content. You can blacklist all countries on which you want to restrict your content, or you can whitelist the countries on which you allow access to your content.

5. **A** (True)

Explanation: Amazon CloudFront can serve both origin and non-origin content. Amazon EC2, Amazon S3 bucket, and Elastic Loud balancing or Route 53 are examples of origin servers, while on-premises web servers are examples of non-origin servers.

6. **C** (Invalidation)

Explanation: Via invalidation API, you can remove the malicious or harmful object before its expiration time from all edge locations. That is an Invalidation request.

7. **A** (Dedicated IP custom SSL) and **B** (SNI custom SSL)

Explanation: With CloudFront, you can use HTTP or HTTPS but if you want to use SSL, then you need to use the default CloudFront URL that is created during the creation of

distribution or you can create a customized URL with your own SSL certificate. There are two separate ways to do Custom SSL depending on budget and outdated browser.

- Dedicated IP Custom SSL
- SNI (Server Name Identification) Custom SSL

8. **D** (Memcached)

Explanation: Memcached is the most commonly used cache engine to store simple data types.

9. **B** (Redis) and **D** (Memcached)

Explanation: Elastic cache supports two in-memory open-source engines:

✓ Memcached
✓ Redis

10. **B** (Redis)

Explanation: Redis engine is used in case of back-ups and data restoration.

11. **A** (Fast Recovery)

Explanation: Replication is one of the best approaches in case of failure of the node. Through this, you can quickly recover the data. It supports high availability, separates out the read, and write workloads. In Memcached, there is no redundancy of data, while in Redis, there is replication.

12. **C** (Memcached)

Explanation: When you need to distribute your data over multiple nodes. It is also useful in those cases when you need to run large nodes with multiple cores and threads.

13. **B** (Redis)

Explanation:

In case of Persistence of key stores, the Redis Cache engine is used.

14. **A** (Route53)

Explanation: Zone Apex domain name is naked or domain name without "www". With Route53, you can configure Alias record to map naked domain name or apex to CloudFront distribution.

15. **A** (PUT, POST, PATCH, and DELETE)

Explanation: CloudFront supports GET, POST, HEAD, PUT, PATCH, DELETE, and OPTIONS HTTP requests. PUT, POST, PATCH, and DELETE requests, responses are not cached in CloudFront.

16. **C** (Memcached)

Explanation: When you need to increase or decrease your system by scaling out, adding, and deletion of nodes, you can use Memcached.

17. **A** (Redis)

Explanation: Redis is a cache engine that is used for complex data types.

18. **A** (AWS Kinesis)

Explanation: Consider the use of Kinesis in the scenario where streaming of a large amount of data is needed.

19. **A** (True)

Explanation: Kinesis is not persistence storage; it basically stores streaming data, then the Kinesis application queries this data for analysis. After analyzing, it stores that data in long-term storage like S3.

20. **B** (3)

Explanation: Data Producers are those that can put data in Kinesis streams. It can be done in three ways.

By the use of Kinesis Streams API, by the use of Amazon Kinesis Producer Library, and in terms of logging data.

21. **C** (1000)

Explanation: In a single shard, you can support a maximum of 1000 PUTS records/sec.

22. **B** (2MB/sec)

Explanation: The capacity of one shard in terms of input is 1MB/sec, and in terms of output, it is 2MB/sec.

23. **C** (Partition key)

Explanation: With the use of sequence numbers, you can pull the data, but identifying which data belongs to which shards can be done by partition key.

24. **D** (B and C)

Explanation: They are the Kinesis stream application that are EC2 instances that perform processing and querying of data via multiple applications running on it. Then they put that process data into some persistence storage.

25. **C** (AWS SNS)

Explanation: Via AWS SNS Mobile push you can push messages to Facebook or WhatsApp, or any other mobile or desktop applications.

26. **B** (More atomic functional units.)

Explanation

Loosely coupled architectures have several advantages, but atomic functional units are the biggest advantage in terms of scalability. These discrete work units can be independently scale-up.

27. **C** (They can enable real-time reporting and analysis of streamed data)
    D (They can accept data as soon as it has been produced, without the need for batching)

Explanation

Kinesis Data Streams can immediately accept data pushed into a stream as soon as the data is produced, thereby minimizing the likelihood of data loss at the producer stage. The data need not be batched first. They can also extract metrics, generate reports and conduct real-time data analytics, so the last two options are correct. Kinesis Data Streams is not a long-term storage solution since the data can only be stored for up to 7 days in the shards. We also cannot handle streamed data loading directly into data stores like S3. For this type of operation, Kinesis Firehose is required.

28. **E** (Simple Workflow Service)

Explanation

AWS SWF is a well-suited workflow system for distributed asynchronous processes involving lead/lag times and processes that are human-enabled.

29. **D** (Dynamic)

Explanation

You may be tempted to use Scheduled because of the traffic patterns, but if we don't get that traffic spike, this could scale needlessly. Dynamic based on certain parameters such as connections CPU or I/O network would be the most efficient way.

30. **A** (KCL)

Explanation

While data can be read (or consumed) using either the Kinesis Data Streams API or the Kinesis Client Library (KCL) from shards within Kinesis Streams, AWS often recommends using the KCL. The KPL (Kinesis Producer Library) will only permit Kinesis Streams to be written and not read from it. You cannot use SSH to interact with Kinesis Data Streams.

Chapter 07: Business Continuity

1. **a** (RAID0)

Explanation: RAID0, also known as striping. It gives the highest write performance because writes are distributed across disks, and no parity is required.

2. **b** (False)

Explanation: Redshift supports one-AZ deployments only, but several clusters can be run in different AZ.

3. **a** (True)

Explanation: With Spread Placement Group and Horizontal scaling, you can reduce the risk of hardware failure in a reasonable way.

4. **c** (Redis)

Explanation: Elasticache for Redis allows multi-AZ configurations, but Memcached does not support it. The other choices are not in-memory cache.

5. **b** (RAID1 with two EBS volumes of not less than 1 TB each)

Explanation: No-fault tolerance for a volume is given by RAID0. RAID1 includes the requisite 2x storage volume space, as well known as mirroring. RAID5 needs at least three volumes.

6. **d** (RPO provides an expectation of potential manual data re-entry for recovery plans.)

Explanation: Recovery point objective (RPO) — is the amount of data your organization is prepared to lose in the event of a disaster. This can inform an expectation of manual data re-entry for BC planners.

7. **a** (Backup and Restore)

Explanation: Simple backup and recovery system will operate with small data and generous RTO / RPO.

8. **c** (Infrastructure)

Explanation: Infrastructure failures are known as broken/failure services or adverse environmental conditions.

9. **b** (Pilot Light)

Explanation: For replication of data, the database is always running, and server images are generated and regularly updated for all other layers. So the different layers are non-active, and in case of failure, the traffic is routed to this environment and makes it active.

10. **c** (Aurora)

Explanation: If you want to use RDS and you cannot use DynamoDB, then use Aurora because it has failover and redundancy capability.

Chapter 08: Deployment and Operation Management

1. **b** (AWS OpsWorks)

Explanation: AWS OpsWork is used to configure and operate the instances of Chef and Puppet because it is a configuration management service. It also aids in the provision of high-level tools for managing EC2 instances. OpsWork can work with any complicated application, regardless of its architectural design. It provides one configuration management for application deployment in a hybrid architecture. It works with both Linux and Windows servers.

2. **c** (AWS CloudFormation)

Explanation: AWS CloudFormation is such a service, which allows you to take a hardware infrastructure and convert it into code. With the help of CloudFormation, you can manage your resource in less time and target only the application on the AWS cloud.

3. **b** (2)

Explanation: Tiers of the ecosystem are classified into two categories;

The web server environment is where web applications are hosted, and HTTP(S) requests are handled.

Web applications are hosted in the working environment, which also performs long-running or scheduled background processing tasks.

4. **d** (IAM roles)

Explanation: With CloudFormation, you can create IAM roles and assign them.

5. **c** (Free)

Explanation: CloudFormation, itself is free; you only need to pay for the resources that you have created in CloudFormation.

6. **b** (JSON) **and d** (YAML)

Explanation: In CloudFormation, when you create a template, the format of the template is JSON or YAML.

7. **a** (2)

Explanation: There are two main elements of the template;

- Mandatory Element
- Optional Element

8. **a** (False)

Explanation: CloudFormation will automatically work out the provisioning order based on dependencies for each resource.

9. **c** (Elastic Beanstalk)

Explanation: Elastic Beanstalk will be a helpful service for those who do not know much about the cloud and only want their environment up and running.

10. **b** (VPC)

Explanation: With the help of CloudFormation, you can enable VPC peering, or you can build multiple VPCs in a single template.

11. **b** (CloudWatch)

Explanation: In Elastic Beanstalk, you are able to access CloudWatch for monitoring purposes and are notified of specific events or health. You can also access log files without logging in to the application server. With the help of Elastic Beanstalk, you can modify the setting of the application server.

12. **a** (Single region for multiple AZ)

Explanation: In Elastic Beanstalk, fault tolerance is not configured for multiple regions, but it will be configured in a single region for multiple AZs.

13. **b** (OpsWorks)

Explanation: AWS OpsWorks allows you to build and manage the stack flexibly and simply along with its linked applications and resources. With the help of OpsWorks, the operational task becomes automated like code deployment, configurations of software, database setups, and server scaling.

14. **b** (Layer)

Explanation: One or more layers in a stack can be used to specify how a group of EC2 instances is configured for a specific task.

15. **c** (5)

Explanation: There is a group of lifecycle events in each layer, which relates to different stages of instance lifecycle.

- the setup
- deploy
- configure
- undeploy
- shutdown

16. **a** (OpsWorks)

Explanation: OpsWork is generally a GUI to deploy and configure the infrastructure fast.

17. **b** (Create deletion policy on those resources)

Explanation: In CloudFormation, you can also specify the deletion policy for resources in the template, or you can define the creation of Snapshots of Volumes and database instances before deletion.

18. **a** (Stack)

Explanation: A stack is a group of resources or is like a container for the resources, which are managed together like ELB, EC2 instances, EBS Volumes, etc.

19. **a** (RDS instance)

Explanation: Elastic Beanstalk has the capability for provision of RDS DB instance. With the help of environment variables, the connectivity to that DB instance is disclosed to the application.

20. **b** (Resources along with its configuration)

Explanation: When you provision resources in CloudFormation, you need to define the list of resources along with the configuration value, which you actually provision.

21. **b** (Automated software releases to production)

Explanation: Continuous Deliver differs from Continuous Deployment because in Continuous Delivery, the Delivery still includes a manual check before releasing to production. Otherwise, the entire process is the same for both of them.

22. d (All at once)

Explanation: All at once- In this deployment method, old version instances are terminated, and new version instances are launched. This deployment method required downtime, but it is the fastest method. Its rollback process is manual.

23. a (Disposable)

Explanation: With the disposable upgrade, a new release is deployed to the new instance and terminate the old instance

24. d (Change sets)

Explanation: You can use change sets to preview changes in CloudFormation, before applying them in order to detect potential collisions or impacts.

25. b (False)

Explanation: In OpsWorks, stacks can be cloned only within the region

Chapter 09: Costing Management

1. **b** (By using Cross-Account Access)

Explanation: Cross-Account Access is allowing access of resources in one account to a trusted principal from a different account.

2. **c** (User)

Explanation: You can create specific Identity and Access Management users within your account that match people in your business instead of providing your root user credentials. Users in Identity and Access Management aren't different accounts; they are just regular users in your account.

3. **d** (2)

Explanation: Identity-based policies can be further classified into two groups;

✓ Managed policies
✓ Inline policies

4. **a** (Resource-based)

Explanation: Permissions policies that are connected to a resource, such as an Amazon S3 bucket, are known as resource-based policies.

5. **d** (Group)

Explanation: You can organize Identity and Access Management users into Identity and Access Management groups and attach a policy to a group. In that case, single users still have their own credentials, but all the users in a group have the permissions that are connected to the group. Use groups for easier permissions management.

6. **c** (AWS Organization)

Explanation: AWS Organizations is an account management service that allows you to consolidate multiple AWS accounts into an organization, enabling you to create a hierarchical structure that can be managed centrally.

7. **a** (Consolidated Billing)

Explanation: One of the key features of AWS Organizations is the consolidation of the billing of all the AWS accounts in your organization, where you have a single AWS account as the paying master account linked with a set of all other AWS accounts to form a simple one-level hierarchy.

8. **c** (Free)

Explanation: Consolidated billing is available at no additional cost.

9. **a** (Reserved Instance)

Explanation: For servers that need to be available all the time and will be continuously running at a known capacity, reserved instances will be the most cost-effective pricing option.

10. **c** (AWS CloudTrail)

Explanation: With the help of Consolidated billing, you can do auditing by use of CloudTrail that is per AWS account and enabled per region by pushing combined logs to the Centralized S3 bucket, but for that, you need to enable CloudTrail in the master account, define a policy for cross-account access and enable CloudTrail in all other accounts.

11. **a** (Volume Discount)

Explanation: Consolidated Billing allows you to get volume discounts on all your accounts.

12. **a** (False)

Explanation: Consolidated billing is not concerned with the provisioning of AWS services in linked accounts, and you cannot provide services on the linked accounts from the paying account.

13. **b** (20)

Explanation: In Consolidated billing, a maximum of 20 accounts are allowed to link to the master account, and in the same organization, two masters (paying) accounts are not allowed.

14. **c** (Resource Group)

Explanation: You may utilize resource groups to organize your AWS resources by assigning a common tag to resources across many services and locations and then view them all together in a customized pane of the AWS Management Console.

15. **d** (Tags)

Explanation: Tags are key-value pairs that are attached to AWS resources. They are labels that you assign to an AWS resource, and they have information about data called "metadata".

16. **b** (On-demand)

Explanation: On-Demand is the least cost-effective pricing option, but the users can save by provisioning a variable level of computing for unpredictable workloads. These types of instances are used during the testing of the application for the first time.

17. **a** (Reserved)

Explanation: Reserved Instances (RIs) enable users to reserve computing capacity for a predictable workload.

18. **b** (Normalization Factor)

Explanation: The normalization factor is a factor of instance type and amount of instance in reservation for finding the size of the footprint of the instance.

19. **a** (Equal)

Explanation: The size of the footprint for the target configuration must be equal to the size of the original configuration. Otherwise, modification requests will not process.

20. **c** (75%)

Explanation: Standard RIs provide a significant discount (up to 75%) compared to the On-demand hourly rate.

21. **b** (Convertible RI)

Explanation: In Convertible RIs, you can change instance families like from t2 to m3, OS like from Linux to windows, tenancy, and pricing option. Therefore, it is the most flexible.

22. **c** (All upfront)

Explanation: All Upfront: Pay the entire reservation charges in advance. There will be no monthly fee during the term.

23. **a** (Spot)

Explanation: Spot instances offer the greatest discounts for workloads that are not tied critical and interruption tolerant. Customers can specify the price they are willing to pay for a specific instance type.

24. **a** (Spot instance+ On-demand)

Explanation: For high availability, you can use on-demand instances and for a cost-effective way, use spot instances. Therefore, for a specific time requirement, you can use a spot instance accompanied by the on-demand instance.

25. **c** (Memory Optimized)

Explanation: For intensive workload, you can use a memory-optimized instance family.

26. **c** (AWS Trusted Advisor) and **e** (AWS CloudWatch)

Explanation: Right sizing is the lowest cost tool that still fulfills a particular workload's technical specifications. The most direct tools for this are CloudWatch and Trusted Advisor.

27. **d** (Get a clear understanding of current costs)

Explanation: You should have a good understanding of current costs. It may turn out that even with financial facts, a transfer to the cloud is not warranted, so the other practices would be waste.

28. **a** (Granular configuration of Security Groups within a VPC)

Explanation: AWS is an account management service that allows you to centrally manage multiple accounts.

29. **b** (Account charges can be tracked individually), **c** (Multiple standalone accounts are combined and may reduce your overall bill), and **d** (A single bill is issued containing the charges for all AWS Accounts)

Explanation: AWS Organizations provide a consolidated billing feature. When enabled and configured, you will receive a bill that includes costs and fees for all of the organization's AWS accounts. Each of the individual AWS accounts is integrated into a single bill, they can still be individually monitored, and the cost information can be imported into a separate file. Having Consolidated Billing will ultimately reduce the amount you are paying as you can apply for Volume Discounts. Use of Consolidated Billing is not charged.

30. **a** (Ensure the model assumes making use of managed services on the cloud.), **c** (If amortization is being used for on-prem assets, using a Reserved Instance cost is more realistic than On-Demand.) and **d** (Ensure that soft costs are somehow accounted for in both models.)

Explanation: Bulk purchases are nearly always cheaper than on-demand, so RIs can be a good proxy. Managed services are going to be more cost-effective than mimicking a pure on-prem server farm. In addition, soft costs like agility or maintenance should be accounted for in the model.

31. **a** (AWS offers agility without large upfront investments.)

Explanation: The primary value proposition regarding price for AWS is that it creates the opportunity for agility using a pay-as-you-go system. Traditional CapEx models make it hard to test new ideas quickly.

32. **b** (If these are Zonal RIs, you first need to modify the zone.) and **d** (If these are Regional RIs, you do not need to do anything.)

Explanation: Regional RIs are not limited to an AZ and can be consumed across a region. Using the ModifyReserveInstances API in the console, zonal RIs can be changed to be used in another AZ.

33. **b** (Use SQS to receive the inbound messages and use a single reserved instance to process them.)

Explanation: For smoothing requests, a buffering pattern is useful. Using FIFO, we can do this with SQS to meet the order requirement. If we only use a spot fleet, we may be outbid and have no available instances. So, we can use an RI.

34. **c** (Overall costs will decrease as soon as we start using cloud assets.)

Explanation: Due to things such as training dual environments lease penalties, consultancy, and planning, costs will most certainly increase during a migration. AWS calls this period the migration bubble.

35. **e** (Purchasing)

Explanation: Except Purchasing, tagging can be used specifically for all of these purposes. But, indirectly, when a tag changes, you can set up a CloudWatch event to trigger some action. That action could be a call to an API to place an order with a supplier.

36. **b** (Leveraging tiered pricing.)

Explanation: Consolidated billing makes it possible for you to understand lower prices on some tiered pricing products.

37. **c** (Dedicated Hosts reserve capacity.) and **e** (Dedicated Instances can run as spot instances.)

Explanation: Dedicated hosts are reserved as you pay for the entire physical network, which cannot be delegated to anyone else. Dedicated instances are available as on-demand, reserved, and spot instances.

Acronyms

AAD	Additional Authenticated Data
ACL	Access Control List
ACM PCA	AWS Certificate Manager Private Certificate Authority
ACM	AWS Certificate Manager
AD	Active Directory
ADM	Amazon Device Messaging
AMI	Amazon Machine Image
API	Application Program Interface
APN	AWS Partner Network
APNS	Apple Push Notification Service
ARN	Amazon Resource Name
ASN	Autonomous System Number
AUC	Area Under a Curve
AWS	Amazon Web Service
AZ	Availability Zone
BGP	Border Gateway Protocol
BLOB	Binary Large Object
CAF	Cloud Adoption Framework
CDN	Content Delivery Network
CGW	Customer Gateway
CIDR	Classless Inter-Domain Routing
CIFS	Common Internet File System
CLI	Command Line Interface
CMK	Customer Master Key
CNAME	Canonical Name
CPU	Central Processing Unit
DB	Database
DBA	Database Administrator
DDoS	Distributed Denial of Service
DKIM	DomainKeys Identified Mail
DMS	Database Migration Service
DNS	Domain Name System
DoS	Denial of Service
DR	Disaster Recovery

DRT	DDoS Response Team
EBS	Elastic Block Store
EC2	Elastic Cloud Compute
ECR	Elastic Container Registry
ECS	Elastic Container Service
EFS	Elastic File Storage
EKS	Elastic Kubernetes Service
ELB	Elastic Load Balancer
EMR	Elastic Map Reduce
ENA	Elastic Network Adapter
ES	Elasticsearch Service
ETL	Extract, Transform, and Load
FBL	Feedback Loop
FIM	Federated Identity Management
FS	Federation Service
GCM	Google Cloud Messaging
GUI	Graphical User Interface
HMAC	Hash-based Message Authentication Code
HPC	High Performance Computing
HSM	Hardware Security Module
HTTP	Hyper Text Transfer Protocol
I/O	Input/output
IAM	Identity and Access Management
IdP	Identity Provider
IDS	Intrusion Detection System
IGW	Internet Gateway
IoT	Internet of Things
IP	Internet Protocol
IPS	Intrusion Prevention System
IPSEC	Internet Protocol Security
ISP	Internet Service Provider
JCE	Java Cryptography Extensions
JDBC	Java Database Connectivity
JSON	JavaScript Object Notation
KMS	Key Management Service
LAN	Local Area Network
MFA	Multi Factor Authentication
MIME	Multipurpose Internet Mail Extensions

MPNS	Microsoft Push Notification Service for Windows Phone
MTA	Mail Transfer Agent
MTU	Maximum Transmission Unit
NACL	Network Access Control List
NAS	Network Attached Storage
NFS	Network File System
OCID	Open ID Connect
ODBC	Open Database Connectivity
OLAP	Online Analytical Processing
OS	Operating System
OSI	Open-System Interconnection
OU	Organizational Unit
PPS	Packets Per Second
Pub/Sub	Publisher/Subscriber
RDS	Relational Database Service
RI	Reserved Instance
RPO	Recovery Point Objective
RTMP	Real Time Messaging Protocol
RTO	Recovery Time Objective
S3	Simple Storage Service
SAML	Security Assertion Markup Language
SAN	Subject Alternative Name
SAN	Storage Area Network
SCP	Service Control Policies
SCP	Service Control Policies
SCT	Schema Conversion Tool
SDK	Software Development Kit
SES	Simple Email Service
SG	Security Group
SLA	Service Level Agreement
SMTP	Simple Mail Transfer Protocol
SNI	Server Name Indication
SNS	Simple Notification Service
SOAP	Simple Object Access Protocol
SOC	Security Operations Center
SQS	Simple Queue Service
SRE	Site Reliability Engineers
SR-IOV	Single Root I/O Virtualization

SSD	Solid State Drive
SSE	Server Side Encryption
SSL	Secure Sockets Layer
SSM	AWS Systems Manager
SSO	Single Sign-On
STS	Security Token Service
SWF	Simple Workflow Service
TB	TeraByte
TCO	Total Cost of Ownership
TCP	Transmission Control Protocol)
TLS	Transport Layer Security
TOGAF	The Open Group Architecture Framework
TTL	Time to Live
TVM	Token Vending Machine
UDP	User Datagram Protocol
URL	Uniform Resource Locator
VERP	Variable Envelope Return Path
VFI	Virtual Function Interface
VPC`	Virtual Private Cloud
VPG	Virtual Private Gateway
VPN	Virtual Private Network
VTL	Virtual Tape Library
WAF	Web Application Firewall
WAM	WorkSpaces Application Manager
WPNS	Windows Push Notification Service
WSDL	Web Services Description Language

References

Data Store

https://do.awsstatic.com/whitepapers/performance-at-scale-with-amazon-elasticache.pdf

https://d1.awsstatic.com/whitepapers/Multi_Tenant_SaaS_Storage_Strategies.pdf

https://d1.awsstatic.com/whitepapers/Storage/AWS%20Storage%20Services%20Whitepaper-v9.pdf

http://jayendrapatil.com/aws-ec2-instance-lifecycle/
https://docs.aws.amazon.com/AWSEC2/latest/UserGuide/ec2-instance-lifecycle.html
https://docs.aws.amazon.com/AWSEC2/latest/UserGuide/putty.html
https://docs.aws.amazon.com/elasticloadbalancing/latest/userguide/elb-ug.pdf
https://docs.aws.amazon.com/elasticloadbalancing/latest/userguide/how-elastic-load-balancing-works.html
https://docs.aws.amazon.com/cli/latest/reference/s3/rm.html
https://docs.aws.amazon.com/AmazonS3/latest/dev/UploadingObjects.html
https://docs.aws.amazon.com/aws-technical-content/latest/cost-optimization-storage-optimization/cost-optimization-storage-optimization.pdf
https://cloudacademy.com/blog/optimize-amazon-s3-performance/
https://aws.amazon.com/blogs/developer/parallelizing-large-uploads-for-speed-and-reliability/
https://docs.aws.amazon.com/AmazonS3/latest/dev/request-rate-perf-considerations.html
https://d1.awsstatic.com/whitepapers/Storage/AWS%20Storage%20Services%20Whitepaper-v9.pdf
https://do.awsstatic.com/whitepapers/Storage/aws-storage-options.pdf
https://www.druva.com/blog/object-storage-versus-block-storage-understanding-technology-differences/
https://docs.aws.amazon.com/AmazonS3/latest/dev/Introduction.html
https://docs.aws.amazon.com/AmazonS3/latest/dev/acl-overview.html
https://docs.aws.amazon.com/AmazonS3/latest/dev/Introduction.html#S3_ACLs
https://docs.aws.amazon.com/aws-technical-content/latest/aws-overview/aws-overview.pdf?icmpid=link_from_whitepapers_page
ttps://docs.aws.amazon.com/AmazonS3/latest/dev/object-lifecycle-mgmt.html
https://docs.aws.amazon.com/AmazonS3/latest/dev/ListingKeysHierarchy.html
https://docs.aws.amazon.com/AmazonS3/latest/dev/PresignedUrlUploadObject.html
https://docs.aws.amazon.com/AmazonS3/latest/dev/uploadobjusingmpu.html

https://docs.aws.amazon.com/AmazonS3/latest/user-guide/server-access-logging.html

https://www.cloudberrylab.com/blog/how-to-enable-and-read-amazon-s3-bucket-logs/

https://aws.amazon.com/about-aws/whats-new/2014/11/13/event-notification-feature-in-amazon-s3/

https://docs.aws.amazon.com/AmazonS3/latest/user-guide/enable-event-notifications.html

https://cloud.netapp.com/blog/ebs-efs-amazons3-best-cloud-storage-system

https://searchdatabackup.techtarget.com/definition/asynchronous-replication

https://d1.awsstatic.com/whitepapers/aws-tco-dynamodb.pdf

Network Design

https://networklessons.com/bgp/how-to-configure-bgp-weight-attribute

https://simpledns.com/help/dns-record-types

https://docs.aws.amazon.com/vpc/latest/peering/what-is-vpc-peering.html

https://docs.aws.amazon.com/vpc/latest/peering/vpc-peering-basics.html

https://www.coresite.com/solutions/cloud-services/public-cloud-providers/amazon-web-services-direct-connect

https://aws.amazon.com/directconnect/getting-started/

https://docs.aws.amazon.com/AWSEC2/latest/UserGuide/enhanced-networking.html

https://aws.amazon.com/blogs/devops/introducing-application-load-balancer-unlocking-and-optimizing-architectures/

https://docs.aws.amazon.com/elasticloadbalancing/latest/classic/introduction.html

Security

https://acloud.guru

https://aws.amazon.com/security/

https://docs.aws.amazon.com/directory-service/index.html#lang/en_us

https://aws.amazon.com/cloudwatch/

https://aws.amazon.com/cloudtrail/

https://aws.amazon.com/cloudhsm/

https://do.awsstatic.com/whitepapers/Security/DDoS_White_Paper.pdf

Migrations

https://d1.awsstatic.com/whitepapers/AWS-Cloud-Transformation-Maturity-Model.pdf

https://d1.awsstatic.com/whitepapers/Migration/migrating-applications-to-aws.pdf

https://d1.awsstatic.com/whitepapers/aws_cloud_adoption_framework.pdf

https://d1.awsstatic.com/whitepapers/Migration/aws-migration-whitepaper.pdf

Business Continuity

https://medium.com/tensult/disaster-recovery-2dd15bea9d39

https://aws.amazon.com/disaster-recovery/

https://www.kecklers.com/aws-domain-1-0-high-availability-business-continuity/

https://d1.awsstatic.com/whitepapers/architecture/AWS-Reliability-Pillar.pdf

https://d1.awsstatic.com/whitepapers/getting-started-with-amazon-aurora.pdf

https://d1.awsstatic.com/whitepapers/Storage/Backup_and_Recovery_Approaches_Using_AWS.pdf

Deployment and Operation Management

https://docs.aws.amazon.com/systems-manager/latest/userguide/sysman-ssm-docs.html

https://aws.amazon.com/systems-manager/features/

https://aws.amazon.com/workdocs/?amazon-workdocs-whats-new.sort-by=item.additionalFields.postDateTime&amazon-workdocs-whats-new.sort-order=desc

https://engineering.klarna.com/simple-canary-releases-in-aws-how-and-why-bf051a47fb3f

https://docs.aws.amazon.com/elasticbeanstalk/latest/dg/environmentmgmt-updates-immutable.html

https://docs.aws.amazon.com/AWSCloudFormation/latest/UserGuide/cfn-whatis-concepts.html#w2ab1b5c15c11

https://docs.aws.amazon.com/AWSCloudFormation/latest/UserGuide/protect-stack-resources.html

https://www.cloudconformity.com/knowledge-base/aws/CloudFormation/it

https://docs.aws.amazon.com/AWSCloudFormation/latest/UserGuide/best-practices.html#cfn-best-practices-changesets

http://jayendrapatil.com/aws-cloudformation-best-practices-certification/

https://aws.amazon.com/api-gateway/

https://docs.aws.amazon.com/apigateway/latest/developerguide/welcome.html

https://aws.amazon.com/config/

https://d1.awsstatic.com/whitepapers/AWS_Cloud_Best_Practices.pdf

http://do.awsstatic.com/whitepapers/Security/AWS_Security_Whitepaper.pdf

https://aws.amazon.com/chime/

https://docs.aws.amazon.com/AWSCloudFormation/latest/UserGuide/aws-template-resource-type-ref.html

https://docs.aws.amazon.com/AWSCloudFormation/latest/UserGuide/template-formats.html

https://docs.aws.amazon.com/AWSCloudFormation/latest/UserGuide/template-anatomy.html

https://d1.awsstatic.com/whitepapers/managing-your-aws-infrastructure-at-scale.pdf

https://docs.aws.amazon.com/AWSCloudFormation/latest/UserGuide/gettingstarted.templatebasics.html

https://docs.aws.amazon.com/AWSCloudFormation/latest/UserGuide/intrinsic-function-reference-getatt.html

https://docs.aws.amazon.com/elasticbeanstalk/latest/dg/concepts.platforms.html

https://docs.aws.amazon.com/opsworks/latest/userguide/gettingstarted.html

https://docs.aws.amazon.com/opsworks/latest/userguide/welcome.html

https://d1.awsstatic.com/whitepapers/managing-multi-tiered-web-applications-with-opsworks.pdf

https://www.chef.io/partners/aws/

Costing Management

https://docs.aws.amazon.com/IAM/latest/UserGuide/id_roles_terms-and-concepts.html

https://docs.aws.amazon.com/IAM/latest/UserGuide/tutorial_cross-account-with-roles.html

https://docs.aws.amazon.com/awsaccountbilling/latest/aboutv2/awsaccountbilling-aboutv2.pdf

https://docs.aws.amazon.com/awsaccountbilling/latest/aboutv2/useconsolidatedbilling-procedure.html

https://docs.aws.amazon.com/awsaccountbilling/latest/aboutv2/consolidated-billing.html

https://www.metricly.com/aws-tagging-best-practices/

https://aws.amazon.com/ec2/dedicated-hosts/pricing/

https://microage.com/blog/aws-ec2-pricing-models/

https://aws.amazon.com/ec2/pricing/reserved-instances/pricing/

https://docs.aws.amazon.com/AWSEC2/latest/UserGuide/reserved-instances-types.html

https://docs.aws.amazon.com/aws-technical-content/latest/cost-optimization-reservation-models/cost-optimization-reservation-models.pdf

https://aws.amazon.com/iam/

https://aws.amazon.com/iam/faqs/

https://aws.amazon.com/premiumsupport/iam/

https://aws.amazon.com/iam/developer-resources/

https://aws.amazon.com/iam/details/manage-users/

https://aws.amazon.com/iam/details/mfa/

https://aws.amazon.com/iam/details/manage-permissions/

https://aws.amazon.com/ecr/

https://aws.amazon.com/identity/

AWS Services

https://docs.aws.amazon.com/AWSSimpleQueueService/latest/SQSDeveloperGuide/welcome.html

https://aws.amazon.com/documentation/sqs/

https://docs.aws.amazon.com/AWSSimpleQueueService/latest/SQSDeveloperGuide/sqs-long-polling.html

https://docs.aws.amazon.com/AWSSimpleQueueService/latest/SQSDeveloperGuide/sqs-dead-letter-queues.html

https://aws.amazon.com/sqs/features/

https://docs.aws.amazon.com/aws-technical-content/latest/aws-overview/aws-overview.pdf?icmpid=link_from_whitepapers_page

https://aws.amazon.com/blogs/mobile/invoking-aws-lambda-functions-via-amazon-sns/

https://docs.aws.amazon.com/sns/latest/dg/AccessPolicyLanguage_OverallFlow.html

https://aws.amazon.com/blogs/mobile/invoking-aws-lambda-functions-via-amazon-sns/

https://docs.aws.amazon.com/sns/latest/dg/sns-lambda.html

https://docs.aws.amazon.com/elasticbeanstalk/latest/dg/concepts-webserver.html

https://cloudkul.com/blog/introduction-to-aws-elastic-beanstalk/

https://docs.aws.amazon.com/elasticbeanstalk/latest/dg/custom-platforms.html

http://docs.amazonaws.cn/en_us/elasticbeanstalk/latest/dg/concepts.platforms.html

https://docs.aws.amazon.com/AmazonRDS/latest/UserGuide/USER_WorkingWithParamGroups.html

https://docs.aws.amazon.com/AmazonRDS/latest/UserGuide/USER_WorkingWithOptionGroups.html

Scalability & Elasticity

https://docs.aws.amazon.com/AmazonCloudFront/latest/DeveloperGuide/distribution-working-with.html

https://docs.aws.amazon.com/AWSCloudFormation/latest/UserGuide/Welcome.html

https://d1.awsstatic.com/whitepapers/Security/Secure_content_delivery_with_CloudFront_whitepaper.pdf

https://docs.aws.amazon.com/aws-technical-content/latest/aws-overview/aws-overview.pdf?icmpid=link_from_whitepapers_page

https://docs.aws.amazon.com/AmazonCloudFront/latest/DeveloperGuide/Introduction.html

https://www.pickaweb.co.uk/kb/cname-can-use-domain/

https://aws.amazon.com/blogs/aws/wildcard-support-for-amazon-cloudfront/

https://aws.amazon.com/about-aws/whats-new/2014/03/05/amazon-cloudront-announces-sni-custom-ssl/

https://docs.aws.amazon.com/AmazonCloudFront/latest/DeveloperGuide/cnames-https-dedicated-ip-or-sni.html

https://aws.amazon.com/cloudfront/

https://aws.amazon.com/caching/

https://do.awsstatic.com/whitepapers/performance-at-scale-with-amazon-elasticache.pdf

https://aws.amazon.com/caching/aws-caching/

https://docs.aws.amazon.com/AmazonElastiCache/latest/mem-ug/Clusters.html

https://docs.amazonaws.cn/en_us/AmazonElastiCache/latest/mem-ug/AutoDiscovery.Benefits.html

https://docs.amazonaws.cn/en_us/AmazonElastiCache/latest/mem-ug/AutoDiscovery.HowAutoDiscoveryWorks.html

https://help.compose.com/docs/horizontal-scaling-for-redis

https://help.compose.com/docs/redis-resources-and-scaling

https://docs.amazonaws.cn/en_us/AmazonElastiCache/latest/mem-ug/Scaling.html

https://do.awsstatic.com/whitepapers/performance-at-scale-with-amazon-elasticache.pdf

https://docs.aws.amazon.com/AmazonElastiCache/latest/red-ug/BestPractices.BGSAVE.html

https://docs.aws.amazon.com/AmazonElastiCache/latest/red-ug/backups.html

https://aws.amazon.com/kinesis/

https://aws.amazon.com/kinesis/data-firehose/

https://aws.amazon.com/kinesis/data-analytics

https://do.awsstatic.com/whitepapers/whitepaper-streaming-data-solutions-on-aws-with-amazon-kinesis.pdf

https://docs.aws.amazon.com/streams/latest/dev/introduction.html

https://docs.aws.amazon.com/streams/latest/dev/key-concepts.html

https://docs.aws.amazon.com/sns/latest/dg/mobile-push-pseudo.html

https://docs.aws.amazon.com/sns/latest/dg/sns-mobile-application-as-subscriber.html#SNSMobilePushPrereq

https://docs.aws.amazon.com/AmazonCloudFront/latest/DeveloperGuide/cloudfront-limits.html

https://aws.amazon.com/cloudfront/faqs/

About Our Products

Other products from IPSpecialist LTD regarding the CSP technology are:

 AWS Certified Cloud Practitioner Study guide

 AWS Certified SysOps Admin - Associate Study guide

 AWS Certified Solution Architect - Associate Study guide

 AWS Certified Developer Associate Study guide

 AWS Certified Advanced Networking – Specialty Study guide

 AWS Certified Security – Specialty Study guide

 AWS Certified Big Data – Specialty Study guide

 Microsoft Certified: Azure Fundamentals

 Microsoft Certified: Azure Administrator

 Microsoft Certified: Azure Solution Architect

 Microsoft Certified: Azure DevOps Engineer

 Microsoft Certified: Azure Developer Associate

 Microsoft Certified: Azure Security Engineer

 Microsoft Certified: Azure Data Fundamentals

 Microsoft Certified: Azure AI Fundamentals

 Microsoft Certified: Azure Data Engineer Associate

 Microsoft Certified: Azure Data Scientist

 Certified Ethical Hacker v11

Made in the USA
Middletown, DE
05 January 2022

57863019R00232